ISRAEL AT THE POLLS, 1981

JEWISH POLITICAL AND SOCIAL STUDIES

General Editors

Daniel J. Elazar   Steven M. Cohen

ISRAEL AT THE POLLS, 1981

A Study of the Knesset Elections

EDITED BY

HOWARD R. PENNIMAN

AND

DANIEL J. ELAZAR

AMERICAN ENTERPRISE INSTITUTE FOR PUBLIC POLICY RESEARCH

WASHINGTON AND LONDON

INDIANA UNIVERSITY PRESS · BLOOMINGTON

Manufactured in the United States of America

Library of Congress Cataloging in Publication Data
Main entry under title:
Israel at the polls, 1981.
(Jewish political and social studies)
Includes index.
1. Israel. Knesset—Elections, 1981—Addresses,
essays, lectures.   2. Elections—Israel—Addresses,
essays, lectures.   3. Political parties—Israel—Addresses, essays, lectures.   I. Penniman, Howard Rae,
1916– . II. Elazar, Daniel Judah. III. Series.
JQ1825.P36518   1986   324.95694'054   84-48482
ISBN 0-253-33011-4
1 2 3 4 5 90 89 88 87 86

CONTENTS

PREFACE   IX
Howard R. Penniman

I. The 1981 Elections: Into the Second
    Generation of Statehood   1
        Daniel J. Elazar
            Labor: Combining Arrogance and
                Nostalgia / 2
            The Sephardic Factor / 4
            The Likud Coalition: 3–2 / 8
            The Crisis of the NRP / 9
            A Jewish-Democratic Synthesis? / 11
            The Arabs Vote Zionist / 13
            What of Dayan? / 14
            The First Begin Government in
                Retrospect / 15

II. Selection of Candidates to the Tenth Knesset:
    The Impact of Centralization   18
        Avraham Brichta
            The Phases of Candidate Selection / 18
            The Nature of the Candidate Selection
                Process / 19
            Conclusion / 30

III. Party Organization and Electoral Politics: The
      Labor Alignment   36
          Efraim Torgovnik
              Background: Emerging Cleavages / 37
              From Defeat to Defeat: 1977–1981 / 43
              The Campaign / 48
              Strategies of the Labor Campaign / 51
              Campaign Organization / 54
              Conclusion / 59

 IV. The Likud   64
          Ilan Greilsammer
              A Brief History of the Likud / 65
              The Ninth Knesset: The Image of the
                  Likud, 1977–1981 / 72
              The Likud's Electoral Campaign / 88
              The Election Results of June 30, 1981 / 95
              Conclusion / 99

  V. The Religious Parties   105
          Shmuel Sandler
              The NRP and Agudat Yisrael:
                  A Comparative Analysis / 107
              The Role of the NRP in the Israeli Political
                  System / 109
              The NRP and Labor: The Origins and
                  Development of the "Historical
                  Partnership" / 110
              Agudat Yisrael and the Israeli Political
                  System / 120
              The Religious Parties and the 1981
                  Elections / 121
              The Religious Parties and the Likud
                  Coalition / 124

VI.   Political Images and Ethnic Polarization   128
       Asher Arian
              Ethnic Polarization   /   129
              Images and Ideology   /   138
              Conclusion   /   155

VII.   Mutual Intervention in Domestic Politics: Israel
       and the United States   159
       Samuel Krislov
              General Principles   /   159
              Israeli Involvement in U.S. Politics   /   163
              U.S. Involvement in Israeli Politics   /   169
              The Straining of the Rules   /   179
              Conclusion   /   181

VIII.   The Role of the Media in the 1981 Knesset
       Elections   186
       Judith N. Elizur
              Image Problem of the Parties   /   188
              Change in Election Law   /   189
              Pattern of Media Use   /   190
              Setting an Agenda   /   198
              Final Phase   /   207
              Conclusion   /   210

IX.   Israeli Foreign Policy and the 1981 Election   213
       Bernard Reich
              Campaign Themes   /   213
              The Campaign Environment   /   218
              Benefits for Begin   /   221
              Begin's Second Administration   /   222
              Policy Continuity   /   229
              Relations with the United States   /   232
              The Shamir Government   /   235
              Future Prospects   /   239

X. Begin's Two-Year Government   244
       Daniel J. Elazar
           The Evacuation of Eastern Sinai / 245
           The Likud's Domestic Agenda / 246
           Operation Peace for Galilee / 247
           Who Really Brought About the Massacre
              Investigations? / 249
           A Turning Point for the Sephardim? / 251
           Begin and Sharon: The Crisis of
              Confidence / 253
           Problems in the Coalition Ranks / 254
           Conflicts within Agudat Israel / 255
           Lesser Parties / 256
           From Begin to Shamir: The Implications
              of Herut's Succession Struggle / 257
           The State of Democracy in Israel / 263

APPENDIX: KNESSET ELECTION RESULTS, 1949–1981   266
    Compiled by Richard M. Scammon
GLOSSARY OF POLITICAL PARTIES   269
CONTRIBUTORS   273
INDEX   275

PREFACE

Israel at the Polls, 1981: A Study of the Knesset Elections is another in the continuing series of volumes on national elections in selected democratic countries published by the American Enterprise Institute for Public Policy Research (AEI). Underlying the series is the belief that public policy makers and students of elections in any democracy can profit from a knowledge of electoral laws and practices in a wide variety of democracies. The greater their understanding of the political consequences of the conduct of elections in other countries, the deeper their insights into the impact of electoral rules and practices at home will be.

As of mid-1984 the *At the Polls* series included volumes on at least one and as many as three elections in the following countries: Australia, Canada, France, West Germany, Greece, India, Ireland, Israel, Italy, Japan, New Zealand, three of the four Scandinavian democracies, Switzerland, the United Kingdom, and Venezuela. A dozen more individual country studies are in progress. AEI has also published two comparative books on referendums, one on *British Political Finance, 1830–1980*, and *Democracy at the Polls: A Comparative Study of Competitive National Elections*. The latter examined the rules and character of elections in some twenty-eight countries. In process is a volume for a new *At the Polls* series that will include chapters on competitive elections held each calendar year in countries with populations of two million or more. The first book will cover the 1983 democratic elections and will appear in 1986.

The 1981 Israeli elections, in Daniel Elazar's words, "offered clear confirmation that Israel has now entered its second generation of statehood. . . . Israel may or may not have a basically two-party system now, but what is clear is that it does have two parties capable of contesting for control of the government." Elazar's comments were stimulated by the second victory in four years for the Likud and its leader, Menachem Begin.

The two Likud victories followed nearly fifty years of dominance by the Labor Alignment and its precursor, Mapai, over Israeli government and politics. Evidence that this half-century of power might be broken appeared in the 1973 election results but at the time went largely unnoticed. In that year the Likud won thirty-nine seats, an increase of thirteen over the twenty-six secured by Likud's predecessor, Gahal, in both 1969 and 1966. The Alignment received fifty-one seats in 1973, a decline of five from their 1969 total. Asher Arian's analysis of Israeli polling data over several decades shows a gradual national shift to the right that began in 1962.

The two major coalitions together won 73.7 percent of the 1981 vote. The total vote won by the other parties that had gained the 1.0 percent minimum vote required to receive at least one Knesset seat was 21.1 percent. Another 5.2 percent of the vote was "wasted" on the very small parties. The combined two-party vote in 1977 was only 58.0 percent, largely because the Democratic Movement for Change, made up primarily of politicians who broke away from the Alignment, took with them 11.6 percent of the vote and fifteen Knesset seats.

In the past, Israeli parties and politicians have frequently taken advantage of the simple legal requirements for presenting candidates to the voters. This has been a factor in the proliferation of parties competing for votes and seats, a proliferation that also limited the votes received even by the dominant Mapai and later the Alignment. Three recent developments may have increased the likelihood that the Alignment and the Likud will continue to capture the lion's share of the popular vote and therefore of Knesset seats.

First, the very fact that elections are more frequently viewed by the voters as a contest between the giants—a view fostered both by the media and by the voters' own experience—leads more voters to choose either the Likud or the Alignment rather than "waste" their votes for a small party whose chances of becoming part of the winning coalition are uncertain. Shmuel Sandler provides statistics in his chapter on the religious and other small parties that illustrate this point. The figures show that in 1981 the vote for most religious parties dropped sharply from the 1977 level while the Likud vote went up by just about the same amount. Sandler cites polling data that suggest that in the last few days of the 1981 campaign lesser parties of both the left and the right lost support to the Alignment or to the Likud. Arian, also drawing on polling data, argues that voting for small parties "was a luxury that [voters] could not afford since the elections were between two large forces."

Second, the major parties increasingly dominate the communications media, because of government rules and bigger budgets. The 1981 rules for free time on Israel's television network assured the

large parties a greater advantage over the smaller parties. In previous
years any party with at least one seat in the Knesset was automatically
given 10 minutes of television time plus another 4 minutes for each
seat held by the party in the outgoing Knesset. The new rules grant
6 minutes of time for each party seat. In her chapter on the media
Judith Elizur points out that the Alignment in 1981 would have received 138 minutes of television time under the old rules, but under
the new rules received 202 minutes for its thirty-two seats. The Likud
share for forty-two seats went up from 178 minutes under the old
rules to 262 minutes under the new. Since the Democratic Movement
for Change did not field a slate in 1981, the third largest party was the
National Religious party, whose twelve seats entitled it to 58 minutes.
All but two of the remaining parties received no more than 22 minutes of free television time. Because the costs of producing a program
are borne by the party, only the largest organizations or those financed by a wealthy patron can afford to make good use of their television time. New parties, of course, have no seats in the Knesset, and
so they have no access to television.

The cost of newspaper advertising has to be shouldered by the parties, so, once again, the two large organizations have a great advantage. In 1981 the Alignment and the Likud each greatly outspent all
lesser parties combined for advertisements that appeared in the four
major Hebrew newspapers. Their campaign funds were great enough
that on election day the Alignment ran fifty-nine ads while the Likud
bought an astounding ninety-five. Every student of elections knows
that a small difference in the expenditures of the two major parties
has little impact on the election results. On the other hand, the lack of
funds to buy any ads and the lack of Knesset seats to assure a reasonable amount of television time prevent the public from even recogniz-
ing the names of most parties. Only a party like Agudat Israel can expect to consistently win four or five Knesset seats with a restricted
budget and limited access to television. Agudat Israel is more or less
secure because its religious followers constitute the source of nearly all
of its votes. Large sums of money would add few votes, and a reduction of funds would cut little from the party's support.

The third development of recent years that may help preserve the
dominance of the two big coalitions is a division within the society that
until recent years has been little discussed. Mapai and later the Alignment were established by the Ashkenazic Jews who came to Palestine
in relatively large numbers during the first three decades of the twen-

tieth century. They were the builders of most institutions in Israel and controlled its politics. Further, as Arian points out, they could expect outside support because the Ashkenazim constituted 85 percent of the world's Jews, most of whom lived in Europe or America.

The other 15 percent of the world's Jews are Sephardim, some of whom have more recently come to Israel, primarily from North Africa and the Arab countries of the Middle East. In Israel today they make up 55 percent of the Jewish population, but because of the age differential between the Ashkenazim and the Sephardim, the former still constitute a slight majority of Israeli voters—a situation that will soon change.

In the last election, and to a more limited degree in 1977, this division was a political issue. Sephardic Jews felt they were treated as outsiders who were not given an equal opportunity in political or other public affairs. They resented their status and many viewed the Alignment as an Ashkenazic instrument for perpetuating this inequality. Many perceived Begin, although an Ashkenazi, as another Jew who was treated as an outsider. They identified with him and he with them. Their votes certainly helped the Likud win control of government in 1977 and in 1981. Begin's commitment to tradition and his support of the religious groups also struck a responsive note among many Sephardim who showed little of the commitment of earlier settlers to democratic socialism and did not share the opposition to religion held by some earlier settlers and leaders of Israel. In the 1981 campaign Ashkenazim-Sephardim tensions became an issue that was tied to other problems, such as the demonstrations against Alignment leaders in public meetings. The division was sharpened by comments of Labor spokesmen that to the ears of the Sephardim—and often of others—sounded offensive and demeaning. Whatever its importance for other purposes, this heightened sense of division, recognized by both parties, helped drive more Sephardim to support the Likud and strengthened some Ashkenazim in their allegiance to the Alignment.

In spite of developments that have recently encouraged Israeli voters to support the major coalitions, there is no guarantee of a two-party system in either the near or the distant future. Israel is beset by so many problems and so many different views about their solution that these differences plus the country's open electoral system may at least postpone a two-party development. This in no way minimizes the importance of the 1977 and 1981 elections in making clear that the Alignment can no longer presume it will control the government.

Nine authors have contributed essays to this volume. Elazar introduces the volume with a discussion of the 1981 campaign, the continuing strength of the Likud, and the difficulties confronting some of the traditional parties. Elazar also concludes the study with a discussion of the role of Menachem Begin during the first two years of the Likud term. Avraham Brichta describes the current methods of selecting candidate lists and offers some possible alternatives. Efraim Torgovnik discusses the Labor Alignment's campaign and its problems. Ilan Greilsammer describes the successful efforts of Begin and the Likud to gain reelection. Shmuel Sandler examines the campaigns and the difficulties of the religious parties. Asher Arian draws on polling and electoral data in his analysis of the election and its results. Samuel Krislov analyzes the interrelations of politics of Israel and the United States. Judith Elizur discusses the media and the election, including changes in the rules for television time for the parties and the parties' use of newspaper advertising. Bernard Reich looks at the impact of the election on Israeli foreign policy. Richard M. Scammon provides the electoral data for the appendix.

I owe thanks to many persons in Israel and the United States for their assistance while this document was being planned and written. I am particularly obligated to Daniel J. Elazar, who identified a number of excellent contributors and agreed at a very late date to take on responsibility for the concluding chapter. Because of his assistance at all stages of the book's preparation, I was pleased that he accepted my invitation to be co-editor of this second volume.

HOWARD R. PENNIMAN, General Editor
At the Polls Series

ISRAEL AT THE POLLS, 1981

I

THE 1981 ELECTIONS
INTO THE SECOND GENERATION OF STATEHOOD

Daniel J. Elazar

The most important aspect of the 1981 elections is the clear confirmation they offered that Israel has now entered its second generation of statehood, and that its political system has turned away from the alignment of forces which was formed in the generation before the rebirth of the Jewish state and which prevailed during the whole first generation of statehood. Israel may or may not have a basically two-party system now, but it is clear that it does have two parties capable of contesting for control of the government. The Labor Alignment (in Hebrew *Ma'arach*) has not yet learned this truth, which is one of the reasons why it lost in 1981 and why it remains in disarray.

When the Labor Alignment was defeated in 1977, it had enjoyed two generations of political hegemony, having come to power in the prestate Jewish *yishuv* (literally, settled community) in the late 1920s and having consolidated its political hold in the early 1950s shortly after the establishment of Israel in 1948. From the mid-1930s until its defeat, it effectively had no rival, so much so that political scientists writing about Israel classified Israeli party politics as a multiple-party system with a single dominant party.[1] Thus the shock to Labor was even greater than it might have been had it been involved all along in a competitive situation.

The changeover took place because of generational changes in the voting population. Beginning with the 1965 elections, the trend to the Likud among new voters entering the lists was clearly visible. In the intervening sixteen years, those voters have become the majority. In that respect as well as in others, the 1977 and 1981 elections can be viewed as critical elections in Israeli history.

Labor: Combining Arrogance and Nostalgia

Labor's leaders still persist in acting as if Labor is the only legitimate governor of the state and that it was the height of affrontery for the Likud or anyone else to challenge its control of the government. If there was anything that turned moderate voters who were not among the strong pro-Likud, pro-Begin forces away from Labor it was that arrogant attitude on the part of the Labor Alignment, which came through in its campaign at every turn. However much electioneering may involve efforts at dissimulation, in Israel it tends to be exceptionally honest and straightforward in the sense that the truth will out. Every television presentation and virtually every speech of the Labor Alignment displayed clearly for all who would pay attention how much the Labor camp saw itself as ruling by right and how little had changed as a result of its defeat four years ago.

The Labor Alignment attitude was manifested in several ways. It was most visible in the Alignment's campaign rhetoric, which openly suggested that the Likud was "by nature" unable to govern and that it was therefore necessary to restore the natural governors of Israel, namely the Labor Alignment, to power. This rhetoric was so blatant that it could not help but reach every segment of the population— indeed, it was intended to do so.

A second aspect of this arrogance was to be found in the way that Labor leaders believed the public opinion polls of the last half of 1980, which seemed to show the Alignment winning a majority of seats in the Knesset. Even the most unskilled political science student would have avoided falling into that trap, considering that the percentage of undecideds in each of those polls was no less than a third of the total electorate and frequently was as high as half. Closer inspection of the published polls, available to any newspaper reader, also revealed that most of the undecideds had supported the Likud in 1977 and could easily be brought back into the Likud camp were there to be a change in their perceptions of the effectiveness of the government.

Apparently, all of this escaped the Labor leadership, encouraging them in a chain of erroneous assumptions that led them to conduct their campaign with extraordinary overconfidence until quite late in the game and to alienate potential coalition partners by acting as if their absolute majority in the Knesset was assured. This was particularly telling in connection with the religious camp, whose participation has been necessary in every lasting governing coalition since the establishment of the Israeli party system. In the precampaign period, Labor adopted a strongly secular stance, openly attacking religious party participation in the government as bringing about deleterious actions of one kind or another and endorsing changes in the status quo that governs relations between the religious and nonreligious in the state, thereby making it virtually impossible for the religious parties to contemplate a coalition with Labor. This was, of course, of crucial importance after the election, when the virtual tie between Labor and the Likud could have been broken either way had the religious parties seen themselves in a flexible position. Labor, however, had effectively ruled itself out of the ball game through its arrogance before the elections were even called. In the aftermath of the Labor defeat, this was one of the major internal criticisms levied against the party leadership.

Another manifestation of Labor arrogance was in their callow attitude toward the Sephardic Jews, who already constituted a majority in the country and whose support has become increasingly necessary for victory. Most visible in this regard were the numerous uncomplimentary expressions directed against Sephardim as a group, associating them with undesirable lower-class behavior. These were, presumably, individual slips of the tongue, but as video tapes shown after the elections revealed, the overall tone of the Labor leadership toward the Sephardic population was patronizing at best and often downright hostile. In a television documentary series analyzing the elections, prepared and narrated by television commentators widely believed to be strongly pro-Labor in their sympathies, there was extensive footage of Shimon Peres, Haim Bar-Lev (Labor's defense minister designate during most of the Campaign), Haim Ben-Shahar (finance minister designate), and other party leaders in confrontational situations with predominantly Sephardic audiences in which the candidate's patronizing or contemptuous manner was obvious to one and all and evoked the expected reaction. One can only assume that this was standard behavior on the part of Labor campaigners.

Part of this arrogance was associated with a strong tendency toward nostalgia in the Labor camp, manifested quite clearly at the Labor party convention and even reflected in some of the popular songs written by Labor supporters during 1981. The essence of this nostalgia was that Israel somehow had lost its pioneering and socialist ideals of the prestate years, presumably as a result of changes that had taken place during the thirty years of statehood and because of the immigration of a population (implicitly the Sephardim) that did not share the old ideals. It is true, of course, that the same could have been said of the Ashkenazim who arrived after the state was established—and to many of both communities resident in Eretz Yisrael even before 1948. This nostalgia for the socialist idealism of that period cannot be separated from the nostalgia for the days when an overwhelming Ashkenazi Labor establishment ruled Israel.

Perceptive observers of the scene, watching the conflicts and the bickering among the Labor leadership and mindful of the scandals which had brought down the Labor Alignment in 1977, could only consider the irony of this nostalgia, since Labor's failures were the responsibility of the generation which had been born in Israel (e.g., Moshe Dayan and Yitzhak Rabin) or who had immigrated to the country before 1948 (e.g., Peres and Bar-Lev) and who were, therefore, the products of socialist Zionism. In other words, they are presumably the best and brightest children of what was presumed by them to be the elite generation of the Zionist enterprise in Israel.[2]

This kind of attitude made it easy for Menachen Begin and the Likud to capitalize on their greatest strength, namely, their role as spokesmen for the outsiders. Thus the government in power was able to win the substantial vote of those citizens who felt themselves excluded by Labor's attitude. In no segment of the population was this more true than with the Sephardic Jews, especially those from Arab countries.

The Sephardic Factor

Most Sephardim still see themselves as outsiders, because that is how they have been labeled by the Labor-dominated Israeli establishment. Hence their easy identification with Menachen Begin, the perennial outsider, and their pleasure in seeing him press the Labor camp unceasingly.

Many people have been puzzled by the attraction between Begin, in many respects the quintessential Polish Jew, and the Jews from the Arab world. This sense of being on the outside is one powerful reason but, beyond that, their mutual admiration should be a lesson to all who believe the myth that there is inherently a great gap between the Jews of Eastern Europe and those of the Mediterranean world. The idea of this gap, which is widely held, especially in the establishment, is a myth developed by that segment of Eastern European Jewry that sought to forget its own traditional past and arrogated to itself the designation "Western" while tagging their Mediterranean brethren with the appellation (or should one say epithet, for that is really what it is) "Oriental." In fact, as those who come from the real West well know, both groups are Easterners; the difference is that one group came from Eastern Europeans and the other from the Arab countries. Both fully share the habits and outlook of the East.[3] Thus affinities between them should not be surprising. Nor should it be surprising that there is an effort to resist recognition of those affinities on the part of those who wish to protect, through a mythology, what they perceive as their superior status.[4]

There is much confusion abroad with regard to the Sephardic factor, based upon an image of "the two Israels" that was developed over more than three decades. That image is in part reflected in the spurious distinction between "Western" and "Oriental" Jews. It is given concrete form in the suggestion that there are class differences between Ashkenazim and Sephardim *per se*.[5] While it is true that the bulk (perhaps as high as 90 percent) of the bottom tenth in socioeconomic status among Israeli Jews is of Sephardic origin, it is not true that the bulk of the Sephardim are on the bottom rungs of the ladder. Sephardim cover the range of income and status positions in Israeli society and include wealthy bankers, industrialists, and property owners, the President of the State of Israel, a large population of middle-class shopkeepers, substantial numbers of attorneys and middle-level managers, and a large blue-collar population. It is true that Sephardic Jews do not yet reach the universities in percentages equal to their share of the population, although the percentage who do is rising steadily. This has certain impacts on status but not necessarily on income. Among the wealthiest Sephardim in the country are contractors and merchants who encourage their children to go directly into the family business. In sum, the situation is far more complex as well as quite different than the mythology makes it out to be.[6]

All this is not to obscure the polarization that is beginning to develop in the country. Perhaps if there were real differences between Ashkenazim and Sephardim of the kind imputed, the gap would be of a different order, but the fact that these differences are more reputed than real merely intensifies the hurt of the Sephardim at being excluded. There were many examples of this during the campaign. One will suffice. Eliahu Nawi, the longtime mayor of Beer Sheba who is of

Iraqi origin, was promised by Shimon Peres a safe (Israelis call it "realistic") place on the Labor Alignment Knesset list. In the end, because Peres had overpromised seats in the precampaign period, when he assumed that the Alignment would win over sixty seats, Nawi was put very far down on the list. He approached Peres to ask why he had been excluded, only to be told that the list already was overloaded with Iraqis. Nawi's response was: "I arrived in Israel seven years before you, yet you are an Israeli and I am still an Iraqi." It is this attitude of the Labor establishment which is the source of polarization and bitterness, the sense of cultural and political rather than economic deprivation, of being pigeonholed by country of origin if one happens to come from the wrong country.

Contrary to some lurid newspaper accounts, Jewish Israel is not divided into "two nations," not into two cultures, and not even into two societies. The degree to which Jews from all parts of the world have integrated into one society goes far beyond the kind of divisions which get headlines at election time. Nonetheless, there is a growing division. I am not sure what to label the phenomenon. It essentially consists of those who believe that the country was theirs by right, and still would be if they could go back to the old ways of the socialist *aliyot*, and there are others who believe that the country belongs to all Israelis with nobody having a special claim by virtue of seniority. It is a division between those who patronize and those who are patronized, those whose particular culture is considered the correct standard, regardless of how good or bad it may be, and those whose particular culture is considered quaint and picturesque or "ethnic," no matter how good or bad it may be.

That this division cuts across parties and camps does not prevent the patronized from seizing upon one party in particular as coinciding more closely with their present interests. In any case, this situation is likely to get worse before it gets better; but bad as it is likely to get, it does not represent a fundamental split in the nation, as it has sometimes seemed to outsiders. The Sephardim have already developed too many legitimate channels, including the Likud, through which to express themselves and advance in public life not to expect to come into their own in the near future. What the 1981 elections highlighted is the true character of Sephardic grievances—not economic, but cultural and political—and the ability of Sephardim and Ashkenazim to forge alliances to gain political power.

Beyond the headlines, one can see the new synthesis developing.

Politically, it is built around a group of outstanding young Sephardic leaders in the Likud, all of whom have emerged from the development towns. David Levy, who started as the head of the works committee in a textile mill in Beit Shean, a small development town in the Jordan valley, and is now contesting for the number two position in the Likud government, is the most prominent example of this phenomenon. He has long since transcended the vulgar jokes which four years ago mocked his Moroccan background. Not only does he dominate the Herut party "machine," he has also become an accomplished and moving public speaker in his own right, sought after for his clarity of expression (he seems to share the strong inclination among Sephardim to value clear, elegant, and precise Hebrew, a matter of overt Sephardic pride at least since the formation of the Sephardic version of the prayer liturgy nearly a millennium ago). But he is not alone. David Magen, mayor of Kiryat Gat; Moshe Katzav, mayor of Kiryat Malachi; and Meir Shitreet, mayor of Yavna, all now Knesset members as well, represent a new and immensely capable power bloc. Each has a story to tell about how he tried to break into the Labor party (or its predecessor, Mapai) at the outset of his political career and was rejected with prejudice by a shortsighted establishment.

This is a sign of the times. Having achieved economic stability and even success in having gained power roughly proportionate to their share of the population in local communities where they represent majorities or substantial minorities, the Sephardim are ready for a great leap forward in public life. In the months following the elections, young Sephardim in their thirties and forties who hold public positions—mayors, vice-mayors of cities and towns, local councilmen, school principals and vice-principals, deputy directors general of various government departments and public corporations—have met to discuss their political future. These leaders, who represent the equivalent of upper middle-level management in the business world, see the time as right to claim what they believe to be their due, namely, the opportunity to advance into the upper echelons of public life in Israel.

With the exception of Tami (of which more below), these groups of young Sephardim are making their demands within the present party political framework, where they are succeeding in the Likud, and may even succeed in due course in the Alliance, although they are at least one step further removed from success there than in the Likud. These are the people to watch as the politics of the second generation of Israeli statehood unfolds. Since the best opportunities for these people lie with the Likud, their advancement is likely to strengthen that party's majority and ability to hold onto the reins of government.

Culturally, like most such syntheses in democratic societies, the Ashkenazic-Sephardic synthesis is not likely to emphasize the highest elements of the various cultures which have been brought to Israel but, at best, their respective middlebrow elements. That is both the glory and the dilemma of contemporary society. Israel, at least, still has standards, and Israelis can tell the difference between better and inferior forms of cultural expression, whatever their origin.

The Likud Coalition: 3–2

What of the details of the election results, what do they mean? The basic message is a massive swing away from Labor. True, the Labor Alignment won forty-seven seats in the voting and then added another by persuading Shulamit Aloni of the Citizens' Rights Movement to join their Alignment, but that merely brought them back to the combined total of Labor and the Democratic Movement for Change of four years ago, itself a far lower figure than the Labor Alignment had normally won in its heyday. Moreover, several of those forty-seven seats were the result of a large Arab vote for Labor, of which more below.

On the other hand, the Likud gained over and above what it and Ariel Sharon's Shlomzion party, which subsequently merged with it, won in 1977. It did so despite the secession of the Likud's right wing to form Tehiya and part of its La'am faction to form Telem. At least four of the five seats won by those two parties must be added to the Likud total to get an accurate picture of the result. Moreover, most of the thirteen seats of the Religious camp represent people committed to a coalition with the Likud in the way that the National Religious party (NRP) was once committed to a coalition with Labor. In effect, the Jewish vote went three to two against the Labor camp.

The Labor leadership may wish to fool itself that it has regained its strength, by misreading the polls just as they did in 1980 when they thought victory was in their pockets. While the possibility that they may win an election in the 1980s cannot be ruled out—after all, a Likud disaster is always possible—the polls since the elections have, in fact, showed the Likud gaining and Labor losing even more seats. From the perspective of long-term trends in the Israeli polity, Labor may well have peaked in the 1981 elections. There is almost no one left to draw into its fold. This is a bitter pill to swallow for those who still believe themselves to be to the manor born, but nothing will change in Labor's prospects until this truth is perceived.

That is not to say that the Likud vote consisted only of Begin's faithful. Perhaps half of its seats were gained from those who happily voted Likud. The other half, I would suggest, were gained through the votes of those who held their noses and decided whom they disliked least. That is a slender reed upon which to build a new majority, but, in the Likud's favor, one of the reasons that most of those voters disliked the Likud least was because of an affinity for the nonsocialist camp. Hence, they are more likely to become Likud voters over time than to shift to Labor. By and large, their opposition to the Labor camp had to be balanced against their dislike for the Likud leadership, including Prime Minister Begin. In other words, they could have been persuaded to vote for an alternative had there been an acceptable one available, but Labor did everything possible to alienate those voters.

The Crisis of the NRP

What of the Religious camp? Did they lose as badly as it seemed at first glance? Yes and no. The camp as a whole dropped from a maximum strength of seventeen to thirteen, a loss of four seats for what was generally considered the most stable bloc in Israeli politics. The NRP absorbed the entire loss—its strength was cut in half, losing seats to the Likud and to its offshoot, Tami, the breakaway party of Religious Affairs Minister Aharon Abu-Hatzeira, who, to build a communal list, tried to capitalize on North African resentment over his trial and, to a degree, succeeded. Agudat Yisrael, on the other hand, held its own and, because of the virtual tie between the two large parties, plus the skills of its leaders, much enhanced its bargaining power.

In other words, 1981 was a decisive turning point for the religious camp in the way that 1977 was decisive for Labor. The religious parties presumably are reassessing who and what they are, just as Labor should have done four years ago. At this writing (1983), it is unclear whether they will be any wiser than Labor. The NRP has a particularly difficult row to hoe. After winning twelve seats in 1977 under the effective dominance of the Young Guard (its strongest faction in 1981), its new leadership was filled with thoughts of expanding its base to become the Israeli equivalent of the European Christian Democratic parties, in other words, a broad-based, religiously oriented political alignment capable of contesting for governmental power and not simply continuing as a balance wheel between the two large parties as in the past. The NRP went so far as to welcome a delegation from the Christian Democratic Union of West Germany in 1980 as part of its initial exploration of the possibilities.[7]

Those hopes have been rudely dashed, at least for the moment. Is this effect temporary? Is it a case of overreach? These questions have occupied the minds of the NRP leadership. One look at Zevulun Hammer's face the night after the 1981 elections was enough to reveal the agonizing reappraisal he was undergoing, especially after having gained effective control over the party, moving it toward a more hawkish position, and then losing all those seats to the Likud, Tehiya, and Tami. The first two succeeded in outbidding the NRP on hawkishness and the last cut into its Sephardic vote.

It is no secret that Interior Minister Yosef Burg's faction in the NRP would have preferred a coalition with Labor. But they are on the decline, with the Young Guard clearly dominant within party ranks, especially after the breakaway of the Abu-Hatzeira faction. This means that the NRP is not likely to turn toward Labor in the near future, barring unforeseen developments.

The Young Guard itself is now rent by internal troubles that emerged before the elections and which have been exacerbated by the failure to maintain, much less increase, NRP strength. Some of the Young Guard's troubles stem from the growing view among faction members that the faction's leaders, Hammer and Yehuda Ben-Meir, now deputy foreign minister, have become as autocratic as were the older factions against which they revolted a decade ago. These people, heavily represented among the academic supporters of the NRP, were unable to make much headway prior to the 1981 elections but since the June debacle have attracted more respectful attention within party ranks.

More important is the movement now taking place among Sephardic members of the party to organize and demand their rightful role within the party and in party-controlled government offices. It is likely that the NRP is the most Sephardic of Israel's political parties other than Tami. According to reports, some 70 percent of the registered party members are Sephardim. At the same time, since Tami broke away there have been no Sephardim in the party's top leadership or in government positions under the party's control. This has led to considerable resentment and, increasingly, to efforts on the part of the party activists of Sephardic background to organize themselves to demand their share in time for the 1984 elections.

A Jewish-Democratic Synthesis?

Curiously enough, however, there is an outside chance that this development may provide the basis for the kind of broad, traditionally oriented party alignment which could compete for the government that Hammer and company envisaged. Tami is the key here. Its origins were something less than noble, involving, as they did, the ambitions of Aharon Abu-Hatzeira; the blatant intervention of Nissim Gaon, a rich Diaspora Jew of Sephardic background whose interest in Israel reflects his own ambitions; and a barely disguised appeal to the North African Sephardic segment of the population. Nevertheless, the ideological trappings in which the party wrapped itself fit perfectly into what is needed for the building of such a coalition.

Tami advertised itself as the movement for tradition in Israel (that is its name), an appeal to Sephardim who are traditional rather than Orthodox and, as such, the first recognition of the *masorati* (traditional) Jews as a potential force in the country. Its emphasis on positive involvement with Jewish tradition on something other than an Orthodox basis and on mutual respect among all the communities in the state was telling, so much so that, had the bearers of those banners been different people, the banners themselves might have attracted even more voters. Should Tami prove to be more than a vehicle for its leaders' ambitions, it could lead the way to the development of a party which could later align itself with the NRP and begin to build a "Jewish Democratic" force.

No one should underestimate the power of the idea which Tami embraced. Menachem Begin did not, since he embodied it in his own person to become a classic "Jewish Democratic" leader. His emphasis on Jewish tradition as the cornerstone of Israel's "civil religion" was a dominant element in his public stance (and one of the bases for his appeal to Sephardic and religious voters). It betrayed a serious concern—derived from Vladimir Jabotinsky, his mentor—for the continuity of Jewish tradition in the Jewish state and for other than Orthodox religious grounds through an appropriate synthesis of civil and religious elements. Few other Likud leaders have reflected that synthesis (David Levy is the exception), which was one of the reasons that Begin was far more popular than they.

The emergence of an articulated and well-formed civil religion in Israel, which draws heavily on traditional Jewish sources and gives them expression in a traditional manner, has been a striking aspect of the Israel of the past decade. This civil religion differs significantly from the one fostered by Labor hegemony earlier in the Zionist enterprise when the Zionist socialists sought to take traditional Jewish forms and infuse them with clearly secular content.[8] The emergent civil religion in Israel selectively takes traditional forms with their traditional content and attaches them to the civil society. This trend reflects the demise of the old ideologies which flourished during the modern epoch but which have become increasingly irrelevant in the post-modern world, and the revival of concern for traditional religion also characteristic of our times.[9] In that respect, the contemporary Israeli experience is simply a Jewish variant of a worldwide phenomenon.

Begin's emphasis on traditional Jewish behavior on the part of the prime minister was a powerful factor in his own attractiveness to a large number of Jews in Israel who wanted to see that kind of "Jewish Democrat" synthesis as the cornerstone of the Jewish state. If the Likud can be infused with it, the party will secure the power that the NRP Young Guard and Tami also seek.

There is a long way from a Jewish democratic synthesis to a desire for Orthodox hegemony, as the postelection coalition bargaining once again revealed. The perennial "Who is a Jew" issue once again brought down a general sentiment on the part of all but the most extreme to avoid the issue, even among those who stood to gain by raising it. Those outside Israel must understand the complexities of this question. For Israeli Jews it is no concession to require conversion according to *halachah* (traditional Jewish law), since that is the only kind of conversion that exists in Israel, nor are more than a handful of Israelis interested in anything else. Were it not for the Diaspora, they could accept the question without perceiving that it cost them anything. The issue is regularly shelved for the sake of worldwide Jewish unity, to prevent permanent divisions in the Jewish people. It has been again.

The advance of Agudat Yisrael in strength and in stature was one of the most interesting phenomena of this election.[10] Because of their skill in using their position, and their essential moderation in the application of that skill, they attracted the admiration of many who were utterly opposed to the kind of Orthodoxy they advocate. For them, the "Who is a Jew" issue, however significant, can be sacrificed in return for additional financial support for their institutions. They are building for the long pull and need funds now far more than they need to win what is, for the most part, a symbolic issue of its effects. Thus, they raised the issue and then, in order to gain a more tangible reward, rather quickly backed off from insisting upon it.

Not only is their bargaining skill admired but, at a time when the NRP appeared to be dominated by nationalist fanatics, the political moderation of Agudat Yisrael in matters of national policy was apparent to all. No "Land of Israel" crusades for them. Indeed, had the Labor Alignment not so deliberately turned its back on the religious camp when its leaders thought it was going to get over half the seats in the Knesset, there might even have been room for Agudat Yisrael to become a partner in a Ma'arach coalition, without seats in the government but providing votes in the Knesset in return for heavy financial support for their institutions and key committee chairmanships.

Agudat Yisrael does raise the hackles of almost everyone else— including especially the NRP—with its demands for exemptions from military service for yeshiva students and teachers and for women in general. This demand is seen as ranging from merely outrageous to downright traitorous.

The Arabs Vote Zionist

Somewhat overlooked in the aftermath of the 1981 elections was the shift in the Arab vote away from the Communist-dominated popular front party and the various lists which have paralleled the several Zionist parties in the Arab community, particularly the Ma'arach. At a time when there were all sorts of reports about how the Israeli Arabs were deserting the state, this trend represented very important evidence to the contrary. In 1981 the major parties included Arabs as integral members and put Arab candidates on their lists, appealing directly to the Arab voters rather than working through their "front" Arab lists as has been the case in the past.

During the first generation of statehood, even those Arabs most committed to developing a modus vivendi within Israel maintained separate party lists. It was generally agreed that they would not be at home within any of the Zionist parties (that is, all the major parties of Israel, except for the Communists), nor were the major parties eager to dilute their Zionist character by accepting Arabs as members. Thus, each of the Zionist parties either established a parallel Arab list or made arrangements to support a separate party established by the Arabs themselves.

The Labor parties were past masters at this, since they had funds and patronage to distribute and Arab politicians understood that they could benefit themselves and their constituents by supporting what was then obviously the majority camp. But, as I noted in the previous volume in this series,[11] even the NRP acquired supporters in the Arab sectors. Those Arabs who wished to demonstrate their anti-Zionism or their rejection of accommodation with Israel voted Communist, even though the Communist party was also led by Jews.

This system began to break down, along with the rest of the party alignment, in the course of the 1970s. Arabs began to vote for Zionist parties and Zionist parties, beginning with Mapam, began to include Arabs as members and even to give them at least symbolic places on their party lists. Integration at this level was more or less completed in 1981. Indeed, an additional problem that the Labor party brought on itself grew out of a promise to an Arab of a safe position on its list. The changing electoral situation and Peres's overcommitting of "safe" seats to the party faithful forced the leading Arab candidate farther down the list. This change led to an angry reaction by the party's Arab adherents, and a subsequent readjustment of the candidate's place on the list.

Perhaps it was because of their integration into the mainstream of the political process that the Arabs overcame their previous reluctance to vote for avowedly Zionist parties. However, an even more likely reason was that they believed that a Ma'arach victory would advance Arab interests (which include Palestinian ones, of course) while a Likud victory would inhibit those interests. They came close to succeeding in putting the Ma'arach over the top in number of seats, although, as suggested above, Labor would still have had a difficult time putting together a governing coalition.

No doubt the Arab vote camouflages a growing Palestinian consciousness among certain sectors of the Israeli Arab population, as well as reflecting a greater willingness to participate in mainstream Israeli politics. Whatever their reasons, the Arabs actually took a big step toward further integration into the Israeli polity, one that should be duly appreciated.

What of Dayan?

Perhaps the biggest loser of all in this election was Moshe Dayan, who was desperately seeking vindication. After some initial excitement, Telem, his new party, soon was understood by all for what it was, a catchall for professional politicians, present and former Knesset members, who had lost their base in other parties and were looking for some way to stay in office. It was a sad collection indeed, where ambition clearly took precedence over talent, even though many of the individuals on Dayan's lists were notably talented. The voters responded accordingly. He kept his corporal's guard of those faithful to him unto death, but no more. Begin rejected Dayan's terms for joining the coalition out of hand. While Telem's two Knesset members voted against seating the new government, Dayan informally committed himself to supporting the government in most matters after its formation. With Dayan's death, Telem lost whatever drawing power it had and its members quite obviously did not know where to turn next.

The First Begin Government in Retrospect

The Begin coalition survived four years in office despite a distinctly mixed record. Its great achievement was, of course, the peace treaty with Egypt, but it was tempered by widespread dissatisfaction in Israel among "hawks" and "doves" alike with the Israeli government's commitment to give up all of Sinai. Many Israelis, including those prepared to make substantial concessions in Judea, Samaria, and Gaza, strongly believed that Israel's security interests required it to maintain control of at least the eastern third of Sinai, and given the fact that the peninsula is virtually uninhabited except by Bedouin who have no ties to either Israel or Egypt, it would have been reasonable to partition it as a buffer zone, or, failing that, to at least have delayed the final withdrawal for a longer period until the peace itself had a chance to take firm root.

The Begin government's greatest failure was in the economic realm, where its rather half-baked efforts to liberalize government economic policy led to an increase in the rate of inflation from some 30 percent annually to over 130 percent. A parallel removal of subsidies on basic foodstuffs, which particularly affected lower-income groups, for a while threatened to bring down the government. This was tempered in the last six months before the election by the policies of Finance Minister Yoram Aridor, then new in office, who, in what can only be described as a series of brilliant moves, managed to temporarily reduce inflation while at the same time encouraging savings and increasing the real income of the average Israeli by a manipulation of tax cuts and the restoration of subsidies. Widely accused of simply playing election politics with the economy, Aridor had a clear economic policy in mind which was designed not only to bring political advantage but to cope with Israel's difficult economic situation. While many of those gains proved temporary and inflation soared again at the end of the summer, Aridor continued to press hard on behalf of his policy of government retrenchment and liberalization of the market.

The only major domestic initiative of the first Begin government, Project Renewal, designed to rehabilitate substandard neighborhoods in which were housed the 10 percent of the population at the bottom of the socioeconomic ladder, most of whom were Likud voters, got off to a very slow start and was the subject of much criticism, particularly on the part of the Israeli press.[12] Nevertheless, it had spot successes in certain neighborhoods. The consequences of these major steps remained to be played out during the second Likud government.

NOTES

1. Cf. Leonard J. Fein, *The Politics of Israel* (Boston: Little, Brown and Co., 1967); Nathan Yanai, *Party Leadership in Israel* (Philadelphia: Turtledove Publishing, 1981); Asher Arian, ed., *The Elections of Israel—1969* (Jerusalem: Jerusalem Academic Press, 1972); Asher Arian, ed., *The Elections in Israel—1977* (Jerusalem: Jerusalem Academic Press, 1980); S. N. Eisenstadt, *Israeli Society* (New York: Basic Books, 1968); Peter Medding, "A Framework for the Analysis of Power in Political Parties," *Political Studies*, 20 (1973), pp. 76–96; Ervin Brinbaum, *The Politics of Compromise* (Rutherford, N.J.: Fairleigh Dickinson Press, 1970); Walter Laqueur, *A History of Zionism* (London: Weidenfield and Nicolson, 1972); David Nachmias, "A Note on Coalition Payoffs in a Dominant Party System," *Political Studies*, 21 (1973), pp. 301–305; Amos Perlmutter, *Military and Politics in Israel* (New York: Praeger, 1969).

2. On this subject treated before the ascendancy of the Likud, see Amos Elon, *The Israelis: Founders and Sons* (New York: Holt, Rinehart and Winston, 1971).

3. On this point, see Daniel J. Elazar, "A New Look at the 'Two Israels,'" *Midstream*, vol. 24, no. 4 (April 1978), pp. 3–10.

4. Sephardic rage at this aspect of their position in Israel is given full expression by Sammy Smooha in *Israel: Pluralism and Conflict* (Berkeley: University of California Press, 1978).

5. Cf. Yohanan Peres, "Ethnic Relations in Israel," *American Journal of Sociology*, vol. 76, no. 6 (May 1971), pp. 1021–1047; and *Ethnic Identity and Inter-Ethnic Relations* (unpublished doctoral dissertation, Hebrew University, Jerusalem, 1968).

6. A good, if somewhat dated, discussion of the subject by one of the Labor establishment can be found in Shlomo Avineri, "Israel: Two Nations?" *Midstream*, vol. 18, no. 5 (May 1972), pp. 3–20.

7. See Shmuel Sandler, "The National Religious Party: Israel's Third Party," *Jerusalem Letter*, no. 24 (October 28, 1979).

8. For an examination of this phenomenon, see Eliezer Don-Yehiya, "Concept of Traditional Judaism in Zionist Socialism," *Kivunim*, no. 8 (Summer 1980), pp. 29–46 (Hebrew).

9. The most important study of this phenomenon to date is Charles S. Liebman and Eliezer Don-Yehiya, *The Civil Religion of Israel: Tradition, Judaism and Political Culture in the Jewish State* (Berkeley: University of California Press, forthcoming). The two authors also published the following articles drawn from their book: "Symbol System of Zionist Socialism: An Aspect of Israeli Civil Religion," *Modern Judaism*, vol. 1, no. 2 (September 1981), pp. 121–148; and "Zionist Ultra-Nationalism and Its Attitude Toward Religion," *Journal of Church and State*, vol. 23, no. 2 (1981), pp. 259–264. See also Daniel J. Elazar, "Toward a Jewish Vision of Statehood for Israel," *Judaism*, vol. 27, no. 2 (Spring 1975), pp. 233–244.

10. For more extensive treatment of this phenomenon, see Daniel J. Elazar, "Religion and Party Politics in the Begin Era," in Robert Freedman, ed., *Israel in the Begin Era* (New York: Praeger, forthcoming).

11. *Israel at the Polls: The Knesset Elections of 1977*, Howard R. Penniman, ed. (Washington, D.C.: American Enterprise Institute, 1979).

12. For examinations of Project Renewal, see Daniel J. Elazar, "Project Renewal: Drawing Sweet from Bitter," *Jerusalem Letter: Viewpoints*, no. 14 (February 23, 1982); "Paint and Paternalism," *The Jerusalem Post Magazine* (December 12, 1980), pp. 10–11; "Yavne is No Longer a Place to Run Away From," *Ma'ariv* (October 10, 1980), p. 19 (Hebrew); "Project Renewal: How to Get Moving Again," *Ha'aretz* (January 22, 1982) (Hebrew); Daniel J. Elazar and Janet Sherman, "Diaspora Community Representatives in Project Renewal: Their Roles and Importance," *Jerusalem Letter*, no. 44 (January 20, 1982); Daniel J. Elazar et al., *Porject Renewal: An Introduction to Issues and Actors* (Jerusalem: Center for Jewish Community Studies, 1980); Charles Hoffman, "The Musrar Connection," *The Jerusalem Post Magazine* (February 19, 1982), pp. 8–9; Moshe Hazani, "Self-Help or Imposed Beneficence? The Central Problem of Project Renewal," *Ma'ariv* (October 15, 1978) (Hebrew) and *Jerusalem Letter*, no. 15 (November 30, 1978) (English).

II

SELECTION OF CANDIDATES TO THE TENTH KNESSET
THE IMPACT OF CENTRALIZATION

Avraham Brichta

The legal provisions defining the process of the selection of candidates to the Knesset are of a limited nature. Minimal statutory limitations govern a party's internal affairs.[1] One legal regulation states that no changes are allowed in the lists of candidates after their submission to the Central Elections Committee and their publication in the *Official Gazette* thirty-five days before the election. The *Fundamental Law of the Knesset* also stipulates that when a member of the Knesset dies or resigns, his place is to be filled by the first unelected candidate on its preceding electoral list.[2]

Besides the very few public law provisions regulating the nomination process, the party constitutions and bylaws state only in very general terms the procedures regarding candidate selection.[3] Moreover, since the courts in Israel are reluctant to interfere in a party's internal affairs, the party bylaws and regulations may be changed or interpreted in many different ways, as we shall see in the discussion of the actual process of candidate selection.

The Phases of Candidate Selection

We have divided the process of candidate selection into two stages:

1. The screening stage, in which the selection committees (usually called nomination or ordering committees), or the national and regional organs of the various parties (such as the party center[4] or the district councils), interest groups, and factions, decide upon the al-

location of the safe seats on the central party lists and upon the rank order or placement of the candidates on the respective party lists. This is the crucial stage of candidate selection since the placement of a candidate on the list determines his chances for election. The nomination, as Benjamin Akzin points out, "is tantamount to recommendation . . . (nomination) does not, as a rule, ensure election, either in law or in fact."[5]

2. In the formal approval stage, existing parties and new parties must submit their lists of candidates to the Central Elections Committee. That committee checks whether the new lists have met the legal requirements by submitting a deposit of 20,000 Israeli shekels (equivalent to $1,000 in 1983) and 1,500 signatures of eligible voters supporting the list. It also requires the validation of candidate signatures on the lists of the parties represented in the outgoing (in this case, the Ninth) Knesset.

Until the elections to the Ninth Knesset in 1977, the rather remarkable stability of electoral support for the major parties enabled them to divide their lists of candidates quite accurately into safe positions, marginal positions, and "unreal" positions. Because the voter casts his ballot for the entire slate with no changes, the first part of the list consisted of safe seats, where placement of a candidate virtually ensured election. This situation changed drastically in 1977, when the Labor Alignment lost nineteen seats, the new Democratic Movement for Change won fifteen, and the Likud gained four. Once again, in the recent elections of 1981, a significant number of candidates in marginal positions were elected: fifteen candidates in places thirty-three to forty-seven on the Alignment list and five members of the Likud in places forty-four to forty-eight. Six candidates of the National Religious party (NRP) who had been assigned seats considered safe—seventh through twelfth—found themselves outside the Knesset when representation of the NRP in the Tenth Knesset was cut in half and only six members were elected.

The Nature of the Candidate Selection Process

Israel's list system of proportional representation, operating as it does within a single nationwide constituency, has a great impact upon the process of candidate selection to the Knesset. Holding the elections for a single constituency requires a centralized process of selection. The selection process therefore has always been carried out by the

central or national party organs. The body that ultimately decides on
the composition of the list of candidates has never been a local or a
district branch, but a nationwide party institution, a central nomination or ordering committee of the center of the party. Furthermore,
since the voter casts a ballot for a list of candidates and may not add or
eliminate names of candidates or change their rank order on the ballot, the whole process of candidate selection is concentrated in the
hands of a relatively small number of party and interest-group leaders
and functionaries. Political scientists analyzing the selection of candidates to the Knesset have usually described it as an extremely centralized, oligarchic, party-dominated, and group-oriented process.[6]
This conclusion coincides with Max Weber's observation that "within a
country-wide proportional list system only two types of nomination
systems and leadership patterns may evolve: *either a charismatic leadership backed by a party machine, or a nomination system based on manipulation
and bargaining by party politicians and functionaries."*[7]

Less oligarchic procedures were used for the selection of candidates
to the Tenth Knesset; the number of people involved in the process
was increased and more elective methods were used. Despite the new
procedures, the selection process has remained basically oligarchic.
This is mainly because the selection of candidates is distinctly a centralized process carried out by the central and national party organs.
Party interest groups, faction leaders, and functionaries maintain a
considerable degree of control.

We also suggest that the process of candidate selection is not only
group-oriented but to a large extent also faction-oriented. Recent
studies of the National Religious party have shown quite conclusively
that the selection patterns in the NRP are faction- rather than group-
oriented, with factions and personalities playing a major role in the
selection process.[8]

In analyzing the role of factions in the process of candidate selection, V. O. Key's definition seems most useful. Key defines a faction as
"any combination, clique or grouping of voters and political leaders
who unite at a particular time in support of a candidate. . . ."[9] Factions may, as Key points out, possess an impressive continuity or may
form only for the duration of one electoral campaign.[10] As in the Italian case described by Raphael Zariski, "to some degree and in some
political contexts . . . factions may be coextensive with political interest groups."[11]

We will use these definitions to show that a faction-oriented selection pattern prevails not only in the NRP but also to some extent in
the Labor party and to a large extent in the two major right-of-center

TABLE 2-1

Model of the Relations between the Electoral, Selection, and Representational Systems

Electoral System		Selection System		Representational System	
Modes of Classification	Major Properties	Modes of Classification	Major Properties	Modes of Classification	Major Properties
Type of ballot	List system	Number of participants and method of selection	Near oligarchical	Type of representatives	Professional politicians and functionaries
Magnitude of the district	Country-wide, single-district	Focus of selection	Centralistic	Level of responsiveness; nature of ties between representatives and those represented	Nonresponsive
Formula to allocate seats in Parliament	Proportional system	Basis of selection	Interest groups and factions	Basis of representation	Party dominant; group- and faction-oriented

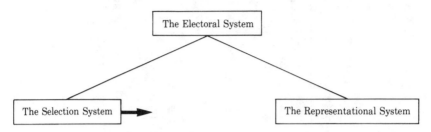

Figure 2-1. Direction of Relations between the Electoral, Selection, and Representational Systems

parties that compose the major components of the Likud bloc. While factionalism in the NRP has an institutional character, the factionalism in the Herut and Liberal parties is more personal and cliquish, and factionalism in the Labor party is presumably temporary, representing the present feud for party leadership.

The model we propose in table 2-1 describes the relations between the electoral system, the selection system, and the representational system within the framework of Israel's proportional electoral list system. In our view, the electoral system is the independent variable defining the nature of the process of candidate selection. Candidate selection, the intervening variable, in turn defines the nature of the representation system, the dependent variable. The direction of the relations between the electoral system, the selection system, and the representational system is shown in figure 2-1.

In order to test the model we will analyze the selection process of the five major parties: the Alignment of the Labor party and Mapam; the National Religious party; and the two major parties composing the Likud—the Herut and the Liberal parties. These five parties together obtained 101 of the 120 Knesset seats in the 1981 elections. We will sum up by explaining why the unique experiment of the Democratic Movement for Change (DMC), that is, the introduction of direct primaries for the first time in the political history of Israel, failed in 1977 and was not reintroduced or readopted by any other group or party, including the Shinui party (one of the founders and major components of the DMC), in the 1981 elections.

The Alignment: The Labor Party and Mapam

The Labor party and Mapam agreed that Mapam would be assigned seven of the first fifty places, considered to be safe seats, on the Alignment's list of candidates. Mapam's candidates were allocated these places on the list: five, ten, nineteen, twenty-five, thirty-three, forty, and forty-six.

Faction- and Group-Oriented Selection in the Labor Party
The rules adopted by the center of the Labor party for selecting the candidates to the Tenth Knesset stated that of the first sixty places on the Alignment list 50 percent be allocated to candidates selected by the district branches of the Labor party and the other 50 percent to candidates chosen by a selection committee elected by the party center. The chairman of the party would also be the chairman of the selection or ordering committee. The rules provided for proper representation of women, for representatives of an auxiliary with members under the age of thirty-five, and for an Arab member of the party. An important provision stated that the candidates who had served in the Knesset for more than two consecutive terms would have to obtain at least a 60 percent affirmative vote in the party center. The rules also stated that the central selection committee would decide upon the rank order of all the candidates and that the list as a whole would be approved and presented by the party center.[12]

According to the rules, a central selection committee was elected, consisting of five members: the chairman of the party (Shimon Peres) and three of his supporters, including the secretary general of the party, and Yitzhak Rabin. The actual power of selection, however, was handed over to a committee of nine, consisting of the leaders of the major party districts (for example, the Tel Aviv, Jerusalem, and Haifa district branches and the leaders of the moshav and kibbutz movements).[13]

Before the selection committee started its work, the center voted to decide the fate of the candidates who had served more than two consecutive terms and thus were required to obtain at least a 60 percent affirmative vote in the party center. This rule, known as the "principle of rotation," was adopted by the second party convention in order to rejuvenate the party's Knesset faction.[14] In the elections to the Ninth Knesset this rule caused the termination of the careers of some veteran senior party leaders and functionaries when, in a personal and secret ballot, the center denied the required 60 percent majority vote to seven of the nineteen candidates seeking renomination to the Knesset. In the elections to the Tenth Knesset, however, to preserve the unity of the party, the chairman of the party and the party leadership decided to ask the members of the center to approve en bloc the candidates seeking renomination. The members of the party center responded favorably and all ten candidates were approved by secret ballot with more than 60 percent of the vote.

The selection process in the Labor party was overshadowed by the intense feud between the faction led by Peres, who gained the support of about 70 percent of the members of the party's convention, and the faction led by Rabin, who was defeated in his bid for party leadership. Nevertheless, Rabin's faction, which obtained only about 30 percent of the vote, demanded the allocation of one-third of the safe seats on Labor's list. After a period of intensive negotiations and bickering between the representatives of the two factions, a compromise was reached that allocated Rabin's followers eleven places among the first fifty-five places on Labor's list (which was the equivalent of the first sixty-three places on the Alignment's list after including Mapam's candidates).[15]

In addition to the factional character of the selection process, the party returned to its traditional pattern of allocating the safe seats to representatives of the various interest groups affiliated with the party. The most striking feature of the process was the rather impressive representation of district branches. Among the first fifty places on the list, twenty were allocated to the representatives of the district branches, eleven to pseudo representatives of the Sephardic groups, seven to the kibbutz and moshav movements, six to women, and an additional number of seats to representatives of the new settlement towns.[16] In the elections to the Tenth Knesset, as in the previous elections, the Labor party kept firmly to its principle of presenting a well-balanced ticket that represented both the main factions and the interest groups.

Mapam
Mapam was allocated eight of the first sixty-three places on the Alignment's list of candidates. The candidates of Mapam were selected by the center of the party by secret ballot. Mapam continued with its group-oriented pattern of selection: four safe seats were allocated to the dominant group, consisting of representatives of the Mapam-affiliated Hakibbutz Haartzi movement, three to representatives of the major city branches, and one to a representative of the Arab sector.[17]

Institutionalized Faction-Oriented Selection
in the National Religious Party

The NRP is a conglomerate of factions. There are three main factions, of which the largest, Lamifne, is a moderately socialist and kibbutz-oriented faction led by Yosef Burg, who is also the leader of the party; the second largest is the Tzeirim (the Young Guard), led by Zevulun Hammer, presently the minister of education; the third largest is Likud V'tmura (Unity and Change), formerly led by Aharon Abu-Hatzeira. In addition there exist a number of smaller factions, such as the Central Faction, the factions of the kibbutz and moshav movements, and the women's auxiliary.

In the elections to the Tenth Knesset the institutionalized faction-oriented system suffered a serious blow as a result of a fierce struggle between two factions, the Tzeirim and the Lamifne. The Tzeirim attempted, without success, to oust the veteran leader of the party, Burg, in order to gain control of the leadership of the party. They also supported Rabbi Haim Druckman, an extreme hawk in political outlook, a keen supporter of the Gush Emunim, and one of the leaders of Bnei Akiva (a youth movement afiliated with the NRP). In attempting to gain the support of the followers of Gush Emunim (a radical group calling for Israeli sovereignty over Judea and Samaria) and of the "Greater Israel movement," the Tzeirim agreed to Druckman's demand to allocate an additional safe seat to a faction that he had established (Eitanim).[18] The executive council of the party decided by a vote of 138 to 116 to adopt the Tzeirim's proposal to assign a safe seat to a second member of Druckman's faction.[19] The positive response to Druckman's demands aroused bitter opposition, mainly among members of the Sephardim. They protested against the under-representation of Sephardic candidates on the party list, claiming that the "unity of the nation" is not less important than the "unity of the land" (the Greater Israel).[20] Finally it was agreed to add a Sephardic representative to the marginal twelfth place on the list.

The Sephardim in the party were not the only ones to be greatly disappointed with the composition of the list. The Likud V'tmura faction strongly protested the exclusion of one of their members from the list and the allocation of the seat to a member of Druckman's faction instead. This, with the very lukewarm party support for the faction's leader, Abu-Hatzeira, when he was standing trial on charges of alleged improprieties in the management of funds in the Ministry of Religious Affairs, led to his disenchantment with the leadership of the

NRP. He subsequently departed from the party and established a new ethnic party, Tami, which succeeded in electing three representatives to the Tenth Knesset.

The breakdown of the factional structure of the party may at least partly account for the serious defeat of the NRP in the 1981 elections. The representation of the NRP was cut from twelve members in the Ninth Knesset to six in the Tenth Knesset. Presumably many former party supporters among the Sephardim switched their support to Abu-Hatzeira's new party; others, with hawkish orientation, preferred to vote for the Likud or Tehiya despite the increase in the power of Druckman's new faction.

The Likud

The selection of candidates to the central Likud list was carried out separately by the three main components of the Likud: the Herut, the Liberal party, and La'am. A prior agreement between the three factions defined the divisions of safe seats in the order shown in table 2-2. The biggest faction, Herut, was allocated twenty-five safe seats, the Liberals were assigned eighteen, and La'am received four. One place number, forty-seven, was given to a former member of the Rafi party who refused to join Moshe Dayan's newly established list, Telem. The following paragraphs represent our analysis of the nature of the selection process in the two main components of the Likud—the Liberal and Herut parties.

Personal and Faction-Oriented Selection in the Liberal Party
The Liberal party may be classified as a cadre party,[21] since it lacks a large party membership. Nevertheless, over the years it has developed a small network of party branches, mainly in the large cities of Tel Aviv, Jerusalem, and Haifa, and is affiliated with some interest groups (such as the federation of industrialists, constructors, merchants, and private farmers) that, due to their socioeconomic and political orientation, traditionally supported the private-enterprise-oriented Liberal party.

The selection of candidates in the Liberal party was carried out predominantly by factions organized around the leaders of the party. In the elections to the Tenth Knesset the leaders of one faction were Avraham Sharir, formerly the secretary general of the party and the minister of tourism ater the 1981 election, and Gideon Pat, the minister of trade and industry also in the postelection cabinet. At the head of the second and larger faction stood Simcha Ehrlich, the party

TABLE 2-2

Allocation of Safe Seats among Three Main Components of the Likud

	Safe Seats
Herut	1, 3, 5, 7, 10, 12, 14, 16, 19, 20, 22, 24, 25, 27, 29, 30, 33, 34, 35, 39, 40, 41, 43, 45, 48
Liberal	2, 4, 6, 9, 11, 13, 15, 17, 21, 23, 28, 31, 32, 36, 38, 42, 44, 46
La'am	8, 18, 26, 37

chairman and deputy prime minister after the 1981 victory, and Yitzhak Moda'i and Moshe Nissim, both of whom then held leading positions in the party and served in the cabinet. The coalitions between leaders are quite fragile, however, and splits between them and their followers are quite common. Within the two main factions a number of safe seats were allocated to the representatives of the Sephardic groups, to the Private Farmers Union, to a representative of the Liberal party workers faction affiliated with the Histadrut, and to a representative of the women's auxiliary.

In an attempt to challenge the party leadership, the party's center decided to uphold a previous decision requiring members of the Knesset who have served for two consecutive terms to obtain a majority of at least 60 percent affirmative votes from the center of the party. The council also decided that the first candidate of the Liberal party (second on the Likud list) would be elected by a separate vote by the party center. No quota of safe seats would be allocated to representatives of the workers faction, and all candidates would be selected by the center in a secret and personal single ballot.[22]

In a special session the Liberal party center selected Simcha Ehrlich for the first place (second on the Likud list). Though challenged, Ehrlich, the party leader, won easily. Ehrlich received 72 percent of the vote while his challenger, the mayor of Ramat Gan, received only 28 percent. Then the center proceeded to vote for the seventeen candidates who would appear, together with Ehrlich, among the first fifty candidates on the Likud central list. The rank order of the candidates was decided according to the number of votes each of them received in the secret ballot taken by the center.

The vote taken by the 245 members of the party center resulted in the renomination of the party leaders. All of them received the required 60 percent of the center's vote. The vote in the center was also interpreted as the personal victory of Yitzhak Moda'i, whose faction obtained the largest number of safe seats.[23]

Herut

The Herut party may also be classified as a cadre party, lacking an elaborate network of branches or a significant number of dues-paying members. Lester Seligman has elsewhere stressed the populistic appeal of the party, namely, that the party does not appeal to specific organized groups as do the sectarian parties, nor does it aggregate a myriad of interests as do the pluralist parties.[24]

The struggle over the selection of candidates involves factions and personalities, mainly those historically affiliated with the prestate underground movements, the Etzel and Lehi, of whom most are also active members of the Tel Aviv district branch. Some of the candidates were supported by such leaders of the party as Yitzhak Shamir, David Levy, and Yoram Aridor, and in some cases by the undisputed leader of the party, Menachem Begin. A small number of candidates was selected by the Jerusalem and Haifa district branches and a few others were selected as representatives of the Sephardic groups.

A special session of the center of the party, comprising about nine hundred members, carried out the selection of candidates, in two phases. In the first stage members of the center, voting by secret ballot, selected a panel of thirty-five candidates, chosen from about seventy whose candidacy had been submitted to the party. Then the center selected the head of the list, Begin, who was selected unanimously in an open ballot. Finally the center decided upon the rank order of thirty-five candidates by a personal and secret vote in five separate ballots. In each round the seven candidates receiving the most votes were selected.[25]

The method of selection in the Herut, in effect since the elections to the Ninth Knesset, has proven to be a distinct improvement over the prevailing patterns of selecting candidates. It has conveyed real power of selection to the members of the center and at the same time introduced a method whereby a fairly balanced ticket could be formed. It has corrected the misrepresentation of any major faction in the process of selection, since the members of the center can consider their vote at each stage of the crucial balloting. When the head of the Jerusalem branch was not selected after the second ballot, the members of the center from Jerusalem threatened to boycott the election campaign; as a result of their protest the Jerusalem district branch candidate received the largest number of votes on the third ballot.

Why the Primaries Failed: The Democratic Movement
for Change in the 1977 Elections

The DMC was established a few months before the elections as a result of a merger between Shinui (Change) and several other groups under the leadership of Professor Yigael Yadin.[26] In the political sphere, one of the DMC's major demands was reform of the electoral system, a major change in the nomination procedures and in intraparty democracy. True to their commitment, the DMC introduced, for the first time in Israeli politics, the direct and closed primaries to elect its candidates to the Ninth Knesset. The leadership of the DMC had high hopes and attached great importance to the primaries. One of the founders of Shinui, writing in the party periodicals, expressed this sentiment:

> . . . the elections [primaries] in our movement ceased to be our own matter. What we are going to do in March 1977 [the date of the primaries] will be a matter closely watched and examined by the whole public. If we succeed, the new democratic system which we are promoting will succeed. If, God forbid, we fail, this will be also the failure of the idea [of a new intraparty democracy] and a victory of the [old] nomination-committee system.[27]

Amnon Rubinstein, a leader of the DMC, also pointed out that the success of the new primary system depended not only on selecting to the list able people capable of attracting great voting support, but that it was also important to obtain a "balanced ticket":

> It is important that our team [of candidates] will include people of various ethnic groups, men and women, young people and people from various regions of the country . . . we should prove that a "balanced ticket" can be achieved not only by nomination committees but also by direct primaries.[28]

The primary system in the DMC failed, however, to produce a balanced and representative list of candidates. No woman was elected to the first fifteen places on the DMC list of candidates. Only one representative from the Sephardic groups gained a seat, while two Druse candidates were elected. The leaders of the former Shinui movement—the progenitors of the DMC—elected only two candidates among the first ten, while the Free Center newcomers elected three.

The results of the primary caused great dismay in the DMC. There was even a demand to alter the outcome of the primary in order to achieve a more balanced ticket. This proposal was considered but rejected by the party's Secretariat.[29] On the other hand, the leaders of the old established parties rejoiced. The comments made by a member of the Labor Central Committee in a debate regarding Labor's own nomination procedures were typical:

> There is no such thing as a perfect democracy. We have seen what has come out of the "super-democracy" in the DMC. They have wound up with an unrepresentative list based on two elements, the Druse and the Ashkenazi.[30]

Why did the primary system in the DMC fail to produce, as its initiators hoped, both a *democratic* and a *representative* system? The answer is simple: Primary elections generally are not representative of the whole party, much less the whole electorate. Direct primaries offer great advantages to well-organized factions within the party, provided that the number of party members participating in the primary is small. This was exactly what happened. The case of the election of two Druse candidates provides an illustration of how the primary system worked and could be exploited by well-organized groups. It was quite easy to get the small number of votes needed for the twelfth place on the list from the Druse community, which still maintains extended-family (*hamula*) ties. It is interesting to note that the DMC received fewer votes from the Druse community in the elections to the Knesset than each of the Druse candidates obtained in the primaries.

Because the unrepresentativeness of primaries has been a rather widely discussed issue in the United States, it might have been foreseen by the leadership of the DMC.[31] In the Israeli case the problem is more acute because the failure of its initiators to achieve a balanced ticket contradicts the very nature of the Israeli group-oriented electoral system.

Thus the adherence of the DMC leaders to the idea of the primaries that resulted in an unbalanced ticket has, to a certain extent, discredited this theoretically most democratic of nomination systems in a country whose political culture still puts a great emphasis on the value of representativeness.

Conclusion

The selection process in the two major blocs, the Alignment and the Likud, and in the largest religious party, the NRP, remains basically oligarchic, despite an increase in the number of participants involved in the selection process. Before the elections to the Ninth Knesset, the nomination of ordering committees of the major parties were composed of ten to twenty members; in the elections to the Ninth and Tenth Knessets, they grew to several hundred members in the central organs of the major parties, voting by personal and secret ballot. Selection, even within the larger bodies using more elective methods, is carried out by party activists and functionaries who are loyal to the leaders of the party and to the major factions and interest groups which are thus open to control and manipulation. As Nathan Yanai observed: "Nomination by a secret ballot in a permanent party body is compatible with clique politics. . . . The secret ballot in a small and permanent party body is also open to considerable manipulation."[32] In the Labor party the democratic provision that would enable new candidates to enter the Knesset by requiring a 60 percent affirmative vote in the party center for candidates who have served for more than two consecutive terms in the Knesset was easily circumvented by the decision to vote for these candidates en bloc. The Tzeirim faction of the NRP had no great difficulty persuading the majority of the 254 members of the party's executive council to promote the candidacy of a member of Druckman's faction instead of the Likud V'tmura faction.[33] Similar methods have enabled the leaders of the factions in the Liberal party to overcome easily the 60 percent barrier required for renomination of those who have served two consecutive terms in the Knesset; they have enabled the leaders and functionaries of Herut to preserve safe seats for themselves on the list and to maintain a safe seat for the head of the Jerusalem branch.

In analyzing the oligarchial nature of the nomination process, we find Elazar's model of the three different types of oligarchy most useful.[34] Elazar classifies oligarchic political control as single-element, multiple-element, or representative oligarchy. In a single-element oligarchy, one group, such as businessmen or politicians, monopolize the decision-making process and the distribution of rewards. In a multiple-element oligarchy, a coalition comprises different elements, each of which has its own sources of power and can exercise maximum control only in conjunction with the other group or groups. In a representative oligarchy, representatives come from all, or nearly all, the different elements within a political system.

Two major properties relevant to our discussion characterize a representative oligarchy:

> A representative oligarchy is not polyarchic because it is not readily open to new interests seeking a share in its power.[35]

> Gaining representation in a representative oligarchy is more difficult than gaining representation in any polyarchic system, though access to members of the oligarchy is relatively easy. By ensuring at least indirect representation of the interests of the excluded elements until it is ready to co-opt their leaders, a representative oligarchy has a great staying power.[36]

In the Israeli context the single-element oligarchy is found only in the very small parties such as Shulamit Aloni's Ratz, Dayan's Telem, Rubinstein's Shinui, or in the monoethnic Tami, and distinctly ideological parties such as Rokach on the extreme left and the Tehiya on the extreme right. In these cases (not discussed here), the selection process is tantamount to self-selection of the leadership group.

The multi-element oligarchy prevails in Mapam (a predominantly two-element oligarchy consisting of the Kibbutz Artzi and the party professionals' urban sector); in the Mafdal (the NRP, a predominantly five-element oligarchy, consisting mainly of the Lamifne, Tzeirim, Likud V'tmura, and the kibbutz and moshav factions), and in the Liberal and Herut parties, the two major partners of the Likud, where the multiple oligarchy is based mainly on a number of personal, clique-type factions.

The Labor party closely resembles a type of representative oligarchy in which a large number of competitive elites, such as the party machine, the district branches, the kibbutz and moshav movements, women, and ethnic groups, are represented. Access to the members of the Labor party oligarchy is relatively easy, although the penetration of new groups is quite difficult. The Labor party oligarchy also demonstrates a great staying power.

From our data we conclude that candidate selection within Israel's framework of a proportional, single-district list system is an oligarchic process concentrated in the hands of the party, interest groups, faction leaders, and activists. Even the introduction of the secret ballot in the larger party bodies "left the mass membership of the party out of the process of nomination and *made the activists' group interest paramount.*"[37]

Candidates are not selected by the members of the party in the various districts or by direct primaries, nor are they directly responsible to the electorate of a constituency. Candidates are instead responsible to party and faction leaders and the interest groups they represent. Ties with the party membership and voters and responsiveness to their demands are virtually nonexistent. Group-oriented and institutionalized faction-oriented selection prevails in mass parties, with their elaborate party organization and large membership. A candidate selected by these parties articulates either the interests of a specific group, representing a sectarian party (for example, Mapam), or the interests of a number of groups, that is, a pluralist party (for example, the Labor party or the National Religious party).

On the other hand, a loose clique-type selection process prevails in the cadre parties. These populist parties, lack elaborate party organization and have a limited dues-paying membership. They have no specific group orientation, unlike Herut or other parties loosely connected with the rather heterogeneous interest groups active in the private sector. Because of the conflicting interests of the members, these groups do not represent a united front, as does the Liberal party.[38]

Some argue that true democratization of the candidate selection process would require the adoption of a direct primary system or the selection of candidates in each district by a nominating convention composed of members of the district party branches. This would involve the decentralization of the electoral and selection systems, either by territory (dividing the country into a large number of constituencies), or by allocating the safe seats to the various sectors within each party and then allowing their members to select their own candidates independently.

Democratization of the selection system would bestow greater influence on the most active segments of the electorate and on a larger number of party components (district branches or sectors).[39] Selection by district branches would also result in better representation of the Sephardic population. Since this population is, to a considerable extent, concentrated in a few areas (development towns, for example, or certain quarters of the big cities), it is reasonable to assume that a district-regional constituency system would increase Sephardic representation substantially and thus end the quite pronounced under-representation in the Knesset. Finally, in a more decentralized system, the diminishing influence of central nomination bodies and national party oligarchies and factions would probably also attract younger and independent candidates to run for office.

NOTES

1. In this regard, the situation in Israel is similar to that prevailing in most Western democracies. See Austin Ranney, "Candidate Selection," in David Butler, Howard R. Penniman, and Austin Ranney, eds., *Democracy at the Polls* (Washington and London: American Enterprise Institute, 1981), pp. 76–82.

2. "The Knesset Fundamental Laws 712–1957," *Laws of Jerusalem* (Jerusalem, 1957), p. 69, paragraph 43.

3. For a more elaborate treatment, see Avarham Brichta, "Gius Maumadim La Knesset: Haheibet Haformali" [The Nomination of Candidates to the Knesset: The Formal Aspect], *Netivei Irgun veminhal*, nos. 2–3 (July 1973).

4. The party center is the highest organ of the party and is roughly equivalent to the Republican or Democratic national committees. The centers of major Israeli parties are large bodies of several hundred members who have been elected by the party's national convention.

5. Benjamin Akzin, "Election and Appointment," *American Political Science Review*, no. 3 (September 1960), pp. 705–714.

6. See Benjamin Akzin, "Israel: The Knesset," in J. Meynoud, ed., *Decisions and Decision Makers in the Modern State* (Paris: UNESCO, 1967); Moshe M. Czudnowski, "Legislative Recruitment under Proportional Representation in Israel: A Model and a Case Study," *Midwest Journal of Political Science*, vol. 14 (May 1970); Avraham Brichta, "The Social and Political Characteristics of Members of the Seventh Knesset," in Asher Arian, ed., *The Elections in Israel—1969* (Jerusalem: Jerusalem Academic Press, 1972); Emanual Gutmann and Jacob Landau, "Political Elite and National Leadership in Israel," in George Lenczowski, ed., *Political Elites in the Middle East* (Washington, D.C.: American Enterprise Institute, 1975); Myron A. Aronoff, "The Power of Nominations in the Israel Labor Party," in Asher Arian, ed., *The Elections in Israel—1973* (Jerusalem: Jerusalem Academic Press, 1975); Efraim Torgovnik, "Israel: The Persistent Elite," in Frank Tauchau, ed., *Political Elites and Political Development in the Middle East* (New York: Shenkman, 1975). For a different interpretation, see: Steven A. Hoffman, "Candidate Selection in Israel's Parliament: The Realities of Change," *The Middle East Journal*, vol. 34, no. 3 (Summer 1980), and Giora Goldberg, "Democracy and Representation in Israeli Political Parties," in Asher Arian, ed., *The Elections in Israel–1977* (Jerusalem: Jerusalem Academic Press, 1980).

7. Max Weber, *Politics as a Profession* (Hebrew translation by Dr. Elizer Shmueli) (Tel Aviv: Schocken, 1961), p. 63 (emphasis added).

8. See Yael Yishai, "Factionalism in the National Religious Party: The Quiet Revolution," in Arian, ed., *Elections in Israel—1977*, pp. 57–75; Elizer Don-Yehija, "Yetzivut vetmurot Bemifleget Mahane: Hamafdal vemhapechat Hatzeirim" [Stability and Change in a Camp Party: The NRP and the Youth Revolution] *Medina, Mimshal ve-Yachasim BenLeumyim*, no. 14 (1979), pp. 25–53.

9. V. O. Key, Jr., *Southern Politics in State and Nation* (New York: Alfred A. Knopf, 1949), p. 16.

10. Ibid., p. 33.

11. Raphael Zariski, "Party Factions and Comparative Politics: Some Preliminary Observations," *Midwest Journal of Political Science*, vol. 4 (1960), p. 29.

12. *The Israeli Labor Party, the Procedures for Electing the Candidates to the Knesset* (Hebrew), presented to the Center on April 24, 1981.

13. See *Yediot Ahronot* (Hebrew evening daily), May 15, 1981.

14. *Minutes of the Second Labor Party Convention*, session 1, February 23, 1977, p. 38.

15. *Yediot Ahronot*, May 15, 1981.

16. M. Meisels, *Ma'ariv* (Hebrew evening daily), May 8, 1981.

17. For a detailed description of the selection process in Mapam see ibid.

18. *Ma'ariv*, May 11, 1981.

19. Ibid., May 12, 1981.

20. Ibid., May 12, 1981.

21. Maurice Duverger, *Political Parties* (London: Methuen & Co., 1967), vol. 1, chap. 2.

22. *Ma'ariv*, May 3, 1981; May 4, 1981; May 8, 1981.

23. Ibid., May 22, 1981.

24. Lester G. Seligman, *Leadership in a New Nation: Political Development in Israel* (New York: Atherton Press, 1964), chaps. 3 and 5.

25. See *Ma'ariv*, May 3, 1981; May 15, 1981; May 17, 1981; and May 21, 1981.

26. A well-known public figure, Yadin was a member of the Agranat Committee of Inquiry of the Yom Kippur War blunders and the second Chief of Staff of the Israeli Defense Forces.

27. *Kav Hadah* (New Line, monthly publication of the DMC), no. 13 (February 1977), p. 3.

28. Ibid.

29. For a brief description of the dispute, see A. Tirosh, "The Great Revolution in Israeli Politics," *Yadan Ma'ariv* (Ma'ariv Almanac), pp. 28–29.

30. *Minutes of the Central Committee of the Israeli Labor Party* (Hebrew), February 25, 1977, pp. 12–13.

31. See Austin Ranney, "Primary Representatives," *Midwest Journal of Political Science*, vol. 12 (May 1968), and idem, "Turnout and Representation in Presidential Primary Elections," *American Political Science Review*, vol. 66 (March 1972).

32. Nathan Yanai, *Party Leadership in Israel* (Ramat Gan and London: Turtledove Publishing, 1981), p. 37.

33. The actual vote was 138 votes supporting the Tzeirim proposals and 116 against (*Ma'ariv*, May 12, 1981).

34. Daniel J. Elazar, *Cities of the Prairie: The Metropolitan Frontier and American Politics* (New York: Basic Books, 1970), chap. 5, pp. 206–218.

35. Ibid., p. 210.

36. Ibid.

37. Yanai, *Party Leadership*, p. 37 (emphasis added).

38. Goldberg claims that "methodological weakness caused Lester Seligman to label the Liberal Party populist, despite its typical sectarian character. . . . Although the Liberal Party's Knesset members are the direct representatives of business. . . ." In Arian, ed., *The Elections in Israel—1977*, p. 116. Goldberg's argument has no methodological weakness. He simply states that the Liberal party Knesset members are the direct representatives of business without proving it. The members of the Liberal party in the Tenth Knesset are almost all party activists, however, and none of them was selected as a representative of a specific group by any of the official bodies of that group. Moreover, the representatives of the industrialists and merchants associations have often complained that the Labor government was promoting their interests better than the government of the Likud.

39. Goldberg claims that "changing the electoral system to a geographical basis is not a necessary condition for democratization. . . . Therefore the proposed change to a constituency system can increase the representation rate of geographical units—but there is no evidence that such a change can democratize the system or decrease the underrepresentation of women, orientals and the young generation." Goldberg is right! There is no such evidence because there has not been such a change. For Goldberg's argument see Arian, ed., *Elections in Israel—1977*, p. 115.

III

PARTY ORGANIZATION AND ELECTORAL POLITICS
THE LABOR ALIGNMENT

Efraim Torgovnik

The 1977 electoral loss of the Labor Alignment was the first since the establishment of the state in 1948. It was viewed by the party as a mishap that was likely to be corrected in the 1981 elections. This perception arose from an assessment that the Democratic Movement for Change (DMC), which was responsible for drawing many voters away from Labor in 1977, was unlikely to survive.[1] Changes in social structure, party identification of voters, and public response to the party and its leaders received little attention from the Alignment. These changes and the emerging cleavages they signified had wide-range consequences in the 1981 election campaign, when Labor regained many of the votes it had lost to the DMC in 1977 but not enough to enable it to return to power.

The 1981 election campaign has given rise to much speculation about the emergence of deep class and ethnic cleavages in Israel.[2] Analysts were surprised by the many votes for the Likud party from less affluent groups and by the large number of votes for Labor from more affluent voters. It was also a surprise that the majority of voters of African or Asian origin (easterners) voted Likud while the majority of those of American or European origin (westerners) voted Labor.[3]

These dimensions of the Israeli election of 1981 probably reflect various social changes and cleavages. They may also be viewed as expressions of political cleavages involving ephemeral policy and leadership.

Social scientists view structural cleavages as corresponding to class divisions. A political cleavage may or may not correspond to these

36

often cohesive divisions. Similarly, ethnic divisions need not correspond to class divisions. Political cleavages in Belgium and some aspects of American ethnic divisions are cases in point. A political cleavage is likely to transcend the structures emanating from class divisions.[4] An example may be the groups that arise from disagreement over a leader or leadership.

One aspect of this analysis deals with the question, Can expressions of social and political cleavages be identified within a political party?

Cleavages inside a political party are often reflected in factions organized on the basis of ideology or policy. They may draw their strength from a defined clientele inside or outside the political party. They retain their viability through a distinct organizational structure, and they maintain a state of conflict with competing groups within the party. Their main concern is the conflict over leadership of the party.[5] A proliferation of groups in a political party beyond established factions is likely to reflect increased cleavage and conflict and an inability to resolve conflict and reach consensus.[6]

It is not common to speak of class (or ethnic) politics within a political party. Neither is the expression of social divisions inside a party widely recorded. The reason is clear. Parties, especially mass parties with a fractionalized structure, attempt to emphasize consensus rather than division. People are more likely to be attracted to a mass party that advances common goals than to a party that openly conducts a struggle over group goals. Parties encourage the modification of behavior, and conflicts over group goals are channeled through factional politics and rules of conflict resolution. Efforts to hide divisions within parties from the public, however, do not negate their presence.

This analysis of Labor in the years 1977–1981 and its electoral campaign in 1981 is organized as follows: (1) the background of events and changes in Israel that affected the Alignment before and after the 1977 electoral defeat; (2) its organization after the 1977 defeat and the extent of social and political cleavages and their expression inside the party, especially conflicts between groups and the resolution of those conflicts; and (3) the organization of the 1981 campaign.

Background: Emerging Cleavages

For the nineteen years from the establishment of Israel in 1948 to 1967, Israelis were occupied with implementing Zionist goals: immigration, security, and nation building. While these goals were being proclaimed by the leaders of the Mapai Labor party, the party through its apparatus and support organizations mobilized the masses and provided an abundance of support for its leaders and the unchallenged goals.[7] Menachem Begin and his followers and the groups that preceded his leadership were outside the mainstream of consensus groups because of differences in ideology, style, and political tactics.[8] Furthermore, Begin was the victim of a deliberate and effective delegitimization campaign conducted by David Ben-Gurion. Begin's ideas of a greater Israel were considered odd at best after the establishment of the state and given the political consensus reached over the partition of Palestine into an Arab state and a Jewish state. In nation building and immigration Begin could add or say little, in view of the scores of new cities that were established by successive Labor governments and the growth of Israel's population, which more than doubled in the years 1948–1954 alone. Signs of division and disaffection, such as a violent ethnic riot in Haifa in the early 1950s, were relegated to the courts as criminal activities. Inside their party Prime Ministers Ben-Gurion, Levi Eshkol, and Golda Meir acted within the bounds of defined groups and the constraints of democracy, but they enjoyed a great deal of freedom of decision. The 1956 Sinai War campaign, for example, was engineered and planned almost single-handed by Ben-Gurion and subsequently received wide public support and acclaim.

In 1967 Israel fought the Six-Day War, which ushered in its greatest victory. Sinai and Gaza, the Golan Heights, and the West Bank came under Israeli control. These areas provided military buffer zones. They also provided a sense of security that had been absent. But this victory was also the harbinger of a series of political cleavages.

The Six-Day War eliminated the traditional concern for security; although the issue remained central, it was seen in altogether different dimensions. Before that war, Begin's idea of a greater Israel was generally ignored. The acquisition of the new territories was a challenge to the idea of the partition of Palestine, and it gave Begin and his party a new legitimacy. Although most Israelis viewed the acquired territories as a security buffer, their continuing control by Israel blurred the distinction between security concerns and Begin's nationalistic rationale for retaining the territories. The 1967 war also brought Begin into a national unity government, which overnight legitimized his link with major national and security issues.

At the outset of the Six-Day War, Moshe Dayan was made minister of defense at the demand of many people, including Begin, and as a result of populist pressures, including street demonstrations. This event had wide ramifications. It was the first major demonstration by the Labor leadership of inability to make decisions on key appointments, a crucial matter for a political party. Dayan's appointment signified a change in leadership. In 1965 he had headed a group of second-line Labor leaders in an attempt to delegitimize the traditional Labor leadership, but his efforts failed. Secession from Labor followed, and a competing party, Rafi, was established, which included Shimon Peres, Ben-Gurion, Dayan, Gad Ya'acobi, Yitzhak Navon, Chaim Herzog, and many others.[9] The populist movement that brought Dayan to power in 1967 and the changes in the Labor leadership that followed did not fail to alert people of varied socioeconomic status and ethnic origin to the possibilities of direct participation in decision making.

Uniting Labor Groups

In 1968 the Labor Alignment was formed. It included the little alignment of 1965, consisting of the former Mapai, identified with Eshkol, Meir, and Abba Eban, and Achdut Ha'avoda, whose leaders were Yigal Allon and Yisrael Galili; Rafi, headed by Peres, Dayan, and Ya'acobi; and Mapam, a leftist Labor party. Together they make up the Labor Alignment (Ma'arach).

Labor unity had always been an aspiration in the various Labor wings. It could not be achieved earlier, in the days when Labor groups actually commanded a majority in the Knesset[10] but were sharply divided ideologically. It became a reality, however, at a point of transition in Israel after the Six-Day War and the changes in Labor resulting from a reduction of the role of socialist ideology in the conduct of the state's affairs. It was a time when the country was already in full swing toward statism—a state approach to the provision of public services for all. In essence, this meant the slow disappearance of practices dating from the prestate period, when many public functions were provided by voluntary Mapai-dominated particularistic organizations, a practice that strengthened the Mapai and the Histadrut (General Federation of Labor).

The unity of Labor under the Alignment was most likely an effort to forestall the previously latent divisions that emerged in the wake of the military success of the 1967 war. The efforts to unite the parts of Labor that had previously cooperated to various degrees ignored the divisiveness introduced into the structure of the Labor Alignment. Each partner in the Alignment had a different view of what was to be

done with the newly acquired territories, and each group became institutionalized under the Alignment agreement, which for all practical purposes gave each a veto right in matters of policy. The party,
which in the past could rely on leadership to inspire consensus, faced
a brokerage leadership that had to give in to the parts to secure their
support for a course of action. Competing groups known as hawks
and doves cut across existing groups and factions, and emphasis could
only be put on current policy, not on long-range goals, ideology, or
political conceptions.[11] Labor unity allowed small fractions of the
party to define its major interests. Finally, Labor unity came in the
wake of new markets in the vast Arab territories, which ushered in
economic prosperity.

Taken together, these dimensions signified (1) a change in the
party's ability to act coherently; (2) a shift of emphasis from nation
building and domestic development to foreign relations; (3) a not altogether conscious change in the definition of Israel's role in the
Middle East; and (4) a de facto wider territorial definition of Israel,
beyond the international consensus that was the basis for Israel's establishment in 1948 as a state. Finally, continuing Arab intransigence
in refusing to recognize Israel accentuated the domestic behaviors
described. The effects of foreign policy on domestic policy were somewhat stronger than in the usual interaction of these two kinds of
policy.[12]

Reduction of Policy Differences

Labor's actual policies in the territories appeared more and more in
line with the Likud's preaching. As a matter of ritual Labor continued
to insist that ideological differences existed and that there were distinctive Labor policies. Various formulas that Labor advanced to explain itself were watered down by such actions as the establishment of
scores of settlements in the West Bank, the Gaza Strip, and Sinai.
There was an effort to explain these activities as reflecting a policy of
creating de facto security borders. A common formula differentiated
between historic Jewish rights to inhabit the West Bank and the understanding that political exigencies would eventually force withdrawal.
The Alignment, however, could not offer a new outlook or rationale
for the 1980s and could not let go of its old rhetoric.

Labor unity enabled different voters to view the party differently.
Those who wanted a tough policy in the territories and their retention
by Israel could identify, until 1977, with Dayan. The more moderate
voters could identify with Pinchas Sapir, then finance minister, or

with Eban. What Labor was not aware of was that differential identification would legitimize outside parties and the movement of voters outside the Labor camp. This became apparent in surveys that persistently showed public opinion moving to a more hawkish position.[13] Israel became progressively a country with a single political issue. Domestic issues, policies, and ideologies were not central. The Alignment had to seek its uniqueness in what was more clearly the domain of the Likud: the scope of the State of Israel.

Golda Meir, who led the Labor confederate structure, demanded and generated outward consensus, but she was apparently not able to generate new existential definitions of ideologies for the party. Labor became a catchall party.[14]

Succession under Pressure

In 1973 a major crisis beset Israel after the surprising military attack by Egypt and Syria. The October 1973 Yom Kippur War reverberated throughout the socioeconomic and political systems. Security buffer zones proved themselves, but the sense of security vanished. Israel's international position became more precarious than ever before. Economically the country entered an inflationary spiral. The Alignment showed an inability to replenish its leadership from within the party after the political unrest of 1973.

The 1973 war generated a deep credibility gap between the public and the Labor government leaders, and protest movements were formed by people who returned from the war. Key party figures such as Sapir and Yehoshua Rabinowitz, on whom Meir had always relied, openly disagreed with and disavowed the party's official stand on security and peace.[15] The Likud continued to grow and gained thirty-nine Knesset seats, up from twenty-six in the previous election.

Unrest and political divisions were shown in various ways: (1) The legitimacy of leaders was challenged. (2) The public questioned old notions of security policy. Israelis who were used to quick and relatively easy victories were shocked by the 1973 war, which was prolonged along borders considered to be the ultimate in defense. (3) The social gap between rich and poor became very salient. One expression of this was an electoral gain in the Histadrut of the militant Black Panther groups. Generally the cleavage between the haves and the have-nots was linked to ethnic divisions. It became a pertinent issue that people of Asian or African origin were generally the poorest.

Yitzhak Rabin was chosen by the Labor party as candidate for prime minister in the wake of the social and party divisions. He was an outsider, the candidate of what remained of the party machine headed by Sapir and Rabinowitz, and he replaced Meir, who had resigned under popular pressure. Rabin lacked the authority of previous leaders, however, and his knowledge of party politics was small. He lacked experience in government, and many felt free to compete—a practice unheard of in Labor politics.

Rabin's candidacy was intended to (1) ward off public criticism, (2) establish a new consensus in the party, (3) signify the party's openness to change, and (4) prove the old guard's ability to control the appointment of leaders. The party machine was actually engaged in warding off the onslaught of Peres for the party leadership. Peres correctly assessed the growing weakness of the machine.[16]

The government of Rabin, the first Israeli-born prime minister, was plagued by the post-1973 war inflation, and he was not what his political mentors had expected. He did not provide the expected youthful leadership; neither could a machine appointee by a symbol of change. Indeed, the party under Rabin failed to forestall the delegitimization of the Alignment especially for a great many people of high socioeconomic status, who in 1977 provided the DMC with fifteen Knesset seats.

Rabin's military background was, of course, important during this period. But his lack of party experience prevented him from gaining support, and the machine that appointed him could not provide it for him. The fractionalized Alignment moved toward a confederate structure even in the government. Allon, as foreign minister, and Peres, as defense minister, along with Rabin constituted a troika in policy, but they did not provide coherence.[17] A leader who does not enjoy the full authority that would result from agreement on his rule seems to encourage strong factional and group struggle.

As the 1977 elections approached, Labor faced the delayed public reaction to the 1973 war and the vigorous DMC, which mobilized former supporters of the previously dominant Alignment, including members of the business and military establishments and the Labor political elite. Rabin's government was plagued by a series of mishaps, which included instances of corruption, the suicide of a government minister, the leaking of party secrets about the modes of election financing, and eventually the implication of Rabin himself in a criminal court case involving his wife's illegal possession of foreign currency. Rabin resigned immediately before the elections, and Peres headed the Labor slate, which was relegated to being the opposition after nearly thirty years at the helm.

Given all these factors, one could hardly agree with the Labor assessment of the 1977 elections as a mishap due to the DMC's success. The Alignment presented itself as a troubled organization, having a weak ideological base and lacking a coherent structure able to mobilize support.

From Defeat to Defeat: 1977–1981

Two major struggles over legitimacy occurred between the 1977 and the 1981 national elections. One was the effort of Begin and his Likud goverment to become entrenched in Israeli politics, the other the numerous and relentless attempts by Peres to gain legitimacy inside the Labor party.

On the evening of May 17, 1977, the two major parties awaited the election results. Spirits in Labor party headquarters began to fall as soon as the television announced the results of its survey conducted near the polls. As the elections results came in and confirmed the television survey, a group of first- and second-line Labor leaders loudly lamented the fate of hundreds of directorships in public companies. The Likud, they argued, would become entrenched in government through appointments. These seemingly trivial concerns at a historic moment for Labor indicated what was already well known: Labor had become to a great extent a party of machine politics with the power to provide material rewards, which increased its support from the economic and social establishment. Labor's political success was interwoven with economics. That is how it had kept many loyalists and mobilized numerous followers. But in the 1977 elections it did not succeed in this most rudimentary of political acts. Its branches did not function with a momentum that would maintain its dominance, and its network of economic enterprises did not prevent its abandonment by followers and voters. In this sense, it was a party that could not mobilize resources, and, according to Giovanni Sartori, such a party is not likely to win.[18]

The Legitimacy of Leaders

After the 1977 defeat Peres was left with a huge party campaign debt and scores of wage earners in the Labor party headquarters. He was free, however, to reorganize the party and reestablish its ruling institutions. He became the only spokesman for the party, as he led Labor's thirty-two Knesset members into the new and unfamiliar role of opposition.

Peres did not establish a new party. Neither did he too much favor his former Rafi followers. He wanted the old kind of Labor party but under his leadership. This ambition exacted a heavy price. He had to spend nearly four years in a bitter battle for legitimacy and in an effort to achieve consensus on his candidacy. He had won a personal victory by becoming the party's candidate for prime minister, but he never achieved consensus on his candidacy. There are many interpretations of this. The political explanation is that Peres was never forgiven for his part in the 1965 secession from Labor and the formation of Rafi. His action then in liaison with Dayan and Ben-Gurion was a blow from which the Labor party never recovered. The challenge to the party at that time was over succession, among other things, and over the ability of younger party activists to penetrate party positions without bending to the party machine. Political machines cannot tolerate such things. Peres became the candidate without the aid of the machine, and its remnants could not aid him because they no longer controlled the party. After 1977 competition for leadership became public and at the mercy of factions and groups.

The struggle for leadership before the 1981 election campaign involved formidable forces, among the most active being the kibbutz movements, Ichud Hakvutzot Vehakibbutzim and Kibbutz Hameuchad. These groups had longstanding privileges in Labor. Their collective mode of life and their preference for the public interest over the private gave them a unique place in the party. The kibbutzim were also strengthened by their long existence as a symbol of the pioneering spirit in the settlement of Israel. In recent years, however, the kibbutzim have had little influence in the country. Settlement pioneering has become the domain of other groups, such as the extreme Gush Emunin, which settle the territories. In the party political arena, however, the kibbutz groups struggle like any others for their share of positions and influence in the Labor party and the Histadrut. The high prestige they enjoy inside the Alignment is merely a resource in their political struggle. Throughout the existence of kibbutzim as an impressive social experiment, they have understood the value of the link between power and their unique representation of societal norms.

In the eyes of the kibbutz movements, Peres was bred on city politics. Before his 1981 bid for leadership, he had never depended on a kibbutz movement for promotion or advancement. It was sufficient then that he was one of Ben-Gurion's lieutenants. Now Peres needed and wanted their support, however, and even their affection. That support could have given him the legitimacy that only the kibbutzim can bestow on a Labor leader in Israel. Finally, it should be noted that the kibbutz movement is very successful economically. This rather embarrassing economic success of the collectivist movements generated many internal pressures and tensions. But for the forthcoming elections of 1981 it was clear to Peres that these movements were likely to help the party with its heavy debts and provide resources for the campaign.

The Ichud kibbutz movement did not directly compete with Peres. Its leader, Moshe Harif, supported Peres against the wishes of part of the movement. His strategy was to head an alliance of important party figures who would impose their will on Peres. Being linked to the historic Mapai, Harif became the head of this coalition. His ambition was to unite the two kibbutz movements. This put him in competition with Yigal Allon, the leader offered as an alternative to Peres by the Achdut Ha'avoda faction, which is dominated by the Kibbutz Hameuchad movement. In his support for Peres, Harif could hope for the defeat of Allon, which would prevent him from combating Harif's ambition to lead the kibbutzim. Allon's death placed Harif squarely in the Peres camp and at the head of a unified kibbutz movement.

With Allon's sudden death, the Kibbutz Hameuchad movement and the Achdut Ha'avoda faction found themselves suddenly without a leader capable of competing with Peres, and they hastened to support Rabin as their candidate for party leadership. His dislike of Peres was by then known and growing daily. It was a personal feud, with roots, according to one observer, in 1962, when Peres was deputy defense minister and Rabin deputy army chief of staff.[19] Its political roots were in 1974, when Peres challenged Labor's political machine and its candidate for prime minister, Rabin, and thus prevented Rabin from gaining a united party stand on his candidacy. Rabin never became the leader of the kibbutz movements or of the Achdut Ha'avoda. He was their choice for the political arena. For a former prime minister to be the second choice of a faction is perhaps the clearest testimony to the fact that Labor had been overcome by factions. It signified Rabin's lack of a political base. He was described, however, by the Allon faction as the bearer of the Allon heritage. Immediately after the 1981 elections, however, there were signs that Rabin was taking an independent course of action somewhat different from the stand of the kibbutzim.

Rabin's challenge to Peres was unsuccessful, but it left its ugly mark on the Labor party. Rabin fought Peres in party forums and in a smear campaign in the press. Front groups published daily smears about Peres, said to be financed by the kibbutz movement. In August 1979 Rabin published a book of memoirs in which he described Peres and his period in the Defense Ministry in the most derogatory terms. The Likud made much use of this book in the 1981 election campaign.

The feud between Rabin and Peres cut across the traditional party factions and groups. Being mainly a struggle for dominance and party leadership, with few programmatic elements, the feud legitimized further party factions. Before the final confrontation between Rabin and Peres, new groups were formed, each hoping to be able to tip the scales of decision in favor of the winner and receive credit for doing so. Yachdav was led by the Tel Aviv branch of Labor and the Beit Berel group was led by the party secretary of the Jerusalem Alignment. The two branches had cooperated before the establishment of these two groups, and they showed many gains; for example, party districts were allocated more representation in ruling institutions and in the party Knesset slate.[20] Yachdav became the backbone of the Peres party campaign. Many of its figures were advanced to important party positions. The Beit Berel group leaned in part toward Rabin but essentially attempted to become a group that would force Peres to accept various dictates. Its main efforts focused on the appointment of Ya'acov Levinson, head of the Workers' Bank, as finance minister. Through him the group hoped for major influence in the party. This was a promising strategy, and the Beit Berel coalition briefly included Harif of the kibbutz movement. The coalition was strong, especially because it crossed factional lines. But it was weakened once Allon challenged the leadership of Peres. The coalition could not last while Allon, a kibbutz leader, was opposed by Harif, who supported Peres.

Finally, Yachdav and Beit Berel demonstrate the group basis of the Alignment. Their major preoccupation was coalition building. Yachdav opted for new people, argued for more direct election to office, and championed the cause of the periphery, the development of towns, and indirectly the ethnic part (easterners) of the party. Beit Berel relied heavily on the more established wing of the party: the kibbutz movement and previous Labor government officeholders.

By the time the Labor party convention was held, on December 17–18, 1980 Peres's hard work had paid off: 70 percent voted for him and 30 percent for Rabin. In two previous Rabin-Peres confrontations, in 1974 and 1977, Peres had lost by forty-four and forty-one votes. Rabin's followers argued in 1980 that he had received the support of 30 percent, and indeed they were right. Peres's victory only meant that future spoils and party positions would be divided on a 70/30 basis. Peres's huge vote was reduced to a formula to determine the division of power and spoils. Peres did not become the agreed leader of the whole party, and his victory was not viewed as a determining decision of the Alignment. Instead, the factionalism of the party was strengthened.

The important consequences of the Rabin/Peres feud were that the Alignment went to the elections with a candidate for whom there was no full party consensus and whose credibility was challenged by a former prime minister, Rabin, and that the new cleavage positioned the party around two camps, named after Peres and Rabin. The true societal tensions involving age, ethnicity, and religion did not receive much attention from the party.

Conflict Resolution

Clearly the mode of conflict and its resolution were not what they had been in Labor. Neither was succession handled as in the past. Labor's election loss in 1977 appeared to have set the party into a pattern of increasing conflict. The party lacked the cohesiveness of purpose it had exhibited when in power. The lack of an authority-wielding party machine became apparent and led to open public competition; rival groups emerged, each seeking supporters and coalitions.

Many social divisions penetrated the party, of which ethnic assertion was perhaps the strongest. It is estimated that nearly 50 percent of the Labor Central Committee consisted of people of Asian or African origin. Similarly, the religious/secular conflict was present in the background, and the divisions of old-timers and new immigrants became salient when people of the development towns attacked the kibutzim for their wealth and overrepresentation in the party and their paternalism toward the new development towns.[21]

The Labor party thus entered the campaign with disadvantages. It was clear to the public that internal opposition to Peres had not disappeared, in spite of the 70/30 formula for division of spoils between Peres and Rabin. And social and ethnic cleavages had found their way into the party.

Labor chose an old way to placate ethnic demands. It allocated more places on its Knesset slate to candidates identified with certain ethnic groups. But in 1981 this was hardly convincing. The issue was important because in 1977 nearly one-half of the voters of African and Asian background had voted Likud. The Likud had attracted their votes with only seven African and Asian candidates on its Knesset slate (among them the popular David Levy, the construction worker who became one of the Likud's great assets), but they were considered more representative of the grass roots than those on the Labor slate.

The Campaign

As long as there are elections, parties will continue to struggle with the question whether to raise issues that are popular at the expense of issues that have little saliency but reflect a party's principles. Issues that a party stresses in its election campaign are usually a reflection of the popular and the desired. As I have shown elsewhere, however, issues also reflect resolution of intraparty conflicts.[22] An election issue may also be a manipulative device.[23] The important thing to note about a party's campaign policy is that it is often far from consistent with the desire to win. Research on electoral campaigns deals with the types of issues used by a party and the styles of appeal that it adopts, an approach that captures the strategy of the party during the campaign.

In discussing the Labor campaign, it is important to note that an Israeli factionally based party is not free to adopt just any kind of campaign. The factions of the party, for example, may insist that their policy position be heard and seen during the campaign. A different influence is exerted by those who administer the campaign. The Alignment faced a number of social and political situations that affected its campaign. I briefly note these and then proceed to analyze the campaign organization, the issues, and the confrontation with the Likud.

The Campaign and Social Change

Given the fractionalized base of the party, the mutual dependence of its parts, and the inherent veto power of its components, the Labor organization and ideological structures proved unable to respond to the social and political changes that have occurred in Israel since the 1967 and 1973 wars. Among these changes were the following:

Public opinion moved to the right and became more hawkish. In 1973, 31.4 percent of the public said that they would refuse to return any part of the Arab territories captured in the 1967 war. In

1981 that proportion rose to nearly 51 percent.[24] About 40 percent said they would return only a small part of the territories. In all elections since 1969 fewer Israelis have wanted to return all the territories. In 1969 some 17 percent classified themselves as right wing; in 1977 that proportion rose to 25 percent. More people identified themselves with the center and fewer with the left during these years. In 1981 the Likud was viewed more as a hawk's party than was Labor: 32 percent said the Likud was hawkish, and only 8 percent said the same of Labor. But 31 percent considered Labor dovish.[25] Given the public's own hawkish tendency, the perception of the Alignment as dovish was not encouraging to its campaign managers, who were not free to emulate the Likud's hard-line stand.

The demographic changes that took place did not help Labor. The young voters were clearly more hawkish, probably in great part because of their continual exposure to wars with Arab states. Table 3–1 shows the vote in the past four elections by age group.

The ethnic vote had also swung against the Alignment (see table 3–2).

Labor suffered from negative public perceptions, most likely attributable to its many years in power and its continuous dominance of the Histadrut. Labor leaders reported repeated reference to them as if the Alignment were still in power.[26] Table 3–3 gives some indication of the negative images, which were certainly not an asset during the campaign. The table compares the ideal image of a party among the voters with their image of each of the major parties.

TABLE 3-1

Vote for Labor Alignment and Likud, by Age Group, 1969–1981
(Percent)

	Labor Alignment				Likud			
Age	1969	1973	1977	1981	1969	1973	1977	1981
Under 25	40	39	20	21	36	44	51	47
25–39	54	37	25	32	30	44	34	37
40–49	61	48	38	30	25	35	29	45
50 and over	62	54	53	40	21	23	23	30

SOURCES: Public opinion surveys May–June 1981. Thanks are due to Professor Asher Arian for making data available. For comparative data see Asher Arian, *Elections in Israel*, 1973, 1977, and Central Bureau of Statistics, *Election Results*, Jerusalem.

TABLE 3-2

Vote for Labor Alignment and Likud, by Place of Origin, 1969–1981
(Percent)

	Labor Alignment				Likud			
Origin	1969	1973	1977	1981	1969	1973	1977	1981
Asia/Africa	51	32	21	23	32	43	37	36
Europe/United States	61	47	68	38	20	20	21	18
Israel	55	21	10	40	26	37	9	47

SOURCE: See Table 3–1.

TABLE 3-3

Party Image: Ideal versus Labor Alignment and Likud, 1981

Party Image	Ideal	Labor Alignment	Likud
Right/left	55/13	28/40	77/7
Innovative/outdated	61/15	26/48	31/42
Young/old	52/10	17/51	28/35
Eastern/Western	11/11	6/47	18/25
Experienced/inexperienced	86/4	79/4	38/45
Looks after the people/			
looks after itself	89/3	43/37	31/45
Honest/corrupt	90/0	35/39	57/18

SOURCE: See table 3–1. This table is based on responses to a survey of voters on a seven-point semantic differentiation scale by the Bureau of Applied Social Research during March–April 1981.

These developments, changes, and images came about in an evolutionary fashion. Most important, they occurred within a stable and nonviolent political system. The 1981 election campaign was not the opportunity to face major issues; for example, the old identification of eastern voters with Labor as a party that established Israel had changed. Left/right perceptions had changed in the past two decades. The wars had given rise to a new set of symbols and political beliefs. People viewed the political party system in different ways, without the consensus that had previously existed. The 1981 elections confronted Labor with a Likud that had succeeded in legitimizing itself as a competitor. This was probably the most significant change in Israeli politics, because until 1977 no party except Labor was able to form a government. Since 1977 this has changed. The literature refers to this as a loss of dominance, which, of course, involves changes in psychological as well as political attitudes.[27] Labor was not fully alert to all of this. Many features of its campaign indicated that Labor had assumed that its past psychological dominance had not withered.

The Likud was legitimized by a series of events: (1) It formed a government in 1977. (2) Begin and the Likud brought a peace treaty with Egypt to Israel after thirty years of war. (3) Leaders such as Dayan and Ezer Weizman gave the Likud credibility and respectability. (4) In social welfare policy the Likud spoke popular capitalist rhetoric and continued old Labor welfare-state policies. It even surpassed Labor in social legislation and passed a special law of income guarantee and a disablement law.[28] It also provided for high school education. (5) Attempts at structural changes in the economic domain that were undertaken by the first and second ministers of finance of the liberal wing were put down by Begin's populist Herut. The new Likud policy provided inflation and the best of two worlds: the high government expenditure led to expanded social programs and higher standards of living. (6) The Likud showed flexibility. On the one hand, it created an atmostphere of continuity by retaining most personnel of previous Labor governments. On the other hand, it appointed three successive ministers of finance in its search for an economic policy.

In the campaign of 1981 the repeated message "We are on the right path" summarized the Likud's search for legitimacy. It also offered a subtle hint of the many benefits provided by the Likud's "election economics" and hence tended to establish the priorities among issues for the voters. Most important, the election economics signified the dominance of the Herut group in the Likud under the leadership of its Labor Federation wing, headed by Levy and Finance Minister Yoram Aridor. Aridor's appointment did away with all traces of the less directed economics associated with his predecessors, Simcha Ehrlich and Yigal Hurvitz.

It was against this background of events and changes that the Alignment undertook its 1981 campaign. Not all indicators were unfavorable for it. Early surveys indicated that in December 1980, six months before the elections, only 25 percent of the public was satisfied with Begin. In May 1980 the Likud would have have won only twenty-six Knesset seats and Labor sixty seats.[29] This was when Weizman noisily resigned from his post as minister of defense and before Aridor's election economics replaced Hurvitz's economic recovery policy.

Strategies of the Labor Campaign

One major campaign strategy of Labor was an attempt to reestablish itself in the minds of the voters in its past image as psychologically dominant: a united, responsible, mainstream party. This underlying approach or attitude was salient throughout the campaign and proved ineffective, especially in light of concrete events. The Rabin/Peres feud and the city/kibbutz conflict were public and could not be hidden. During the last week of the campaign the party, under pressure from unfavorable polls, announced that Rabin would be defense minister at the expense of Haim Bar-Lev, who had been assigned to this post. To change horses in midrace is not what campaign strategists would advocate. The effect of this move on the voters will never be known. The change made it clear, however, that the campaign managers believed their support to project a united, solid party did not carry much weight with the public.

The second major strategy of the Alignment campaign was an effort to discredit Begin and his Likud party as a passing episode. This attempt to delegitimize Begin and the Likud was not very effective. Begin was the unchallenged leader of a ruling party, while the Labor candidate was in the opposition and was challenged from within his own party in the most public, venomous, and hateful manner.

Begin's leadership had been legitimized in nearly four years at the helm because he was linked to the peace treaty with Egypt under the Camp David Accords. After Camp David, the Likud became sufficiently entrenched that it could even absorb with little damage the resignation of two of its stars, Dayan and Weizman. The legitimacy the Likud had gained in its first two years in power was strongly aided by Dayan's withdrawal from Labor and his entrance into the Likud government. It appears that the Alignment misread many of the public surveys, which showed dislike of the Likud government and led Labor to believe that the delegitimization process would be easy. What was forgotten was that a party in power has many ways to manipulate public opinion. The following are examples:

As the campaign of 1981 approached, Yoram Aridor was appointed the Likud's minister of finance. He reasoned that inflation has psychological features and that lowering prices by edict might induce actual price reductions. The closeness of the elections made this policy of planned incongruity suspect as a manipulative election policy. It involved massive reductions in taxes on heavily taxed consumption items, such as television sets. Furthermore, it included a generous short-term government savings scheme, which began to affect the cost-of-living index. The Alignment referred to all this on television and in the press, in leaflets, and at public meetings as "election bribes" and election "miseconomics."[30]

At the height of the campaign, President Anwar Sadat of Egypt flew in for a summit meeting with Begin. It was not clear why this meeting was held during the election campaign, but clearly it helped the Likud.

Labor was left aghast in the middle of the campaign by the precision air attack launched on the Iraqi nuclear plant by Israel. The raid took place three days after Sadat's visit, giving rise to speculation about collusion between Israel and Egypt, which of course helped the Likud. The justifiable pride Israelis felt in their air force would have remained differentiated from the Likud government. But Labor also criticized the raid, and this cost it many votes.[31]

These situations showed that the Likud, after only four years in government, had learned to use its governmental power to increase its party power through electoral politics. National policy became a campaign issue. Usually campaign debates over specific policies are not attractive to the voters. What the Likud did was not to debate policy but to make and execute it. It left to the Alignment arguments over the correctness of the policy. It is very likely that when three popular policy acts of the Likud government were compared by the voters with the rhetoric against them advanced by Labor, the former came out ahead.

Specific policy stands and arguments have little chance in campaigns against general symbolic arguments or acts. This has been widely noted in research on election campaigns.[32] Examples of the national symbol-evoking campaign are numerous; Begin apparently understood the importance of symbolic rhetoric. In justifying the raid on Iraq, he argued publicly with the U.S. secretary of defense and reminded him of the million and a half children killed in the Holocaust. Peres and Herzog, head of information for Labor, were accused of aiding, by their criticism of the Iraqi raid, those in the United States who placed an embargo in Israel. In short, Begin made the Alignment look unpatriotic. Indeed, in one of his last public appearances, Begin urged the crowds to reduce the Alignment to twenty-eight seats in the Knesset so that they might learn how to be a loyal opposition for the people of Israel.

Campaign Organization

The Labor campaign organization reflected the party's many divisions and groups, which had previously asserted themselves during the Rabin/Peres feud. The confederative structure made discussion of campaign strategy virtually impossible. For example, followers of Rabin at campaign headquarters constantly complained about his lack of exposure on the party's television presentations. The relatively little time allotted to each party on public television was competed for by the major factions, groups, and campaign organizational subdivisions. One result of this competition was a bureaucratic takeover, which prevented complete paralysis. Few of the leaders appeared on television; the director of information of the campaign filled most of the time. As the campaign progressed, Moshe Harif, the kibbutz leader, became the czar of Labor television, and his strong hand was apparent. It is alleged that he acquired his position because of a threat by his group to withdraw kibbutz resources from the campaign. This could not be verified, but he received his appointment at the height of the campaign, and kibbutz manpower subsequently became very visible in the branches.[33] Clearly, a victory for the Alignment would have been credited to Harif and the kibbutz movement, which also had one of its people as deputy campaign manager, the second most important post in the campaign organization. It appears that the competition among Labor's divisions and groups found expression in the campaign management and even in very technical divisions of campaign work. This fierce competition was a result of the feeling of impending victory.

The push-and-pull atmosphere was heightened by the fact that the campaign organization was separate from the regular party apparatus—a bureaucracy that replicated the party's regulars and its field network and competed with them. This arrangement was perhaps necessary given the various party groups and the impressive array of personalities who rallied to the Alignment's "return to responsibility" slogan. As impressive as this array of people was, they were not the rank and file of Labor, and their ascension to key posts in the campaign indicated to the regulars that in case of victory the spoils were not likely to go in their direction. Thus their incentive to work hard was greatly affected.

Major Campaign Issues

The major foreign policy issues involved two levels of discussion: the general and the specific. The broader issue was Labor's conception of

Israel as a small state, of which the immediate electoral implications were the many arguments against the Likud's conception of a greater Israel. This was actually an old debate between Labor and Begin and his people. The Alignment's effort to make the issue salient during the 1981 elections was consistent with its general leaning on its past to win the hearts of the voters in the present and control the government in the future. The campaign against the Likud's idea of a greater Israel constituted Labor's major ideological stand. It was the vehicle for Labor's differentiation with the Likud and its definition of Israel as a relatively large power in the Middle East. But the Alignment's arguments against the Likud's alleged extremism were brought forth at a time when Begin had agreed to return all of Sinai to Egypt and had had public confrontations with hard-liners formerly of his own party, such as Geula Cohen, which modified his image.[34]

Ideological statements were supplemented by a debate over specific policies. Labor attempted to show that the Likud's plan for administrative but not political autonomy in the West Bank was not likely to succeed, and engaged in very detailed arguments dealing with the agreements involved. Labor had one general idea with which to excite the public: the Jordanian option, Labor's proposal to solve the West Bank problem by waiving sovereignty to Jordan. But this issue lacked sufficient force vis-à-vis the Likud's autonomy plan, which would retain Israeli sovereignty and was a part of the then popular peace plan.

The Alignment's efforts to challenge specifics of the Likud's autonomy plan, especially arguments that it would lead to a Palestinian state, were not credible. It is, of course, possible that Begin's autonomy plan will lead to a Palestinian state. But this outcome was too hypothetical and too threatening to make sense during the election campaign. Begin and the Likud are not viewed by the Israeli public as friends of the Palestinians. Their long dedication to what Labor calls the greater Israel gave them credibility on the Palestinian issue and therefore paradoxically provided them with a flexibility in policy that the Alignment lacked. Labor had laid a trap for itself in the issue of autonomy. It had to outdo the Likud and take a tough policy stand, which could easily be interpreted as hawkish. It thus exposed itself to accusations by its own followers of being too much like the Likud. A campaign on specific policy positions appears unlikely to be effective against a ruling government.

A major effort of the Labor campaign was a comparison of the leaders of Labor with those of the Likud. The Alignment published huge advertisements featuring pictures of its leaders next to Likud leaders and asked who was more fit to be, for example, minister of defense,

Ariel Sharon of the Likud or Haim Bar-Lev of Labor. This, like other features of the campaign, reflected the Alignment's inability to view the Likud as a legitimate party in Israeli politics. The Labor campaign decision makers may have become victims of a longing for their glorious past, when the party under Ben-Gurion had succeeded in making Begin look like the leader of a lunatic fringe. In 1981 this could not be done to Begin, the Prime Minister of Israel, and this tactic especially did not work with the masses. The Labor comparison of leaders boomeranged. Three years in power had given Likud leaders sufficient credibility. Even worse for Labor, the Likud responded by contrasting the consensus about Begin as the leader of his party with the conflict and rift over the leadership of Peres. Indeed, as the campaign progressed, the entire Likud campaign was carried by Begin alone and against Peres alone. Furthermore, as it became apparent in public surveys that the lower socioeconomic groups were leaning toward the Likud, the appearances of Begin in public squares became more and more frequent and effective.

A "Reactive" Campaign

The effort of the Alignment to initiate debates over issues, leaders, and the quality of personnel was very short. The latter part of the campaign was what I call a "reactive" campaign. Labor could initiate very little and for the most part had to improvise in response to the Likud's issues. Elsewhere I have referred to a similar situation as one of system-generated election issues.[35] The difference between the two types can be stated as follows. In a reactive campaign events are dictated practically daily by the opponent's actions. Control of television time enhances this type of campaign. System-generated issues are basic issues raised and made salient by opponents that a party would not otherwise choose to emphasize. A reactive campaign can have positive or negative consequences for a party. It is a quick game, and the scoring is immediate. Overall, Labor scored well during the reactive campaign.

The reactive campaign began as a response to Begin's public speaking style, which usually had somewhat agitating if not inflammatory aspects.[36] In Begin's efforts to mock his political opponent, he would get carried away. In response to audience adulation, he would openly challenge the Syrians to dare not to remove missiles that they had moved into Lebanon, and he publicly gave notice to the American mediator, Philip Habib, to remove the missiles from Lebanon or else.

Labor argued that all this was demagoguery which stirred up the masses, was motivated by the elections, but did very little for Israel. The reactive campaign against Begin and the personal challenge to him were justified by the Alignment as a response to election violence. The violence began in public squares and came to be directed against Peres during his appearances. In a number of communities it reached unprecedented heights, and it became the key issue of the campaign. Labor reacted to it quickly and raised its salience. A scare tactic was undertaken by Labor in its television commercials. Because under Israeli election laws no public figure can be shown on regular television during the election campaign, the Alignment used its television time to show Begin at his own election meetings. By showing excited crowds along with violent scenes at Peres's meetings, Labor was able to associate Begin and the Likud with the image of extremism. This reinforced Labor voters and fitted in well with the image the Alignment and its leaders had of the Likud. Although Labor's efforts to brand Begin and the ruling Likud as extremists had failed in the early part of the campaign, Begin's rhetoric now made violence and extremism a prominent election issue. For the Likud this was a disadvantage. It was a basic issue, built up daily and generated by the campaign, that the Likud would have preferred not to face. Labor's reactive campaign strategy at this point was summarized in its derogatory slogan "Vote Anyone but the Likud." The slogan was intended to contribute to delegitimizing the Likud and to reinforce Labor voters.

The Campaign and Social Divisions

As Labor realized its potential gains from the issue of campaign violence, it neglected all other issues. It failed, however, to distinguish between mere rowdyism and real violence. It referred to noisy Begin fans as fascist and Khomeiniistic. These and other reactions began to polarize the voters between the more educated, well-to-do people of European or American (and Asian or African) background and the less educated and affluent Asian or African (and European) votes. It was around the campaign issue of violence that a thesis about class cleavages and politics was born.

I argue that the cleavages that became so salient during the campaign were not the reflection of a structural division of Israeli society. One explanation is to be sought in the personalities involved in the campaign. It is well known in Israel that Begin is successful in articulating issues for people of lower socioeconomic strata. His hawkishness is appealing to them, and so is his rhetoric, as well as his sensitivity to the Jewish heritage and to religious symbols. Begin generally made no demands on people to change their personalities, trades, world outlook, or traditions, as Zionist ideology and its Labor spokesmen had in the past. He talked tradition and popular policy. Perhaps Begin's attraction for the masses is based on his being perceived first and foremost as a prime minister sensitive to Jewish symbols.

What appeared alarming to political analysts during the campaign, however, was the division into "we" and "they" that emerged between the two major parties as a result of the party leaders' rhetoric. The television broadcasts of Labor during the campaign also emphasized this division, but the Alignment did not, of course, bargain for the ethnic overtones that the "we" and "they" division carried. As violence grew during public appearances by Peres, for example, the difference between Likud and Labor followers was described in terms of two cultures. Later this was explained by Labor leaders as meaning different political cultures. But during the campaign it was viewed as a phrase with ethnic connotations.[37]

Another example of the "we" and "they" division was Peres's persistent effort to organize Labor after its 1977 defeat. He succeeded in bringing back many former Labor supporters who had voted for the DMC in 1977. But especially impressive during the 1981 campaign was the public identification of many well-known writers, actors, journalists, and intellectuals with Peres and Labor. These usually mild and politically uninvolved persons helped in the polarization involving perceptions of ethnic and class cleavages. Never directly, but by using cues that all understood, Avraham B. Yehoshuah, the writer, for example, admonished Labor for distributing as a campaign tactic flowers that were trampled on near the Tel Aviv bus terminal. His words were immediately interpreted as directed against people of a distinct background and origin. At a major Alignment rally with Peres present, it was publicly asserted that Labor had the officers of the crack army units and Begin's Likud did not. The cue was clearly understood. These people and Labor spoke nostalgically of Eretz Yisrael Hayafa, Israel the Beautiful, referring to past dedication, pioneering deeds, and devotion to ideals. Labor was held up as heir to those who had done so much for Israel. Once again it became clear who was excluded from these images. Even the language became prey in the election campaign to ethnic sensitivities and to symbols. Examples are numerous. A popular entertainer as master of ceremonies at a Labor rally referred to Likud voters in terms usually applied to uncouth, common persons. At a Likud rally the next day, Begin repeated the derogatory references, and the interpretation that they referred to Jews of Asian or African origin was soon widespread.

These events, however, were not clear ethnic or class politics.[38] They involved ethnic sensitivities. The actual voting results helped to reinforce the interpretation of class politics. True, the results show several clear-cut ethnic differences. For example, in some age groups there were about twice as many voters of one major ethnic group (Asian-African) for the Likud as for Labor. This ethnic division reflected a very special type of politics, however. Ethnic cleavages and politics are usually reflected in issues of religion, language, culture, and quotas, but these were not present in the 1981 campaign. The issues of that campaign somewhat transcended the normal acrimony found in election campaigns. The various ethnic incidents, however, indicated a more general undercurrent of disaffection, the results of which are seen in the election results since 1969 (table 3–2).

Labor may have stimulated ethnic sensitivities by emphasizing events from the past, deeds that many of the eastern Jews were not a part of because they were not in Israel at that time. Many reacted to Labor negatively because it was the party in power when they or their parents went through hardships in their first years in Israel. They felt very little nostalgia for those early years. Many believed that Labor was responsible for whatever social gap remained, and others' reactions may be explained in psychological terms as reactions to an old authority figure. Yet during the election campaign both major parties fed the underlying tensions over certain sensitive symbols. Only when the issue of campaign violence threatened the Likud were efforts made by many, including Begin, to modify the competition.

Conclusion

The 1981 election campaign was a completely new experience for Labor. For the first time in thirty years it faced an opponent that had been in power for nearly four years and had used state resources skillfully before and during the election campaign. It faced a relatively disciplined party with an agreed-upon, relatively popular leader who carried the entire campaign virtually single-handed. Never before had Labor leaders faced such a situation. Peres attempted to oppose this Likud with a party unwilling to present a united front on either policy or leadership. At the critical period of the elections Labor was busy with campaign organization.

In foreign policy the Likud could offer the voters peace and hawkishness together—an ominous combination to an Alignment accused of being a party of four wars with a less than popular dovish wing. In economics the Likud's campaign stressed the policy that had raised the standard of living and offered reduced taxes on consumer goods. In the social domain it continued the welfare-state policies of the past and even launched various new social laws, such as urban neighborhood renewal.

The efforts of Labor to explain in great detail the evils of the Likud's economic policy, the dangers of the peace movement and its accompanying autonomy plan, and the return of the Sinai desert buffer zone were not effective. Neither were the detailed arguments against the bombing of the Iraqi nuclear plant. Labor presented itself in position issues. These are not as effective with voters as dramatic issues and rhetoric with symbolic overtones, such as peace or Begin's justification for Israel's bombing of Iraq: he described the danger of the nuclear plant to Israel's children.

Was the final vote a reflection of the ethnic and class politics that emerged during the electoral campaign? This question is still open to debate. Given the division of the vote by ethnic group and the well-known correlation between low income, education, and ethnicity, the temptation among analysts is to label the 1981 vote a class vote.[39] But my interpretation is that the polarized vote lacked many of the characteristics and issues of class politics. The election and its results revealed ethnic groupings in the two major parties rather than a class cleavage with a clear solidarity structure. The personalities and symbols of the campaign reinforced the ethnic division, but the campaign was mainly a further step in a voter realignment that is traceable to the mid-1960s and is a growing issue in each successive election. The ethnic divisions of the voting reflect issues of party identification and party stability rather than the stability or instability of Israel's social structure. Israeli politics in 1981 was not based on ethnic divisions, although the election campaign and results had many ethnic characteristics. One purely ethnic list—Tami—won only 45,000 votes. One supporting piece of evidence for this thesis is the very special attention given in both parties to "ethnic" figures on their slates. The ethnic issue was carried mildly into the Alignment and almost not at all into the Likud. One of the Labor factions—the Yachdav group—championed the cause of more representation for the *edot* ("ethnics") and for the development towns—which means more representation for eastern Jews. But this was not a major, exclusive issue of the Yachdav group.

Finally, Labor faced the problem of a negative public image. As late as May 1981, one month before the election, Labor was viewed more negatively than was the Likud (table 3–3).

What really pulled the Alignment up in 1981 was the issue of violence that emerged, which gave way to a reactive campaign that involved both major parties and left out the others. It contributed to the demise of some of the small parties which benefited Labor. In the election similar proportions voted for the Likud and Labor. Both made electoral gains. Labor's gains were dramatic, but the Likud formed the government.

To sum up, the reactive electoral campaign, developed by the Alignment around the issue of violence, had a number of effects: (1) It gave Labor an opportunity to assert itself in an otherwise Likud-dominated campaign. (2) It enabled the Labor campaign organization to work coherently and with little group dissension. (3) It polarized voting groups and consolidated the Labor vote. (4) It also had a strong boomerang effect in regard to groups that Labor needed in order to win.

A reactive campaign develops around issues that have a high potential of moving voters' emotions. As such it differs from a campaign in which the issues that emerge do not force the parties to change their original campaign strategies. In a reactive campaign a party must react. Is a reactive campaign waged mainly by an opposition party? Clearly the criterion that high emotion is involved excludes a one-sided conclusion. In 1981 violence forced the Likud to respond to Labor as much as Labor responded to the Likud. The Likud forced Labor to a debate over the need for Sadat's visit and over the bombing of the Iraqi nuclear plant. But essentially these were ephemeral campaign issues. The violence during the campaign and its accompanying ethnic overtones set the pace for the reactive campaign, which did not subside until after the elections.

NOTES

1. Efraim Torgovnik, "A Movement for Change in a Stable System," in Howard Penniman, ed., *Israel at the Polls: The Knesset Elections of 1977* (Washington, D.C.: American Enterprise Institute, 1979).

2. Cf. Asher Arian, "The Electorate: Israel, 1977," in Penniman, *Israel at the Polls*; and Asher Arian, "Elections 1981: Competitiveness and Polarization," *Jerusalem Quarterly* (Fall 1981), pp. 3–27.

3. See "The Campaign and Social Change," below.

4. Seymour Martin Lipset and Stein Rokkan, *Party Systems and Voter Align-ments: Cross-National Perspectives* (New York: Free Press, 1967).

5. Efraim Torgovnik, "Party Factions and Election Issues," in Asher Arian, ed., *The Elections in Israel—1969* (Jerusalem: Jerusalem Academic Press, 1972); and Alan Zuckerman, *The Politics of Factions: Christian Democratic Rule in Italy* (New Haven, Conn.: Yale University Press, 1979).

6. Sigmund Neuman, ed., *Modern Political Parties* (Chicago: University of Chicago Press, 1956); and Giovanni Sartori, *Parties and Party Systems* (Cambridge: Cambridge University Press, 1976).

7. Yonathan Shapiro, *The Formative Years of Israel's Labor Party* (London: Sage Publications, 1976).

8. Yaacov Shavit, *Revisionism in Zionism* (Tel Aviv: Yariv, 1978); and Dan Horowitz and Moshe Lissak, *The Origins of the Israeli Polity* (Tel Aviv: Am Oved, 1977).

9. With the ascension of Peres to the leadership of the Labor party, the Rafi group no longer exists formally, although in division of positions former factional considerations are taken into account.

10. In 1965 all Labor groups together had sixty-three members of the Knesset.

11. This situation is probably responsible for further factionalization of the Labor Alignment, whose consensus is dependent on ephemeral policies on security and peace.

12. See, for example, Henry A. Kissinger, "Domestic Structure and Foreign Policy," *Daedalus* (Spring/Fall 1966), pp. 503–29.

13. See discussion below and Arian, "Elections 1981," p. 11.

14. Y. Mendilow, "Party Cluster Formations and Multi Party Systems," *Political Studies* (December 1982).

15. Efraim Torgovnik, "The Election Campaign: Party Needs and Voter Concerns," in Asher Arian, ed., *The Elections of Israel—1973* (Jerusalem: Jerusalem Academic Press, 1975).

16. Peres's decision to confront the party machine candidate Rabin is proof of the machine's emerging weakness.

17. It should be noted that in the early 1970s, when peace efforts were made and aired by the U.S. representatives, William Rogers and Henry Kissinger, competition between these persons introduced difficulties into the negotiations. In the domain of economics these three leaders joined hands in support of lowering the standard of living and cutting inflation.

18. Sartori, *Parties and Party Systems*, p. 200.

19. Shlomo Nakdimon, *Yediot Achronot*, December 19, 1980.

20. Proceedings of party convention 1980. The discussion here is also based on personal observation of the proceedings.

21. The first major confrontations between the kibbutzim and the development towns was in the 1977 elections.

22. Torgovnik, "Party Factions and Election Issues"; and Torgovnik, "The Election Campaign."

23. Cf. James Barker, ed., *Readings in Citizen Politics* (Chicago: Markham Publishing Co., 1970), esp. pp. 80–90; Richard Rose, *Influencing Voters: A Study of Comparative Rationality* (London: Faber and Faber, 1967). See also Edward Carmines and James A. Stimson, "The Two Faces of Issue Voting," *American Political Science Review*, vol. 74, no. 1 (1980), pp. 78–91.

24. The figure for 1973 is based on Torgovnik, "The Election Campaign." Figures for 1981 are provided by a published survey of PORI and the Israeli Labor party and by Asher Arian, May–June 1981 surveys.

25. Data provided by Asher Arian.

26. Based on personal observations and interviews. Viewing Labor as a ruling group in spite of its opposition position may not in fact be outlandish. In its years in power, Laborites or those identified with Labor filled many positions in key public economic enterprises. People identified with Labor were associated with the establishment even after the Likud's ascension to power.

27. Cf. Maurice Duverger, *Political Parties: Their Organization and Activity in the Modern State* (New York: Wiley, 1961; London: Methuen, 1964).

28. Income guarantee acts and disablement laws are part of the national system.

29. See *Haaretz*, January 1, 1980; *Yediot Achronot*, May 23, 1980; and survey of Jerusalem Institute for Applied Social Science, *Yediot Achronot*, September 21, 1979.

30. On these economic programs, see *Maariv*, May 8, 1981, August 16, 1981, and October 2, 1981; and *Yediot Achronot*, March 13, 1981 and February 14, 1981. See also minutes of meeting of the party Lishka (executive committee), Tel Aviv, July 7, 1981, p. 6 and passim.

31. See minutes of meeting of party Lishka (executive committee), Tel Aviv, July 7, 1981, p. 6; and cf. Larry J. Sabato, *The Rise of Political Consultants* (New York: Basic Books, 1981).

32. Torgovnik, "Party Factions and Election Issues"; also Donald Stokes, "Spatial Models of Party Competition," in Angus Campbell et al., *Elections and the Political Order* (New York: John Wiley & Sons, 1969), chap. 9; David Butler and Donald Stokes, *Political Change in Britain* (London: Macmillan, 1968), chaps. 8, 15; and Robert Zajonc, "Attitudinal Effects of Mere Exposure," *Journal of Personality and Social Psychology*, vol. 9 (1968), pp. 1–27.

33. Based on personal observation.

34. Their persistent opposition to the Camp David Peace Agreement helped to modify Begin's image.

35. Torgovnik, "Party Factions and Election Issues."

36. Examples of this can be found in threats issued by Begin against Syria's missiles in Lebanon during the Likud party convention and his ad hominem attack on German Chancellor Helmut Schmidt and U.S. Defense Secretary Casper Weinberger. See *Haaretz*, April 30, 1981, and May 22, 1981.

37. Minutes of meeting of party Lishka (executive committee), Tel Aviv, August 13, 1981, pp. 12, 56.

38. Cf. Lipset and Rokkan, *Party Systems and Voter Alignments*, chaps. 6, 7, pp. 1–64.

39. E. Yuchtman and G. Fishelson, "Inequality in Distribution of Income," *Economic Quarterly*, vol. 17, no. 65–66 (1970), pp. 75–88.

IV

THE LIKUD

Ilan Greilsammer

A June 1980 opinion poll conducted by the Modi'in Ezrachi Institute on voter opinions indicated that in the event of immediate elections, the ruling Likud would get only 14.5 percent of the vote and 17 seats in the Knesset (out of 120). Thus, after the visit of Anwar Sadat to Jerusalem, Camp David, and the peace treaty, the party led by Menachem Begin could hope for only a status similar to that of the religious parties, a little more than what the new Democratic Movement for Change (DMC) achieved in 1977. The Likud would become a minor political force, maybe a marginal party. Its leader appeared to be in poor health (he had suffered several heart attacks). In addition, the opinion polls indicated that a Likud led by Defense Minister Ezer Weizman would fare much better than a Likud under the leadership of Begin.

A year later, however, the Likud obtained the most brilliant result of its history. Menachem Begin emerged as the undisputed leader of the party, while Ezer Weizman was entirely out, not even a participant in the electoral competition. The Likud's electoral campaign had been almost completely centered on the personality of Begin, who was presented as a dynamic man in perfect health, a strong man of un-questionable authority. Finally, it was obvious from the day after the elections that the Likud was the only party that might be able to set up a coalition. And indeed, the new Likud government was established in a relatively short time.

Thus, we are presented with a paradoxical double image of the Likud as both a defeated party and a triumphant party. This chapter addresses that paradox. Before beginning an analysis of the Likud's public image between the 1977 and the 1981 elections, we will sum up briefly the history of the three basic components of this party. The

Likud is not a united party: It remains a political bloc, composed of forces that have maintained their own identity, orientations, and interests.

A Brief History of the Likud

The Likud has three main components; other political factors have joined forces with or separated from this core depending on the time and the situation.[1]

The first two elements—Herut (freedom movement) and the Liberal party—have been united in one party since 1965. Diverse and quite dissimilar political forces that united in 1976 in La'am (for the people) joined the other two in 1973. These three components have constituted the Likud until the present day; however, their character has altered noticeably since the decision to form one single list for the 1973 elections. The smallest element—the La'am faction—changed most drastically; yet Menachem Begin's Herut, the dominant party of the union, also underwent considerable transformation resulting from an addition and a defection—the former being the joining of Ariel Sharon after the victorious 1977 elections, and the latter that of Begin's former friends who opposed Camp David and the peace treaty with Egypt. It should be added that during the Ninth Knesset the Likud included a fourth element, Achdut (unity), composed of former members of the small Independent Liberal party led and represented in the Knesset by a single member, Hillel Seidel. This faction has now disappeared.

Herut until 1965[2]

Menachem Begin, commander in chief of the Irgun Tsevai Leumi (National Military Organization, also known by its Hebrew acronym, Etzel),[3] established Herut in June 1948 as a direct continuation of the former guerrilla group. Herut was later joined by former members of another extremist guerrilla group that had fought the British—the Lehi (fighters for Israel's freedom).

On the ideological level, Herut set itself the task of implementing the principles of what had been the Revisionist party, inspired and guided by Vladimir Zeev Jabotinsky.[4] The Zionist-Revisionists had constituted an opposition within the World Zionist Organization and then seceded from it, having criticized the Zionist leaders for the feebleness with which they demanded that the British government

allow free immigration to Palestine. Being antisocialists, they had demanded optimum conditions for private enterprise and were strongly
opposed to the privileged status of cooperative and collective enterprises. Above all, during the 1936–1939 Arab offensive, when the
Hagana leaders were practicing a policy of restraint toward the Arabs,
the Revisionists favored a tough policy and violent counterattacks.
They seceded and founded the Irgun.[5] Thus, from its inception,
Herut appeared as a nationalist Jewish party chiefly interested in foreign affairs, adopting a strongly activist policy. Its main objective was
that the new state should extend across the whole of the land of Israel
within its biblical borders. The ideal of a united and strong Jewish nation and the bond with the Eretz Yisrael Hashlema movement were
Herut's basic principles.

After the War of Independence and the armistice agreements,
Herut became an irredentist party, dreaming of the reconquest, peaceful if possible, of the territories of Eretz Israel, which had been temporarily "abandoned" to Jordan.

This basic goal meant a much harsher foreign policy platform
regarding the Arab countries than that of the socialist and liberal parties. In foreign policy, Herut had a pronounced pro-Western orientation. And its national ideal manifested itself in an intransigent attitude to anything that involved the interests and the honor of the
Jewish people. Herut, for instance, led the opposition to establishing
relations with West Germany.

Herut's strongly antisocialist internal policy provided it and the Liberal party with a common ground. In contrast with the Liberals, however, Herut's first priority was foreign policy, superseding its concern
for economic and social matters. It would have compromised on the
social and economic issues far more easily than on the foreign policy
issues.

In both foreign policy and economic policy matters, Herut found
itself at odds with Mapai, the forefather of the present Israel Labor
party. This antagonism was fueled by the longtime personal animosity that existed between Begin and David Ben-Gurion and by the
grudges accumulated on both sides. After the *Altalena* affair, in which
an Irgun boat was sunk on Ben-Gurion's orders, reconciliation became almost impossible.[6] Ben-Gurion had always promised himself
that he would never form a coalition with Herut (or the Communists).

Herut's first appearances on the parliamentary stage were modest.
In the 1949 elections it received 11.5 percent of the vote and fourteen
seats, which placed it fourth, far behind Mapai. Following a mediocre
campaign in 1951, Herut dropped even lower, receiving 6.6 percent

of the vote and eight seats out of one hundred twenty. At this point, three years after the establishment of the State of Israel, the party was in danger of becoming marginal. It did everything to regain its middle-class electorate and to appeal to the deprived immigrants whose numbers were constantly growing.

Ben-Gurion's announcement in 1952 of negotiations with West Germany for reparations provided Menachem Begin with the opportunity to show his readiness to fight for a cause. Herut battled desperately against the very idea of negotiations, creating a somewhat disruptive atmosphere (marching on the Knesset, and so on). This implacable opposition to contact with West Germany was supported by significant sectors of the population.[7] Herut appeared as the champion of a certain political morality, its leader as a pure and tough man, unwilling to compromise his principles. At a later date he fought over the Kasztner affair, submitting a motion of censure against Moshe Sharett's government.[8]

The elections to the Third Knesset, in 1955, were held against a backdrop of defense and security matters. Herut's activism and its firm stand regarding the Arabs reinforced its popularity. It almost doubled its 1951 results, getting 12.6 percent of the vote and fifteen seats and became the second largest political force in the country, a position it would maintain until its 1977 victory. Its progress was restrained by the prestige of Mapai following the Suez Campaign. Begin could not but congratulate Ben-Gurion for his brilliant handling of the war, which nevertheless did not prevent Begin from violently criticizing the government for its unilateral evacuation of Sinai. Herut's progress in the 1959 elections was minimal; with 13.5 percent of the vote, it gained seventeen seats.

In 1960–61, with the resurgence of the Lavon affair (a security mission that failed in 1954), which split Mapai deeply, Herut intensified its attacks on that party's intrigues. These attacks did not gain much on the electoral plane; the 1961 election results were the same as those of 1959.

This relative stagnation moved Menachem Begin to seek alliance with the other opposition party—the Liberal party. In 1965 the Gahal (Gush Herut Liberalism—"Herut-Liberal Bloc") bloc was formed.

The Liberal Party until 1965

The Liberal party (formerly the General Zionist party) represents a minimally doctrinaire right-wing stream. Its following comes largely from middle-class circles of European origin. It demands more freedom and privileges for private enterprise and a reduction of government intervention.

The 1948 General Zionist party was the direct successor of Faction B of the General Zionists, which developed after World War I. Upon the establishment of the State of Israel, Faction A, led by Chaim Weizmann, formed the small Progressive party.

After 1948, the General Zionists placed themselves in strong opposition to Mapai, criticizing various aspects of Israeli socialism. Only twice throughout the twenty-nine years of Labor rule did the General Zionists agree to join the coalition: in 1952–1955 under Moshe Sharett and in 1967–1970 in Golda Meir's national unity government.

The party's electoral results prior to the establishment of Gahal in 1965 showed an improvement followed by a decline. After making great progress at the beginning of the 1950s, the party suffered a sharp drop in popularity, finding itself in 1961 at its 1949 level.

In 1949 the party received only 5.2 percent of the vote, but it had quite a success in the municipal elections of 1950 and even more so in the 1951 Knesset elections when it received 111,394 votes (16.2 percent) as compared with 22,661 in the previous elections. In the Second Knesset this party, with twenty seats, took second place behind Mapai. Actually, part of its success was related to the country's deeply entrenched economic difficulties. The government's unpopularity on this account benefited the General Zionists. They had campaigned against the bureaucracy, the ministerial inefficiency, the black market, and the high cost of living.

Mapai sought them out as partners for the government. Only in December 1952, after tough negotiations, did the General Zionist party agree to enter into a coalition with the socialists. It got four important ministries (Commerce-Industry, Interior, Communications, and Health) and obtained promises of reform, particularly in the fiscal sphere.

Shortly before the 1955 elections, the General Zionists decided to abstain in the vote on the Kasztner affair. The prime minister resigned, and the Liberals returned to the opposition ranks. From that time on, the party was in a state of decline. In 1955 it received only 10.6 percent of the vote. On the one hand, the economic situation was improving; on the other, a part of the General Zionist middle-class electorate had been disappointed by their party's performance in government. They now turned to an opposition party that promised a more brilliant future: Herut. The General Zionists' luck went from bad to worse. In 1957 they failed in their campaign to change the electoral system. In 1959 they received only 6.2 percent of the vote.

As the 1961 elections came near, the General Zionists were reconciled with the Progressive party, and the two together formed the Liberal party. This moved the formerly separate parties ahead a bit, and the Liberals received 13.6 percent of the vote, seventeen seats.

But coexistence proved difficult. The former General Zionists, growing more and more critical of Mapai, saw no further possibility of compromise with the socialists. They increasingly looked in Herut's direction, becoming convinced that only an alliance with Menachem Begin could bring about the overthrow of Mapai. It was the right moment for such a move—the Liberals and Herut had each obtained seventeen seats in the 1961 elections and were thus able to conclude an agreement on a basis of equality. The former Progressives, on the other hand, though hostile to Ben-Gurion, wanted to continue their alliance with Mapai. They welcomed the replacement of Ben-Gurion by Levi Eshkol in 1963. As for Herut, the Progressives vigorously opposed its foreign policy options.

In April 1965, the majority of the Liberal party (the former General Zionists) voted in favor of a list shared with Begin's new Gahal party. The former Progressives seceded and established the Independent Liberal party.

Gahal until 1973

Gahal very quickly won electoral successes, which only strengthened the intention of its two elements to remain united. Its first public appearance was at the Histadrut elections in September 1965, in which it received 15.3 percent of the vote. This in itself was exceptional, given Labor's traditional quasi monopoly in the syndicate. In the legislative elections the same year, the party received 21.3 percent of the vote, a bit more than the combined support for Herut in 1961 and the General Zionists in 1959.

Menachem Begin immediately installed himself as the incontestable leader of Gahal. Nevertheless, he encountered problems within his own party. In 1967 three Herut members of the Knesset, led by Shmuel Tamir, seceded and established a new party, the Free Center.

On June 1, 1967, Herut and Liberal leaders joined Levi Eshkol's national unity government. Gahal was represented by six ministers. Begin was one of those who demanded, and obtained, Moshe Dayan's appointment as minister of defense.

The experience of being in power (1967–1970) did not harm Gahal—quite the contrary. The party clearly progressed in the Histadrut elections in 1969, and got 21.7 percent of the vote in the Knesset elections of the same year. Gahal was given back its six seats in the cabinet formed by Golda Meir after the elections. The party, however, spent only six months in the coalition. In August 1970 the majority of the cabinet voted to accept the American peace initiatives and to enter negotiations under the auspices of Ambassador Gunnar V. Jaring. Gahal, despite the reservations of the Liberal party, returned to the opposition. This decision provided a clear illustration of Herut's growing control within Gahal. In matters of foreign policy, Herut's (actually, Begin's) decisions were imposed. Thus Gahal adopted a position that opposed any Israeli withdrawal from the Golan, the West Bank, and Gaza and supported the official annexation of these territories.

Until 1973 Gahal gained strength but did not constitute a serious alternative to the Labor Alignment led by Golda Meir. Herut and the Liberals appeared to be frozen within a rigid anachronistic structure, each party apparatus more concerned about self-perpetuation than about coming to power. (This position was very clearly demonstrated in the eleventh congress of Herut when Ezer Weizman tried to introduce a bit of new blood and to question Menachem Begin's absolute power. The party veterans objected strongly, and Weizman was obliged to leave his post as president of the executive.)

Signs of unrest in the country continued to stir public opinion focusing on rising prices, inflation, and the high cost of living. Gahal, and above all Herut, played on the discontent of the population.

The Constitution of the Likud and Its 1977 Victory

Before the December 1973 elections, Gahal succeeded in attracting and organizing other political forces that were equally opposed to the Labor party. The role of General Ariel Sharon in assembling these forces and establishing the Likud was crucial. The Yom Kippur War and the dramatic errors of the government led by Golda Meir served to strengthen the cohesion of the Likud components.

The three parties that Gahal attracted into its orbit represented three original ideological streams of Israeli political life.

First, the devoted friends of David Ben-Gurion, who had followed him throughout his political career: when he seceded from Mapai, when he established Rafi (the Israeli Workers list), and in 1969 when he created the State list. This group was composed of former Labor party members who had increasingly emphasized their national ideals and their desire for an activist policy toward the Arabs rather than their socioeconomic policies. They chose a new direction—bringing them increasingly nearer to Herut, after having decided not to follow Dayan and Shimon Peres in their 1969 reintegration in the Labor party.

Second, the former Herut members who quit the party in 1967—mainly for personal reasons—and founded the Free Center party decided to renew their collaboration with Menachem Begin within the framework of the Likud. In 1974, the Free Center faction of the Likud split when Shmuel Tamir, who was instrumental in bringing about the 1967 schism in Herut, decided to regain his total independence. He would later join the Democratic Movement for Change under Yigael Yadin. Two former Free Center deputies remained in the Likud.

Third, the strongly ideological component of the Likud was the Land of Israel movement.[9] It was composed of people of various political backgrounds, including former extreme leftists and extreme rightists. Their common denominator was an intransigent stance against any territorial concession, especially any relinquishing of lands that were part of Eretz Israel.

In 1976, these three components of the Likud decided to unite in order to have a stronger influence within the larger organization. They constituted the La'am faction. This minor partner of Herut and the Liberals was to be confronted by serious internal problems, precisely because of its heterogeneous composition.

In the 1973 elections, the Likud took a leap forward. It obtained 30 percent of the vote, while Gahal had received only 21 percent in 1965 and in 1969. The Likud appeared for the first time as a dangerous rival to the Alignment.

During the Eighth Knesset, several factors combined to ease the way for the Likud's further progress toward victory in the 1977 elections. One of the main factors was obviously the aftermath of the Yom Kippur War: the revelations of the errors of the Labor government, the protest movements against the Labor establishment, and so on. Furthermore, the period between 1973 and 1977 was marked by some of the most famous scandals in the nation's history, in which several members of the Labor leadership were involved. The top leadership of the Labor party appeared more divided and embattled than ever. Finally, the quick deterioration of the economic situation raised the population's interest in the solutions included in the Likud's pro-

gram to reduce state intervention in the economy, to lessen the Histadrut's power, to impose compulsory arbitration in basic public
services, to give priority to the poorest strata of the population, to establish a national system of health services, and to launch a huge housing program. After a very effective campaign, managed by Ezer
Weizman of Herut, one which emphasized the moderate character of
the Likud's orientation in every field of state policy, the party got 33.4
percent of the vote, and received forty-three seats. Immediately after
the 1977 election, the Shlomzion party, led by Ariel Sharon, joined
Herut, and the Likud reached forty-five deputies.[10]

Menachem Begin succeeded in establishing a government composed of three political forces: the Likud, the National Religious party
(NRP), and the Agudat Israel party. Such a coalition was supported
in the Knesset by sixty-two deputies (including an independent member of the Knesset and Foreign Minister Moshe Dayan). On October 20, 1977, exactly four months after the cabinet was created, it was
strengthened by the addition of the Democratic Movement for Change
and its leader, Yigael Yadin. Until a dramatic schism occurred later in
the DMC, Begin boasted a stable seventy-seven deputies in the
Knesset majority.

The Ninth Knesset: The Image of the Likud, 1977–1981

Without attempting to evaluate the Likud's four years of government,
we could point out the factors that have been considered either positive or negative by the Israeli people. In other words, we will analyze
the elements that might have induced the public to vote in favor of or
against the Likud in June 1981.

Some preliminary observations must be made. First, Israeli public
opinion judges its government's actions very differently from the way
they are judged in other countries. In fact, it may be that the gap between the evaluation of these actions at home and the evaluation of
them abroad has been steadily increasing during the past years. Of
course, some acts or decisions have been perceived in the same way:
For example, the peace treaty with Egypt was generally received as
positive while the repeated quarrels between Israeli ministers, leading
to contradictory decisions, have been condemned in Israel as well as
abroad. But on most issues, the viewpoints diverge: on the multiplication of Jewish settlements in the West Bank, on the prime minister's
strong criticism of foreign heads of state, on the destruction of the

Iraqi nuclear reactor, on the tough decisions toward Arab mayors, and so on. Following each of these events, while Israel was almost unanimously criticized by the international community, opinion polls showed that most Israelis supported their government's decisions.

Second, the impact of these various decisions or events on voter behavior was very different. For example, while Camp David reinforced the Likud's prestige, the rapid deterioration of the economic situation during the same period was much more important to the outlook of the voters. Likewise, in spite of the peace treaty, in the spring of 1979 popular support for the Likud decreased drastically because of escalating inflation. In general, economic factors, and especially the rise in the cost of living, have had a stronger influence on public opinion than international affairs have had. Thus, as has been pointed out by the Labor opposition, the sharp comeback of the Likud a few months before the 1981 elections was primarily attributable to the tax reductions decided upon by Finance Minister Yoram Aridor.

Third, when analyzing the actual impact of various Likud actions, we must distinguish between the various questions asked in the opinion polls: The positive value given to a government decision was not always directly translated on the level of voter inclination.[11] Thus, while there may have been an increase in positive answers to the question "Do you think that Israel's situation is rather good or bad?" there may not have been a comparable vote shift toward the Likud. Likewise, some people may have responded differently to the questions "Do you think Mr. Begin is a good prime minister?" or "Do you think that the government manages the affairs of the country well?" without shifting their voting inclination. For example, during the year 1980, a growing percentage of Likud voters considered the presence of Begin at the helm of the party a negative factor but that did not mean that an equal percentage changed their intention to vote Likud. Therefore, in the following analysis, we will mention only government actions that have had a direct impact on voter inclination.

Finally, when speaking of the Likud government's public image, one must be precise as to which part of the public is intended. Likud leaders certainly did not intend to reach every stratum of the population, since they knew that some strata (for example, kibbutz members) were firmly bound to Labor. Their aims were first to keep or reattract their 1977 voters and then to capture a part of the National Religious party's electorate, a small part of former Democratic Movement for Change voters, young people who would vote for the first time in 1981, and others. Above all, the Likud sought to keep—and eventually extend—its strength among immigrants from Arab countries. Therefore, these Sephardic newcomers were potential voters who must be kept in mind when one studies the positive and negative impact of government actions. After having presented these actions and their impact on the public, we will follow the evolution of voter inclination between 1977 and 1981.

Positive Factors

The Peace with Egypt

The three meaningful events that marked the peace process (Sadat's trip to Jerusalem, Camp David, and the peace treaty) obviously enhanced the prestige of the governing party. Therefore, during the 1981 electoral campaign, Likud leaders strongly emphasized their foreign policy achievements. The campaign on television, in particular, was built around the image of Begin, standing between the American and the Egyptian presidents, and on the images of the Begin-Sadat summits. These extraordinary events allowed the Likud to present itself to the voters as the political force that had convinced the Arabs to recognize Israel, and to say, "We are the party of peace."

It is necessary, however, to emphasize the time gap between the three landmark events of the peace process. When President Sadat came to Jerusalem, the Likud government was five months old. Its prestige was already very high before the visit. Opinion polls indicated that it would obtain an absolute majority in the case of immediate elections. Sadat's visit appeared as a tremendous success for the government, all the more so since it was not yet known if territorial concessions would be made by Israel and which ones.

Before the May 1977 elections, a majority of the population told pollsters that the situation of Israel was "not good." After the elections, the percentage of those who thought it was "good" or "very good" kept growing. During the two days that preceded Sadat's visit, this response rose to 44 percent. And during the following week, it jumped up to 56 percent (which represents the highest percentage of positive responses to that question since the Yom Kippur War).[12] Another indicator was the proportion of those who said that the Likud government managed the country's affairs "well" or "very well." After Begin's trip to the United States in July 1977, it was 70 percent. Two weeks before the Egyptian president's coming to Israel, it fell to 62 percent. But the day before the visit it went up to 75 percent, and in the following two days it reached 87 percent.[13]

For some reasons, Camp David and the peace treaty did not change the Likud's positive image in the same measure that Sadat's visit did: The country was already deeply enmeshed in the economic crisis, the radical decisions taken by the finance minister had failed to produce any result, and the two important foreign policy achievements were somehow overshadowed by a wave of social unrest. Second, the enthusiasm toward the peace process began to be a little more moderate than before: Israel was obliged to evacuate the Sinai settlements and to negotiate an autonomous regime for Gaza and the West Bank. Opposition to these concessions developed within the Likud itself (eventually leading to the secession of some of its members). Therefore, when studying the evolution of voter attitudes during this period, we may observe that Camp David was not able to stop the deterioration of the Likud's image. Immediately after the agreement, opinion polls gave the party forty-six deputies[14] in the case of immediate elections but only thirty-five five months later.[15]

The March 1979 peace treaty had a more positive impact, but not for long: According to the April polls the Likud would obtain forty-four deputies,[16] but four months later, the number fell again to thirty-five[17] and continued to decline until the 1981 comeback.

We may conclude that the peace process reinforced the Likud's image, but not with all the strength and durability possible.

The Multiplication of Jewish Settlements in the Territories
Every survey conducted in Israel during the last years has clearly shown a steady increase in the hawkish feelings of the population. It appeared in the continuous support of the government's firmness in foreign policy matters and especially of the policy of establishing new settlements on the West Bank.[18] Such a mood was felt not only by the Likud, but was reflected by other political parties as well. The Alignment gave prominent status to its hawks on its 1981 election list, and the National Religious party did its utmost to keep its foremost hawk, Rabbi Haim Druckman. The Likud took advantage of this popular wave to reinforce Jewish settlements. In that area, the role of Agriculture Minister Ariel Sharon was crucial. He strengthened existing colonies, established new settlements, built new urban townships, placed observation points in the hills, and transformed military camps into civilian villages. Furthermore, the government was tough in its dealings with the Arab mayors supporting the PLO (for example, in the case of the expulsion of the Hebron and Halkhoul mayors). Finally, it gave a free hand to Gush Emunim's settlement projects.[19]

Such a policy enhanced the Likud's image, and the party reiterated it time and time again during the electoral campaign: "We are on the map" became the Likud's slogan, and the agricultural minister organized tours in the territories for the Israelis who wanted to see first-hand the results of the Likud settlement policy.

Menachem Begin

Public support of Menachim Begin, both as leader of the Likud and as head of the government, fluctuated greatly during the four years of his first term.

In the first months, his authority was very great. He showed his statesmanship qualities during his first trip to the United States. In August 1977, 70 percent of Israelis considered Begin "the best choice for Prime Minister" (Rabin and Peres received only 8.8 and 8.2 percent).

But during 1978 and 1979 the prime minister's prestige steadily declined. He appeared in poor health and had difficulty imposing his authority on his quarreling ministers. Ezer Weizman's charisma grew; Dayan and Weizman increasingly criticized Begin's performance. After Begin's 1979 heart attack, most commentators believed he would resign. A Dahaf poll in January 1980 revealed that the Likud, under Begin, would obtain thirty Knesset seats while it would obtain forty-five seats under Weizman.[20] And in April 1980, only 21.4 percent gave Begin's name in answer to the question "Whom would you prefer as prime minister?" while 29.9 percent gave Rabin's name and 24.7 percent preferred Peres.[21] In July 1980, when the Likud's popularity was at its lowest, polls indicated that it would obtain seventeen seats under Begin but thirty under Weizman.[22]

The greatest asset of the Likud, however, has always been the capacity of Begin to face a crisis. When he was released from the hospital in July 1980, Begin seemed to recover. He announced that he would personally manage the Likud's campaign and that he would address meetings all over the country. He knew that the Likud could win only if he succeeded in reaffirming his own leadership and if he were perceived as a strong man. For this reason he became vehement in his criticism of foreign heads of government, showed his firmness on Jerusalem and the autonomy negotiations, and demonstrated strength on several other issues. The consecutive resignations of Dayan and Weizman also permitted him to reassert his leadership in the cabinet.

Menachem Begin's success in rebuilding his own image can be measured by the enthusiasm of the crowds during the spring of 1981.

When he appeared in public, he was greeted by songs such as "Begin, King of Israel. . . ." The strengthening of the prime minister's popularity was obviously related to the weakness of Labor leadership's public image.

These, then, are the major factors that influenced the public in favor of the Likud. These, however, would not have been sufficient to assure the party's success at the polls without the detaxation measures decided upon and applied during the four months before the elections. We will elaborate further on this electoral economic policy later. In addition to these positive factors (the peace, the settlements, and the prime minister's charisma), we can mention a few others of less importance, for example, the continuing support offered to the Likud by the National Religious party and Agudat Israel, and their assessment that, in any case, they would prefer the Likud as the governing and coalition-building party. Specific local circumstances could also have worked in favor of the Likud, for instance, the administration of two major towns—Tel Aviv and Ramat Gan—by Liberal mayors.

Negative Factors

The Economic Situation

The main factor leading to the deterioration of the Likud's image was the incapacity of the party to stop—or even to bridle—runaway inflation.[23]

It is true that inflation began under the Labor administration. Prices had already begun to rise sharply. For example, in December 1976 the Consumer Price Index was 38 percent higher than one year before; in 1977 the index increased by 43 percent. The original cause of rising prices was the sharp increase in the cost of oil and other products on world markets. But the Rabin government had contributed to the rise by its taxation policies and by yielding to worker pressures for higher salaries.

Economic problems played an important role in the 1977 electoral campaign. The Liberal party proclaimed that the Likud, if it came to power, would carry out an authentic economic "revolution." The Likud entirely rejected the socialist and cooperative features of the Israeli economy: bureaucracy, state interference, Histadrut encroachments on various sectors, state prejudice toward the private sector, and other socialist policies. Taking his inspiration from Milton Friedman's works, the finance minister—and leader of the Liberals—Simcha Ehrlich announced a series of radical decisions on October 28, 1977.

He suggested three objectives: to curb the rate of inflation by restrain-
ing the budget and by suppressing government subsidies of various
basic products, to promote the liberalization of the economy's institutions and to ease administrative procedures, and to improve the balance of trade. To achieve these goals, the government decided

to abolish exchange controls,

to fix a floating exchange rate for Israeli currency,

to increase the VAT (value added tax) rate but to lower indirect taxation of transactions,

to suppress progressively all the subsidies of basic products,

to establish a new tax on import stocks and on specific foreign currency reserves of the banks.

In an article published in *Newsweek*, Milton Friedman called these
reforms "a new Entebbe." By contrast, the Labor opposition harshly
criticized the government and predicted that Ehrlich's policy would
lead to catastrophe.

Today it is widely recognized—even by Likud leaders—that the
October 1977 economic "revolution" was a failure.[24] The two clearest
signs of this failure were (1) growing pressure, inside and outside the
Likud, to replace the finance minister, who finally resigned in November 1979; and (2) a sharp decline in voter support for the Likud.

For the population, the test of the success or failure of Ehrlich's policy was the evolution of the price level, the cost of living. In fact, prices
continually rose, and the cost of living became higher and higher. Inflation increased dramatically. In 1978, inflation ran at more than 48
percent, with a 70 percent rise in health costs, a 65 percent increase in
the fruits-vegetables sector, and a 56 percent jump in apartment costs.
In 1979, in spite of Ehrlich's announcement that the rate of inflation
would go down to 35–40 percent, Israel had 111 percent price rise,
with more than a 165 percent rise in apartment costs.

Why did the government fail to curb inflation? First, it failed to reduce or even to stabilize the growth of state expenditures. There were
some attempts to reduce the budget of the various ministries, but
without result. For example, the repeated requests of the finance ministry to freeze the number of civil servants failed to produce any
noticeable effect. Budgetary limits were not adhered to, budget sup-
plements were requested repeatedly, and the government was obliged

to print money. Second, private consumption did not decrease. Confronted by the steady devaluation of the currency and by price rises, the population bought huge quantities of goods—especially electrical products—to get rid of its cash. The government was not able to resist demands for higher salaries. (Formerly, when the same party led both the state and the Histadrut, social conflicts were tempered.) Salary augmentation and cost-of-living allowances reinforced the inflationary spiral. Suppression of government subsidies caused price rises but did not reduce the buying power of the population. Third, the Likud leaders' liberal principles deprived them of the instruments of control and regulation used by Labor governments: regulation of credit and interest rates, action on the exchange rates, etc.[25]

While the Likud would probably have obtained an absolute majority of seats if elections had taken place immediately after Ehrlich's economic decisions (October 1977), opinion polls indicated that when the finance minister resigned (November 1979) the Likud would have received only twenty-eight deputies (and Labor fifty-eight).[26]

Begin appointed Yigal Hurvitz, head of the La'am faction, in place of Simcha Ehrlich (the new finance minister had previously resigned as minister of trade and industry because he opposed the government's concessions to Egypt). Hurvitz defined his economic policy by this simple phrase: *En li* ("I have not"), which meant that he intended to practice a policy of austerity and answer negatively to workers' salary demands as well as to budgetary requests of various ministers. On November 19, 1979, he disclosed the following decisions:[27]

drastic budgetary reductions, including a freeze of public investment, a reduction of infrastructure investment, a total freeze of civil servant recruiting, a set of sanctions against public institutions that went beyond their budgetary limits, etc.

an end to all government subsidies apart from bread and public transportation

freezing of salaries in the administration

new credit limitations

For several reasons, Hurvitz was not able to achieve his goals.[28] First, it was very difficult to impose such a policy on other ministers. He clashed with every other cabinet member on where, when, and what reductions could be made: with David Levy, minister of housing and absorption, who was eager not to cause more dissatisfaction in the population; with Ezer Weizman, about a limitation of the military budget; and so on. Finally, Hurvitz resigned in January 1981, after a protracted conflict with Zevulun Hammer, the education minister, about the implementation of the Etzioni report, which included pay raises for teachers.

Second, Hurvitz was in office in 1980, which was a preelection year. There was a growing gap between the finance minister's policy and the election preparations of the Likud leaders. The latter (and especially the Herut leadership) were increasingly apprehensive concerning the effects of Hurvitz's policy upon the electorate. The fact that the finance minister was the leader of the smallest component of the Likud increased the defiance of the leaders of the two largest parties. The tension increased until the end of 1980, and Begin was by then obliged to choose between the severe budget proposed by Hurvitz for 1981–1982 and a much more liberal policy, as proposed by his other colleagues for the election year.

When the finance minister resigned, the rate of inflation—during the twelve months of 1980—reached 140 percent. A motion of no-confidence against the economic policy of the government was defeated on November 19, 1980, by a very narrow margin (fifty-seven to fifty-four). Weizman and Dayan voted against the government.

Internal Discord

Beyond the economic situation, strife within the Likud also tarnished the party's public image. We can distinguish among three kinds of internal conflicts:

Conflicts were rife among the three components of the Likud. Throughout the period under discussion, La'am protested against what it considered to be discrimination by the two big parties. La'am asked for a fairer distribution of government posts and administrative functions and also for more adequate methods of nominating the Likud candidates for elections (for example, La'am protested against the Likud nominations for local elections in 1978). The La'am leaders constantly insisted on the necessity of total unification of the Likud. These were vain efforts. There were still several occasions when the Liberal and Herut leaders did not consult with their junior partner and tended to neglect its interests.

However, the harshest conflicts took place between Herut and the Liberal party. Herut, which draws its power from the immigrants from Arab countries with a low socioeconomic level, became increas-

ingly incensed with the Liberals. It ascribed the Likud's loss of prestige
to the negative economic decisions of the Liberal ministers. Since its
inception, Gahal has had a twofold base: Herut's public is the urban
proletariat; the Liberal party's electorate is mainly middle-class and
bourgeois. A kind of class war developed within the Likud during
the Ninth Knesset. It was reinforced by the fact that after the 1977
elections, the Liberal party "monopolized" all the economic ministries
(Herut keeping foreign policy and defense matters for itself). Among
Herut leaders, the idea of dividing the Likud and separating from the
Liberals had several advocates. On the other hand, Liberal leaders
dreamed of a large "liberal center," perhaps to be led by Ezer
Weizman.

The tension between the two parties was exacerbated by the opinion polls. Thus, in May 1979, a Modi'in Ezrachi poll revealed that
among those who intended to vote Likud, 67.7 percent supported
Herut, 7.5 percent supported the Liberal party, 3.6 percent supported La'am, and 21.2 percent supported the Likud as a whole.[29] (At
the same time, the Likud's Knesset faction included twenty-one Herut
deputies, fifteen Liberals, and eight La'am.) Finally, if the Likud
remained united, it was mainly because of the strenuous personal
efforts of the prime minister.

Conflicts were also active within each of the three components:
Herut, the Liberal party, and La'am. One of the distinctive characteristics of Herut since 1948 has been its cohesiveness. Because of its past
as a fighting organization, it was united under its sole leader. A small
opposition appeared only on very rare occasions (as when the Free
Center seceded in 1967).

Until January 1978 this cohesiveness was maintained and even reinforced by the victory at the polls and the visit of Anwar Sadat. But in
January 1978, Menachem Begin was obliged to reveal his proposals to
Egypt, and he announced his readiness to make important concessions (Sinai and the autonomy plan). This provoked the anger of most
of the prime minister's old friends within Herut. The founders of
Herut—more than the new generation in the party—were unable to
accept the idea of abandoning Jewish settlements and the idea of Arab
autonomy in Eretz Israel territories. Such a notion was completely
opposed to the traditional political philosophy of Herut. Begin's most
intransigent old companions (Geula Cohen and Shmuel Katz) established a "circle of Herut loyalists" within the party. This internal opposition grew after Camp David. Some of the prominent leaders of
Herut abstained or even opposed the Camp David agreements when

they were presented to the Knesset. Among the opponents were
Yitzhak Shamir, chairman of the Knesset, and Moshe Arens, chairman of the Foreign Affairs and Defense Committee.

Nevertheless, Menachem Begin succeeded in isolating the intran-
sigents from the rest of his party and in having the "circle of Herut
loyalists" condemned.[30]

Following the peace treaty with Egypt, the "loyalists" undertook
negotiations with a few other anticoncession forces, such as the new
party founded by physics scholar Yuval Ne'eman, Gush Emunim, the
Ein Vered group, and others, and in June 1979 the small group of
Herut "loyalists" quit this party and abandoned the Likud to participate in the creation of the party Tehiya (renaissance). The latter
included in its political program its absolute refusal to any territorial
concessions and its resolution to prevent the evacuation of Sinai
settlements.[31]

The Tehiya schism hurt the Likud for several reasons: first, because
its leaders addressed, ideologically speaking, the same public as the
Likud, that is, Israelis who favored the annexation of the territories
and wished the extension of Jewish sovereignty over the whole of
Eretz Yisrael; second, the Tehiya party incessantly attacked the Likud
and criticized its leader, asserting that Begin's policy was defeatist and
reflected a loss of essential Zionist principles. During the months that
preceded the elections, the Likud leaders became apprehensive about
the effects of Tehiya's campaign on the Likud's electorate, and they
feared Tehiya would wrest a few seats at the Likud's expense.

The Likud's leadership, on the other hand, was harshly criticized by
one of its former members, Ezer Weizman. The latter suggested that
the Likud lacked a true desire to implement the peace treaty with
Egypt and to bring autonomy negotiations to a positive conclusion.
He pointed out the prime minister's "lack of authority" and the "cata-
strophic results" of the government's economic policy. In May 1980, the
defense minister resigned, but he declared that he would like to remain
a Herut member. After he voted in favor of the no-confidence motion
of November 1980, however, his party decided to exclude Weizman
from Herut and the Likud.

Conflict within the Liberal party was less than in Herut, and there
were no secessions from its ranks. However, there were many internal
conflicts in the party. These conflicts were generally personal quarrels, but the Liberals also had ideological conflicts. On the foreign policy level, for example, the hawkish faction of Energy Minister Yitzhak
Moda'i steadily increased its strength at the cost of Vice Prime Minis-

ter Ehrlich's faction. There was also an attempt by the "young guard" to seize power in the party, or at least to lessen its establishment's predominance (for example, in trying to impose limitations on Liberal ministers' nomination on the Likud list). But this offensive was ineffective, and the leadership maintained its supremacy.

Conflict within La'am, because of its heterogeneous composition, arose after the Camp David agreements: Two deputies firmly opposed Begin's policy; the others supported it. This basic divergence on the concessions to Egypt was to provoke a schism in the party. In November 1978, La'am broke in two equal factions, each having four deputies. In the beginning they kept the same name. Afterward, the former deputy of the Land of Israel movement, Moshe Shamir, abandoned the Likud and contributed to the establishment of Tehiya. The faction of Finance Minister Yigal Hurvitz then took a new name: Rafi—the State list, which was precisely the name of the two parties founded by David Ben-Gurion after his departure from Labor. Rafi deputies began to see in Moshe Dayan (who was a founder of the 1965 Rafi) their potential leader and drew nearer to him, until, in January 1981, they quit the Likud, dangerously narrowing the government majority in the Knesset.

Finally, personal quarrels also contributed to the hostilities. Even if it did not follow every political controversy between the Likud's three components—or within them—public opinion was well aware of the poor quality of the relations between ministers. Thanks to the press and to television, the population followed daily the violent conflicts among Likud leaders, the personal attacks, the insults, the bitter strife within the establishment.[32] During the four years of the Ninth Knesset, personal conflicts were countless. Maybe more than any other factor this phenomenon contributed to the deterioration of the Likud's image. The prime minister tried incessantly to put an end to such conflicts, but without success. Of course, personal conflicts and even insults were also part of Labor's government, but they did not reach the same intensity and bitterness.

In conclusion, runaway inflation and internal conflicts within the party were the two major causes of the sharp decline in the Likud's popularity between the summer of 1978 and the end of 1980.

Impact of These Factors on Voters

Various opinion polling institutes regularly asked a sample of the population for which party they would vote if elections were to take place

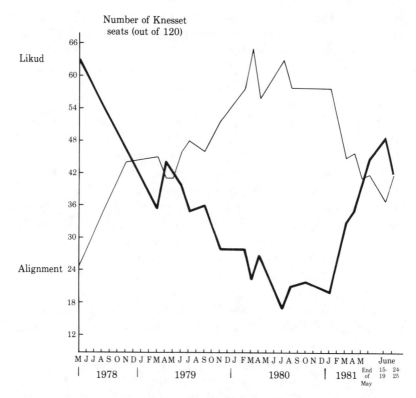

Figure 4-1. Evolution of Voter Inclination
(Modi'in Ezrachi Institute)

on the day the question was asked. In this study, we will give only the
results of Modi'in Ezrachi opinion polls, regularly published in the *Jerusalem Post*.[33] On the basis of these results we have drawn the diagram
shown in figure 4–1 to focus our analysis on the Likud's image.

Clearly, the Likud's popularity began to decline during the summer
of 1978, and Labor's image improved in a parallel manner. Immediately after Camp David, the two big parties would have obtained—
more or less—the same number of deputies (forty-five seats, which is
not very far from the final results of June 1981), and this quasi equality was maintained until May–June 1979. Beginning in July 1979, the
gap suddenly increased, and, according to the polls, the Alignment
would have obtained about ten seats more than the Likud during the
summer.

From October 1979 on, the polls showed that the Likud sank
sharply, and the Alignment might have won a twenty-four-seat advan-

tage in November and a thirty-seat advantage in February 1980. The widest gap appeared in July 1980, when Labor was projected to get sixty-three seats (the absolute majority) and the Likud only seventeen seats.

A slight turn back took place in August 1980: The Likud went up again, while Labor's triumphal ascent seemed to have stopped. Between August and December–January, Labor was predicted to get about fifty-eight seats, the Likud twenty to twenty-two seats.

Then came the real turning point: Five months before the general elections, the Likud went up again, while the Alignment sank even more rapidly than the Likud had in the second half of 1978. This double parallel movement appeared irresistible. At the beginning of May 1981, the two parties were more or less equal, but the Likud continued to increase its strength. It seemed to be at its best between June 15 and June 18. According to the Modi'in Ezrachi poll, it would have obtained forty-nine seats (the Alignment only thirty-seven) if the elections had taken place during that week.

The last opinion poll, which was conducted on June 24–25, gave quite precisely the actual result of the elections: The two parties seemed to be on an equal level. (Only their exact number of seats was not anticipated: forty-two to forty-two according to the poll, forty-eight to forty-seven as the final result. The drastic loss of votes for the small parties had not been foreseen.) Thus, in the late days of the campaign, the Likud's progress was curbed.

Some observations are in order concerning this evolution of voter inclination.

First, all through the period under discussion, the percentage of undecided (those who had not yet decided, or who had decided not to vote, or who refused to say for which party they would vote) was very high. It was particularly high during the peroid of the Likud's decline, when this party seemed to have been abandoned by the public.

In May 1978, a poll conducted by the Hebrew University Institute for Applied Social Research indicated that 40 percent of voters were undecided; in August 1979, it appeared that a third of those who voted for the Likud in 1977 were undecided; in March 1980, there were 30.4 percent undecided; in April 1980, 39 percent; in August 1980, 43 percent. In November 1980, the peak was reached: 46 percent undecided voters.

When the Likud went up again, beginning in February 1981, the percentage of undecided people decreased accordingly. The obvious interpretation of this phenomenon is that the mass of people who "abandoned" the Likud were *not* converted into firm supporters of other parties, especially not the Alignment. They were immobilized, so to speak, and maintained a wait-and-see attitude. Thus, the evolution of voter inclination and the results of the opinion polls, which predicted the Alignment's triumph, were calculated on the basis of a little more than half of the electorate. The success of the Likud was its ability to rally its former 1977 supporters and to convince those undecided people that it was, after all, the best alternative.

Second, some observations on the influence of opinion polls must be made. As in 1977, Modi'in Ezrachi and other institutes announced rather precisely the 1981 results. In general, Israeli polls give a good evaluation of the major trends and changes in public opinion, and both party leaders and the general public considered the polls to be trustworthy. But this belief in their trustworthiness influences voter behavior. During the preelection period, such an influence was felt, at least on two occasions:

> Between March and July 1980, everyone believed that, if elections were to take place immediately, the Alignment would obtain an absolute majority of seats in the Knesset. This would give Labor the possibility to govern alone, without any need for coalition partners. It would be omnipotent. This was certainly not the situation anticipated or desired by those who were dissatisfied with the Likud's management. The fear of the Alignment's omnipotence, as was predicted by the polls, was a major factor in the return to the Likud by many undecided people.

> A similar—but reverse—phenomenon probably occurred during the last week before the elections. A section of the electorate became apprehensive about the continuous ascent of the Likud and wanted to prevent that party's total victory.

Third, we should complement the results of the opinion polls by an analysis of the various elections that took place in Israel between 1977 and 1981. Election results, however, were not always similar to the findings of opinion polls. (Of course, there is a huge difference between trade unions and local ballots on one hand and general elections on the other hand. The opinion polls that we have quoted above deal with the latter.)

The first test was the Histadrut June 1977 elections. The Likud, which obtained 22.7 percent of the vote in 1973, gained only 5.9 percentage points (28.6 percent).[34] This was well below its 33.4 percent in the national elections in May. It is true that the Histadrut electorate is composed mostly of workers, firmly bound to Labor.

Local elections took place in the autumn of 1978. They reflected fairly accurately the public's dissatisfaction with the Likud. While the Likud was pleased to keep its hold on Tel Aviv–Jaffa (even if the Liberal mayor, Shlomo Lahat, was rather independent of the Likud's orientations), it achieved less favorable results in all the other large towns such as Jerusalem, Haifa, Ashkelon, and Petach Tikva. Thus, local elections confirmed the estimates of the opinion polls.[35]

Similarly, some trade union elections confirmed the Likud's decline. For example, at the civil servants' union elections in June 1980, Labor obtained 61 percent of the vote (as compared with 52 percent eleven years earlier, in 1969), while the Likud dropped from 24.4 percent to 18.4 percent.[36] This result was remarkably close to the findings of the Knesset opinion poll that was conducted at the same time.

The last elections that preceded the June 30 Knesset ballot were the Histadrut elections in April 1981. The results deluded the Alignment, because they led that party to believe that it was still preferred by the general population. The Likud got only 26 percent of the vote. But the Histadrut electorate constitutes only 65 percent of the Knesset electorate; furthermore, only 60 percent of Histadrut members went to the polls, and after a campaign that was centered on economic and social problems, not on defense and foreign policy matters (which are the "strong points" of the Likud).[37]

Fourth, the opinion polls conducted between 1977 and 1980 helped clarify the character and personality of the average Likud voter. Even when it was at its lowest level of popularity, the Likud succeeded in keeping a hard core of supporters among certain strata of the population. The average Likud voter generally conforms to the following characteristics:

He is young. Thus, in July 1979, when the Likud got 28.4 percent in the opinion polls, its percentage reached 38 percent in the age group eighteen to twenty-one years old (which is the military service age), but only 15 percent among those fifty-one years and older. When the Likud reached its lowest point, in June 1980, it got only 14.5 percent in the whole population, but it still got 21.6 percent in the eighteen to twenty-one class, while it obtained only 6.5 percent in the forty-one to fifty age group.

He is a sabra (born in Israel), of parents who in general were born in Arab countries. According to pollsters Mina Zemach and

Amiram Yarkoni, in April 1979, 50 percent of the children of immigrants from Arab countries intended to vote for the Likud.

He lives generally in development towns (which were established to
absorb new immigrants from the Arab countries), but a lot of remaining supporters (in the hardcore) live in moshavim (which are
farming communities).

He very often has a low level of education. He attended primary
school but did not attend secondary school, or he dropped out. The
inclination to vote for the Likud clearly lessens when the level of
education grows higher.

He has a rather low income. The Likud has its staunchest supporters among blue-collar workers and shopkeepers; it has a weaker
base among white-collar workers. The inclination to vote for the
Likud clearly lessens when the income grows.

He is very respectful of Jewish religious tradition, if not religious
himself. The Likud—in fact Herut—draws less support among
Israelis who have strong secular orientations.

Finally, the Likud has generally drawn more support from women
than from men; and its has a particular appeal to unmarried
people.[38]

The Likud's Electoral Campaign

When the Likud's popularity reached its lowest point in the summer
of 1980, the leaders of the party decided that a strenuous effort
had to be made to ameliorate this situation. During the autumn,
they made choices on several basic questions, which served to guide
the Likud during the whole electoral campaign. We will first analyze
these decisions and then point out the main features of the Likud's
campaign.

Decisive Options

The Timing of the Elections
Because of public opinion oscillation, the question of whether to hold
early elections was repeatedly discussed by the Likud leaders. On one
hand, they could let the Ninth Knesset continue until the end of its
mandate, which meant that elections would take place in November
1981. On the other hand, the government could submit a bill of dis-

solution to the Knesset and organize early elections. After such a bill is voted, the cabinet becomes a caretaker government, and it cannot be overthrown. For two major reasons, this question had been very frequently discussed in the governing party's leadership.

First, the possibility of new elections was a crucial card in the Likud's fight against Labor. It was necessary to keep the latter in the dark concerning the date of the ballot, to induce the Alignment to begin its campaign too early or too late. The Likud leaders, and especially the prime minister, keep the question hanging. The statements of the ministers on the subject were contradictory.

Second, the Likud leaders truly opposed one another on this question. Some of them believed that the later the ballot, the better it would be for the party. A late ballot would give the government the time to begin several big projects, such as the renewal of poor neighborhoods, the construction of the Mediterranean–Dead Sea Canal, the massive construction of low-rent apartments, and the like. The idea of updated elections was advocated by other ministers when Likud chances appeared brighter (for example, in March–April 1979, immediately after the peace treaty) or worse (for example, in January 1981, after the resignation of the second finance minister and at a time when the government's majority fell to sixty deputies).

Finally, Menachem Begin decided in favor of moved-up elections, to be held on June 30, 1981. The official reason for this decision was that the prime minister did not want to govern on the basis of a frail majority, reinforced in the Knesset by half a dozen lone deputies.[39]

The Themes of the Campaign
One of the Likud's central themes was chosen very early: the Likud's staunch opposition to Labor's "Jordanian option."[40] The Likud would insist that the Jordanian option leads to abandoning Judea and Samaria to Yasser Arafat's hands. The Likud "is the only political force able to bar the way to Labor, which is preparing the ground for a Palestinian State." The argument was summed up in the slogan "Save *Eretz-Yisrael* from Labor." The Likud then focused on Mapam (the left wing of the Alignment) and its dovish orientations concerning the Palestinian problem. In electoral terms, such a theme was to be fruitful, given the hawkish mood of the population.

The Likud decided to confront directly, and on a very personal level, Begin's stature as a statesman in contrast with the image of Shimon Peres. "Don't trust Shimon Peres!" was the second theme of the campaign. The prime minister—although generally a courteous man—attacked his rival rather violently, calling him a liar and a hypo-crite. He had particularly harsh words when the Labor leader decided a few days before the election to replace Haim Bar-Lev with Yitzhak Rabin as defense minister in his shadow cabinet.

On the other hand, Begin was presented as an honest and reliable man, and the Likud placed special stress on the good health of its leader. An important landmark of the campaign was Begin's an-nouncement at the beginning of May 1981 that he had "changed his plans" about his retirement date. He had said previously that he would retire at seventy, which meant summer 1983, after the Tenth Knesset had completed only half of its term. Then, in May 1981 he announced that he would *not* retire at half-term.[41] By serving no-tice that he had changed his mind, Begin achieved several goals. He showed that he was in perfect health; he denied the Alignment's asser-tion that he was cheating his electorate in soliciting a new mandate; and he reminded his political friends that he intended to remain the party leader for the next four years.

Given the detrimental effect of the Likud's divisions, it was urgent that a new image of the party be propagated: one of a united, co-herent, and homogeneous political force. It was essential to put an end to the ministers' quarrels, and Begin enjoined cabinet members to stop fighting one another. Furthermore, the prime minister de-cided to convene a dramatic conference, in order to proclaim the Likud's unification. On April 8, 1981, he announced that delegates of the "three components" would meet a month later. The goals of the conference would be, first, to approve the electoral platform of the united Likud; second, to name the leader of the Likud list (Begin); third, to give the leader the right to choose his ministers as he wished, if the party were to win the elections. The conference met on May 10 and was widely publicized. A "scroll of unity" was signed by the lead-ers of the three factions. However, the unity was rather artificial, since it was agreed that the united Likud would elect its governing bodies only "when the time comes."[42] The Liberal party remained the main opponent to the Likud's total unification, because it feared a seizure of the central governing body of Herut.

Above all, the Likud did its best to promote its "ethnic" image, which was one of a staunch and uncompromising advocate of Sephar-dic Jews.[43] To achieve this goal, the leaders came to several decisions. First, the image of David Levy—one of the main Herut leaders—was put into the spotlight. Levy, a Moroccan immigrant, was very popular among those Jews who came from Arab countries and who could identify with him: He was the father of eleven children; he was not religious but traditionalist; he was formerly a construction worker; he lived in a deprived development town (Beit Shean). Levy's stature was further enhanced during the Histadrut electoral campaign, which preceded the Knesset ballot: "David Levy, a strong man in the Histadrut!" was the slogan. Furthermore, the notion of "the strong man" has always been attractive for this stratum of the population, and it applied to Begin as well as to David Levy.

Because these people were respectful of Jewish tradition, the prime minister stressed his good relations with the religious parties and the government's record in the field of religious legislation.[44] Because they had settled mainly in development towns, these towns were the focus of the Likud's electoral campaign. The party, for example, harshly criticized the "kibbutzim establishment" (the kibbutzim, frequently located near immigrant towns, enjoy a much higher standard of living, provoking the envy and bitterness of the towns' poor inhabitants). Finally, the Likud was successful in giving wide publicity to Labor's maladroit handling of the Jews from Arab countries.

In summary, then, the dangers of the "Jordanian option," the statesmanship of the prime minister, a united Likud, and the defense of the Sephardic Jews were the four central themes of the Likud's campaign.

Which Economic Policy?
After the resignation of Yigal Hurvitz in January 1981, Yoram Aridor of Herut was appointed finance minister. Aridor's policy was completely opposed to that of his predecessor, and he immediately made several popular decisions. His first decision was to order Israel Television to prepare all its programs in full color before January 1, 1982. The tax on color television sets was reduced, which caused sellers to lower prices. In January 1981, only 25 percent of the television sets in Israel were color, and every survey indicated that possession of a color set was a dream for thousands of Israelis.[45]

Following this first step, the new minister undertook a tax-reduction policy on a grand scale. Taxes were reduced on expensive products which most Israelis wanted to buy, such as washing machines, refrigerators, cars, and so forth.

The population received these measures enthusiastically, and the minister followed with other decisions such as:

> granting cost-of-living increments that would *totally* compensate the workers for inflation

making government bonds and savings plans more attractive

curbing the devaluation of the shekel

restoring or increasing government subsidies to basic products

not raising the price of gasoline, even when world oil prices rose

not taxing capital gains and stock exchange profits [46]

In spite of the Alignment's protestations, the finance minister explained his economic policy on television. The opposition asserted that it was a rather unusual step for a minister to use the national media for "party purposes," just before the beginning of the electoral campaign. Later, the minister summed up his policy by these words: "Don't be in too much of a rush to buy today, for tomorrow things may be cheaper still."

Israelis, seized by a frenzy of buying, profited greatly from the tax reductions. Purchases of electric appliances increased dramatically on the eve of the election. Aridor's policy was a major theme of the Likud's television campaign. Not only the Alignment, but also most election commentators based the Likud's comeback on the finance minister's economic measures.

Finally, few choices were made—in the context of the campaign—concerning certain individuals. In the Likud, as in the Alignment, individual personalities played a disproportionate role. For example, Begin decided to entrust his foreign minister, Yitzhak Shamir, with the Likud's campaign management. He decided also to call back to the party the leading industrialist, Ya'acov Meridor—a living example of economic success, the kind of success destined for the state if the Likud won the elections.

When the problem of an eventual reintegration into the Likud of former Herut star Shmuel Tamir was discussed, however, the entire leadership of Herut voted against him. On the electoral level, Tamir would have been a genuine asset for the Likud. But the former leader (with Yigael Yadin and Amnon Rubenstein) of the Democratic Movement for Change was rejected for two major reasons: first, his charisma made him a possible heir of Begin as leader of the party and, second, he advocated positions on Judea-Samaria that were considered by most Likud members to be too moderate.

The Unfolding of the Campaign

Political Violence

One of the toughest campaigns in the political history of Israel, the 1981 electoral campaign was characterized by many violent acts. Violence surged sharply upward at the end of April, during the traditional festival of Moroccan Jews, the Mimouna. In Jerusalem, Shimon Peres and the secretary general of the Histadrut, Yeroham Meshel, were assaulted by youngsters who shouted pro-Likud slogans.[47] As a result, Central Election Committee President Moshe Etzioni issued a warning and asked all parties to refrain from violence. Anti-Likud papers emphasized the tradition of political violence that had marked Herut's history and recalled the street demonstrations against relations with Germany in the 1950s.

During the whole campaign—and especially near the end—the Alignment asserted that the perpetrators of these violent assaults were Likud members or people paid by the Likud. It was not able to prove, however, that it was a deliberate Likud policy to deprive Labor of its right of expression by assaulting speakers at political rallies.

During May and June, the number of disruptive acts multiplied. Most involved a few youngsters gathered in front of Alignment meetings, shouting pro-Likud or pro-Begin slogans that prevented Labor leaders from speaking. The most serious disturbance took place in Petach Tikva, at a meeting to be addressed by the opposition leader. On several occasions, Peres and Rabin had to be protected when they left their political meetings.

From the beginning of May, the Likud campaign managers began to grow anxious about this phenomenon, which could tarnish the party's democratic, open, liberal image.[48] The prime minister repeatedly called on his electorate to refrain from violence, to be patient and tolerant toward the socialist opposition, and not to interfere in the Alignment's meetings. He strongly denied, however, any Likud role in the assaults.

These attempts of the Likud leadership to limit the interference of their militants in the Labor campaign proved ineffective, and the assaults became more and more serious. In the second half of June, the issue of violence became the Alignment's war cry, and the last days of its campaign focused on the equation "Beginism = fascism." The Likud's inability to curb the violence of its own supporters may have contributed to the sudden rise of Labor just before June 30. The assaults negatively affected the remaining undecided voters; and the seriousness of the situation convinced leftist and liberal voters to abandon the small parties (Shelli, Shinui, and the Citizens' Rights and Peace movement) and vote for Labor in an effort to defeat the Likud.

The Media Campaign

The Likud's campaign on radio and especially on television was extremely effective and contributed to its success. From the technical point of view as well as from the standpoint of content, it was much more effective than the Alignment drive. It was a truly professional campaign (the Likud, like the other big parties, was counseled by advertising agencies). One of the most successful aspects of the Likud campaign was its jingle, which told the voter that he "must choose between continuing the move forward or sinking back. The Likud is on the right road." Begin was almost the sole performer in the Likud campaign: He was presented as a dynamic, reliable man, "a family man waxing ecstatic about a favorite granddaughter, and a hard statesman who [didn't] mind a 16-hour workday."[49] This was a very different style from that of Labor, which did not emphasize the personality of Peres. The two other foci of the Likud's radio and television spots were the peace treaty and the Yoram Aridor economic policy.

The high point of the campaign was the Begin-Peres debate on television on election eve. In spite of a few tactical errors (such as too much insistence on statistics, on the Irgun's history, and so on), Begin was effective with his own electorate. For example,

Begin was indignant at Peres's declaration that Labor saw Begin "as simply a party leader, not as a prime minister" (the Likud head knew very well that his electorate was intensely respectful of authority and of titles and functions).

Begin concluded the debate in a very positive and "traditionalist" manner: by asking each side to forgive the other's offenses and by emphasizing the maxim "Love thy neighbor as thyself."

In conclusion, on the level of its "decisive options" as well as in its television campaign, the Likud proved to be very effective. Its strategy was supported by such powerful actions as the attack against the Iraqi nuclear reactor, the criticism of West Germany, and the summits with the Egyptian president. The campaign was totally centered on the personality of Begin. The only failure of the Likud was its incapacity to limit the violence.

The Election Results of June 30, 1981

Global Results

Of the 1,937,366 valid votes, the Likud, which presented the MHL list, obtained 718,941 votes (37.1 percent).[50] The Alignment, which presented the EMT list, obtained 708,536 votes (36.6 percent).

The Likud won 48 seats (out of 120), instead of the 43 seats it previously had, while the Alignment, because of this 0.5 percent gap, won only 47. (However, after the ballot, the sole deputy of the Citizens' Rights and Peace movement joined the Alignment, which gave the latter the same number of seats as the Likud. Furthermore, from the voter percentage vantage, the "new" Alignment exceeded the Likud: it was credited with 38 percent of the valid votes.)

Apparently, the two big parties had very similar overall results. But we shall see in our conclusions that such quasi equality is rather far removed from reality and that the Likud's results were more promising than those of the Alignment.

The two big parties, with a total of 76 percent of the vote, were the only political forces that received votes in almost all the polling stations of Israel. The other parties had a much more concentrated electorate.[51]

With 37.1 percent of the vote, the Likud achieved its best result in the country's history (either as a united party, or as the sum of the former results of its components). In 1977, it had received 35.4 percent (if we take into account the votes obtained by Ariel Sharon's party, Shlomzion, which joined the Likud immediately after the elections). In 1973, after the Yom Kippur War, it won only 30.2 percent of the vote. Thus it seems that the Likud was steadily progressing, even if its 1977–1981 gain (+1.7 percent) was smaller than its 1973–1977 gain (+5.2 percent).

On one hand, the Likud's victory was smaller than could have been expected during the months that immediately followed its 1977 victory: In the second half of 1977 it could probably have reached an absolute majority. The June 30, 1981, result was also less than the Likud would have won if the elections had taken place one or two weeks before, when the political effects of the electoral violence had not yet been felt.

Nevertheless, Likud leaders may rightfully claim that they gained a brilliant victory over the Alignment. First, the idea that the Likud could obtain forty-eight seats in the Knesset was unthinkable during most of the period it governed the country previously. In 1980, the Alignment appeared on the verge of total victory over the Likud. Second, the components of the Likud had their best results in the state's history. Finally, it succeeded in mustering its 1977 voters, while the Alignment, although it recovered from its previous defeat, remained 3 percent below its 1973 result.

Analysis of the Election

The Likud appears to be firmly rooted in urban localities. Its success was greater in cities than in the countryside. Eighty percent of the votes garnered by the Likud came from Jewish towns, as compared to 70 percent of the votes obtained by Labor. Concerning the three biggest cities of the country, the number of Alignment votes exceeded Likud votes only in Haifa. In Jerusalem, the Likud got 41.5 percent of the votes, and in Tel Aviv 40.9 percent.

The Likud achieved impressive gains in polling stations located in the poorest quarters of the major cities, which are generally populated by immigrants from Arab countries. In Jerusalem, for example, while it got only 25.2 percent in the residential areas of Rehavin and Kiryat Shmuel, it obtained 57.8 percent of the votes in the poor quarters of Morasha and Mamila or 57.1 percent in Kiryat Menachem and Ir Ganim. In Tel Aviv, while it gained only 26.3 percent in the upper-income areas of Ramat-Aviv, the University and Afeka, it reached 58.6 percent in lower-income areas such as Kerem Hatemanim, and even 60.3 percent in southwest Tel Aviv.

The Likud obtained its best results in the new development towns; 24 percent of its total votes. In these towns, the most serious rival of the Likud was Tami (the Movement for the Tradition of Israel) of Aharon Abu-Hatzeira, which had the same electorate: Tami got 46 percent of its votes from the development towns (in comparison, these localities account for only 13–14 percent of the Alignment's votes).

In general, while the Likud received 37.1 percent of the votes in the whole population, it obtained nearly 50 percent of the votes in the new towns. This also meant that the electorate of the Likud was rather more concentrated than that of the Alignment: 37 percent of the Likud voters were located in polling stations where this party got more than half of the votes, while the parallel proportion for the Alignment was only 29 percent.

The Likud derived a certain benefit from the sharp decline in the

National Religious party's electorate. It is impossible to ascertain how many former supporters of the NRP voted for the Likud in the last election, but they almost certainly contributed one or two seats to the latter. The Likud and the NRP have distinctive electorates, but they attempt to reach similar categories of the population. In 1981, some of the disgruntled NRP voters turned to the Likud, but most of them voted for Tami (which won three seats). Thus Tami prevented the Likud from obtaining an even better result. These two parties had the highest percentages of voters in the same localities. In addition, they shared most of the votes representing Samuel Flatto-Sharon's supporters in 1977. (In 1981, the Flatto-Sharon got only 0.6 percent of the vote and was not reelected.)

The Likud's results were less impressive in the traditional Alignment strongholds, particularly in the oldest urban localities (established before the creation of the state) and in the residential quarters of the big towns, where the proportion of immigrants from Europe and the United States was higher. Thus, while in the new Jewish towns the Likud got 49 percent of the votes and the Alignment 29.5 percent, they obtained respectively 39.7 percent and 36.8 percent in the older towns. The Likud was even weaker in the kibbutzim, which are firmly bound to the parties of the Alignment. The Likud's best results were obtained in the "new kibbutzim" (2.3 percent) and in the kibbutzim of Hapoel Hamizrachi (bound to the NRP).[52] The Likud fared much better in the moshavim, but there was a huge difference between the Likud's percentages in the older and in the newer moshavim. In the former it got only 14.2 percent of the votes; in the latter, 32.9 percent. Rural and farming settlements, however, contributed only 4 percent of the total votes received by the Likud, while the corresponding percentage was much higher for the Alignment, the NRP, and even Tehiya.

While Tami represented only a minor obstacle for the Likud, the Likud was anxious chiefly about its main objective rival, Tehiya. The Likud even tried, before the elections, to have the required minimum percentage of the total vote, which gives a party the right to be represented in the Knesset, raised from 1 percent to 2.5 percent. But such a reform, which the Likud hoped would hinder Tehiya, was not achieved.

Tehiya, however, which obtained 2.3 percent of the vote and three seats, did not seriously harm the Likud. In the new towns, and particularly in the development towns, the Tehiya did very poorly (1.5 percent). Tehiya wrested supporters from the Likud (and the NRP) only

in the settlements located in the administered territories. The score of
Tehiya in these settlements (23 percent) was ten times higher than in
the whole country. Because of Camp David, the peace treaty, and the
abandonment of the Sinai settlements, the Likud obtained fewer votes
in the territories than it had in 1977. It remained rather strong in
Judea-Samaria (35 percent) and in the Gaza-Sinai area (31 percent).
But it won only 23 percent of the votes in the Golan (the Alignment
reached 49 percent there). It is true that several Golan settlements
were affiliated to Labor and that there was a relatively wide national
consensus on the necessity to keep the Golan. Tehiya faced the same
difficulty as the Likud in the Golan, where it won 17 percent of the
votes and 25–27 percent in the other administered territories.

Aftermath of the Election

Although the Alignment and the Likud each got forty-eight seats in
the Knesset, the Likud was in a much better position to form a government coalition. Among the seven small parties represented in the
Knesset, and which could be potential partners in a coalition, five had
either already declared their preference for the Likud (the NRP,
Agudat Israel, and Tami) or found themselves nearer to the Likud
than to the Alignment (Tehiya and in a certain measure Moshe Dayan's
Telem).

The Alignment could not officially include the Communists in a
coalition. There remained only Shinui and perhaps Telem as possible
partners in a government, and these in any case would not give Labor
a majority. On July 14, after the official publication of the election results, President Yitzhak Navon asked the Likud leader to try to set up
a new government. Menachem Begin declared that he was very op-
timistic and that a government would be presented to the Knesset before July 27, the day of the next Israel-Egypt summit.

It was not an easy task, however. It quickly became obvious that
Telem and Tehiya would not enter the coalition. The former presented unacceptable demands, such as Israel's unilateral extension of
autonomy rule on the territories or the appointment of Dayan as head
of the autonomy negotiations. The latter was too opposed to the basic
principles of the Likud's policy toward Egypt to be a desirable partner.

Therefore, the Likud needed the participation of all three religious
parties: Such a government would have had a base of only sixty-one
Knesset members, and the defection of one party would ruin the

Likud's efforts to set up a coalition (a minority government, although considered usual in many countries, could not last long in Israel).

The main difficulty was the rather strained relationships between the NRP and its offshoot, Tami. After having agreed to coexist in a Likud-led coalition, they fought for the crucial Religious Affairs Ministry, which was thought by each party to be its natural possession.

Furthermore, their indispensability led the religious parties to increase their demands for cabinet seats and for future religiously oriented legislation. Because of these demands, each of the Likud's components also claimed more portfolios. Begin found himself in danger of having an inflated and unworkable cabinet. The NRP religious demands on the one hand induced Agudat Israel to insist on more privileges, while on the other these demands incensed the secularist elements of the Likud.

The two main factors that helped the Likud leader to speed up the three parties' entry into a coalition were Begin's threat to call for new elections, which would probably further reduce the small parties' representation, and the deteriorating situation in the north of the country, with Palestinian bombings of Israeli towns and Israeli counterattacks in Lebanon. On August 4, Menachem Begin reached an agreement with his religious partners, and the day after, a new Likud-led government was presented to the Knesset. Even if each coalition's party had to give up certain demands—the Likud itself relinquished the Immigrant Absorption portfolio, which caused tension within Herut—Begin's new cabinet was unusually large and included the highest number of vice-ministers ever seen in the state's coalition-making history.

Conclusion

The election results for the Likud in June 1981 must be carefully evaluated. In large measure, the Likud's achievement was more significant than that of the Labor Alignment, for at least three reasons.

First, one of the most interesting characteristics of this election was the surprising vote of an important part of the non-Jewish minorities for the Alignment. These Israeli Arabs were generally thought to support Rakah, the Israeli Communist party.[53] A part of the votes received by Labor came, therefore, from a population whose growing Arab nationalist feelings were well known as was its hostility toward any Zionist party. The Arabs who voted for the Alignment did so to

bar a Likud victory. This sector of the population will probably return
to Rakah in the long run and, in any case, cannot be considered by
Labor as a reliable indication of its recovery. On the contrary, even if it
continues to attract a few hundred non-Jewish (mostly Druse) votes,
the Likud is supported mostly by the Jewish population, which is totally identified with the state's interests and future.[54]

Second, even if the Likud did receive the votes of citizens who
feared, above all, the return of the socialists to the government, such a
phenomenon was much more obvious in the case of the Alignment.
The large majority of Likud electors voted for it because they preferred it, because they identified with it, and because they liked its
policies and its leader. This was a case of positive identification. On
the contrary, an important part of those who chose the EMT (Labor)
list did so to prevent the Likud from remaining in office, not because
they liked the Alignment policies or admired its leadership. The best
indication of such an attitude is the complete elimination of the Zionist
extreme left (Shelli), which temporarily lost its constituency to the
Alignment, and the surprisingly poor showing of the two left-of-
center parties, Shinui and the Citizens' Rights and Peace movement,
which also lost a part of their electorates to the Alignment. This was
also the meaning of the slogan *Rak lo Likud* (vote for any party except
the Likud), which was very popular during the campaign in circles
close to the Alignment. To sum up, the Alignment cannot hope to
base its return to power on the totality of the votes it got on June 30,
1981, while almost all the votes given to the Likud were given specifi-
cally and positively to it.

Third, on the demographic level, the Likud is supported by a Jewish electorate that is clearly more dynamic than that of the Alignment.
The population that votes for the Likud may truly be considered the
country's future: Above all, they are the young generation, the age
group 18–21 years old, the soldiers as well as the inhabitants of new
localities, towns, or moshavim, the new immigrants (from Arab countries and also from the Soviet Union), the large families, etc. On the
contrary, the Alignment's voters represent much more the past history
of Israel: older strata of the population, smaller families of European
or American origin, inhabitants of older localities, kibbutzim, etc.

Still, the Likud's campaign and the methods used to achieve its brilliant results show that the Likud may also suffer a setback. Negative
factors could provoke a Likud defeat. The three most dangerous potential problems facing the party are:

The problem of "after Begin." It is indeed hard to see what leader or collective leadership might be able to impose relative cohesion on the Likud's components, a relative cohesion that, until now, has been achieved only with difficulty by the Herut leader.

The basic economic problem. The Likud was not defeated, mainly because of a series of short-run specific economic measures. It is hard to believe that the popular electorate of the Likud would continue to support this party in the next election if inflation continues to escalate at the same rate as it did during the Ninth Knesset.

American and world pressures. These external pressures could drastically increase, obliging Israel to make more concessions. If these concessions were to concern very sensitive areas such as Jerusalem, the Golan, or Judea and Samaria, the whole political spectrum of Israel would be upset and the Likud could hardly escape a profound internal crisis.

NOTES

1. This account is based on the study by Ilan Greilsammer, "Histoire des partis politiques israeliens" [History of Israeli Political Parties], in Bernhard Blumenkranz, ed., *Histoire de l'Etat d'Israel* [History of the State of Israel] (Private edition, forthcoming). See also Benjamin Akzin, "The Likud," in Howard R. Penniman, ed., *Israel at the Polls: The Knesset Election of 1977* (Washington, D.C.: American Enterprise Institute, 1979), pp. 91–114.

2. See, for example, Leonard Fein, *Politics in Israel* (Boston: Little, Brown, & Co., 1967), pp. 88–91; and David Zohar, *Political Parties in Israel: The Evolution of Israeli Democracy* (New York: Praeger, 1974), pp. 48–50.

3. See David Niv, *Ma'archot Hairgun Hatsvai Haleumi*, 6 vols. (Tel Aviv: Klausner Institute, 1965–1979); Menachem Begin, *The Revolt*, 5th ed. (Jerusalem: Steimatsky, 1972); and Eitan Haber, *Menachem Begin: The Legend and the Man* (New York: Delacorte Press, 1978).

4. On the Revisionist movement, see Joseph B. Schechtman and Yehuda Benari, *History of the Revisionist Movement* (Tel Aviv: Hadar, 1970); Ruth Daniela, "Hamiflaga harevisionistit haeretz-Israelit 1925–1935" (M.A. thesis, Tel Aviv University, 1970). On Jabotinsky's life and thought see, for example, Joseph B. Schechtman, *Fighter and Prophet: The Vladimir Jabotinsky Story* (New York: Thomas Yoseloff, 1961). See also Zev Jabotinsky, *Neumim, 1905–1926* (Jerusalem: Eri Jabotinsky Press, 1947); and *Ketavim Ziyonim Rishonim* [Early Zionist Writings] (Jerusalem: Eri Jabotinsky Press, 1949). In the first elections to the Knesset in 1949, the Revisionist party ran its own slate of candidates. Herut won fourteen seats, the Revisionists, none. In 1950, Herut became the Israeli branch of the World Revisionist movement, and its leader, Begin, the leader of the world movement.

5. For a study of the Jewish political forces before the creation of the state,

see Dan Horowitz and Moshe Lissak, *Origins of the Israeli Polity: Palestine under the Mandate* (Chicago: University of Chicago Press, 1978).

6. On June 20, 1948, during the first Arab-Israeli cease-fire, an Irgun ship, *Altalena*, clandestinely reached the shores of Israel, carrying a huge quantity of weapons and ammunition and about 800 young people, some of whom had received military training. When the ship appeared off the shore of Tel Aviv, it was blown up by Israeli artillery.

7. See Nicholas Balbkuis, *West German Reparations to Israel* (New Brunswick, N.J.: Rutgers University Press, 1971) and Inge Deutschkron, *Bonn and Jerusalem* (Philadelphia: Chilton Book Co., 1970).

8. Rudolf Kasztner was a former Zionist leader in Romania and Hungary, who settled in Palestine after the war. He became very active in Mapai. In 1953 he was accused of having collaborated with the Nazis in Hungary. The question of Kasztner's past provoked a government crisis and became a crucial element of the 1955 electoral campaign. Kasztner was assassinated in 1957.

9. On the Land of Israel movement, see Rael Jean Isaac, *Israel Divided: Ideological Politics in the Jewish State* (Baltimore: The Johns Hopkins University Press, 1976), chap. 3.

10. See Dan Horowitz, "More than a Change in Government," *Jerusalem Quarterly*, no. 5 (Fall 1977), pp. 3–19.

11. See the analysis of specialist Louis Guttman in *Jerusalem Post*, November 30, 1977.

12. Ibid.

13. Ibid.

14. *Jerusalem Post*, November 8, 1978.

15. *Jerusalem Post*, April 24, 1979.

16. Ibid.

17. *Jerusalem Post*, September 21, 1979.

18. According to an opinion poll conducted two months before the 1981 election, about 75 percent of the population favored the continuation of the settlement policy in Judea-Samaria. *Jerusalem Post*, May 6, 1981.

19. On this important annexation pressure group, see the recent study by Zvi Raanan, *Gush Emunim* (Tel Aviv: Sifriat Poalim, 1980).

20. *Jerusalem Post*, January 31, 1980.

21. *Jerusalem Post*, April 25, 1980.

22. *Jerusalem Post*, July 1, 1980, and July 15, 1980.

23. On this subject, see the chapter "Change in Israeli Economy" in Ilan Greilsammer, *Israel el l'Europe, Histoire des relations entre la Communaute Europeenne et l'Etat d'Israel* (Lausanne: Centre de Recherches Europeennes, 1981), pp. 120 ff.

24. See *Le Monde*, June 13, 1978, and November 8, 1978; and *Financial Times*, July 12, 1979.

25. See Sever Plocker, "Economic Anarchy," *New Outlook*, vol. 23, no. 5 (July–August 1979), pp. 34–38.

26. *Jerusalem Post*, November 21, 1979.

27. *Le Monde*, November 21, 1979.

28. See *Ecnomic Review* (Bank Leumi), no. 90, 1980.

29. *Jerusalem Post*, May 31, 1979.

30. Menachem Begin's victory in his own party was achieved at a Herut central committee session, in November 1978. See *Jerusalem Post*, November 23, 1978.

31. For an analysis of the characteristics and functions of the two-parties situation on the Likud's right (Tehiya and Rabbi Meir Kahana's Kach), see Ilan

Greilsammer, "Les groupes politiques marginaux en Israel: Caractéristiques et fonctions," *Revue Française de Science Politique*, vol. 31, no. 516, pp. 891–921, 1981.

32. These bitter personal attacks were analyzed in the *Jerusalem Post*, March 1, 1981.

33. The evaluations of voter inclination given by the various Israeli opinion poll institutes are frequently divergent. For example, three institutes asked the same question at the beginning of May 1981 and got the following results:

Modi'in Ezrachi (*Jerusalem Post*): Likud 41, Alignment 41

Pori Institute (Harretz): Likud 36, Alignment 41

Institute for Applied Science Research (Yediot Aharonot): Likud 23, Alignment 34

See the *Jerusalem Post*, May 18, 1981.

34. See the *Jerusalem Post*, June 30, 1977.

35. See *Jerusalem Post*, October 6 and 17, November 8 and 13, 1978. These local elections were characterized by the apathy of the public and a general climate of indifference.

36. *Jerusalem Post*, June 12, 1980.

37. *Jerusalem Post*, April 8, 1981.

38. On the profile of the average Likud voter, see the study by Mina Zemach and Amiram Yarkoni (then directors of the Modi'in Ezrachi Institute) in the *Jerusalem Post*, April 24, 1979.

39. The isolated Knesset members who could have helped the Likud in continuing to govern until the end of its mandate were generally remnants of the late Democratic Movement for Change.

40. This central theme was exposed by Yoram Aridor to Herut militants as early as August 1980. See the *Jerusalem Post*, August 25, 1980.

41. *Jerusalem Post*, May 4, 1981.

42. *Jerusalem Post*, May 11, 1981.

43. According to Daniel J. Elazar, one of the main reasons for the attraction of Begin for Sephardic Jews was his own past as an "outsider" in Israeli politics, which allowed him to present himself as the spokesman of all the outsiders and marginals in Israeli society. See "The 1981 Elections: Some Observations," *Viewpoints of the Jerusalem Center*, August 15, 1981; see also Alain Greilsammer, "Israel, une democratie a repenser," *Les Nouveaux Cahiers* (Paris), no. 66 (Autumn 1981), pp. 1–6.

44. Even if the most religiously oriented bills voted by the Ninth Knesset were initiated by the NRP and Agudat Israel, religious legislation has satisfied a wide segment of Herut's traditionalist electorate. Furthermore, Eliezer Don-Yehiya and Charles S. Liebman observe that Begin has used religious terminology throughout his career. See "Zionist Ultranationalism and its Attitude toward Religion," *Journal of Church and State*, vol. 23, no. 2 (1981), p. 271, note 42.

45. The Central Bureau of Statistics had just indicated that, during the first nine months of 1980, the number of television sets sold to the public had declined by 19 percent. *Jerusalem Post*, January 14, 1981.

46. For an exposé of the economic orientations of the new minister, see the *Jerusalem Post*, January 20 and 25, 1981.

47. *Jerusalem Post*, Aprl 28, 1981.

48. The manager of the Jerusalem Likud campaign, Y. Matsa, publicly declared: "The whole subject of political violence could hurt us. . . . We want the whole thing out of the headlines." *Jerusalem Post*, June 18, 1981.

49. *Jerusalem Post*, June 3, 1981.

50. The results quoted in the following pages are taken from the Central Bureau of Statistics, *Results of the Elections to the Tenth Knesset (30.6.81), First Detailed Conclusions*, Jerusalem, October 1981.

51. Polling stations in which neither the Likud nor the Alignment got any votes represent only 1 percent of all polling stations in the country.

52. In 1977 the Likud had obtained much better results in the kibbutzim: 3.1 percent in the old (prestate), 4.2 percent in the new kibbutzim.

53. See Alain Greilsammer, *Les Communistes Israeliens* (Paris: Presses de la Fondation Nationale des Sciences Politiques, 1978).

54. Results of the Likud in non-Jewish settlements: 3.3 percent in the towns; 5.2 percent in "urban localities"; 7.8 percent in large villages; 11.4 percent in small villages; and 10.1 percent in Bedouin tribes.

V

THE RELIGIOUS PARTIES

Shmuel Sandler

If the 1977 election results were marked by a major upheaval in the Israeli political system—that is, Labor's defeat at the polls for the first time in the history of the Jewish state—the 1981 elections marked another significant political transformation. The National Religious party (NRP; in Hebrew, Miflaga Datit Leumit, or Mafdal)—the largest party in the religious camp—lost half its Knesset representation and consequently was reduced from a medium-sized to a small party. Although the 1981 elections did not favor the smaller parties in general, the fact that Agudat Yisrael, the second largest religious party, maintained its parliamentary strength and even came very close to increasing it from four to five seats[1] (see table 5–1) indicates that the NRP's decline cannot be attributed merely to a general political trend. Moreover, the total elimination of the third religious party—Poalei Agudat Yisrael (PAY), whose positions on national issues were closer to NRP than to the Agudah—as a result of the 1981 elections also supports the need for a more profound inquiry into the religious camp.

In the June 1981 elections the NRP's parliamentary strength was slashed in half—a marked decline especially since the Mafdal had demonstrated a stable record of winning ten to twelve seats from its inception. This phenomenon was also striking in terms of Israeli politics in general, which is not accustomed to such a sharp decline on the part of a major political force, well established and rooted in public life. Obviously, there were immediate visible factors to explain the drastic shift of voters. The appearance of two other semireligious parties that competed with the Mafdal for its traditional constituency definitely contributed to the defeat (see table 5–2). Tehiya (Rebirth), the ultranationalist party which drew much of its strength from Gush Emunim, attracted many of the traditional and potential supporters

TABLE 5-1

**Final Results of Elections to the Ninth and Tenth Knessets
for Major Religious Lists**

List	1977			1981		
	Popular Vote	Per-cent	Seats	Popular Vote	Per-cent	Seats
National Religious Party	160,787	9.2	12	95,232	4.9	6
Agudat Yisrael	58,652	3.4	4	72,312	3.7	4
Poalei Agudat Yisrael	23,571	1.3	1	17,090	0.9	—

SOURCE: The Central Bureau of Statistics, *Results of Elections to the Tenth Knesset*, Jerusalem, October 1981, pp. 6–7.

TABLE 5-2

Final Results for Tehiya and Tami

List	Popular Vote	Percent	Seats
Tehiya	44,700	2.3	3
Tnuat Masoret Yisrael	44,466	2.3	3

SOURCE: The Central Bureau of Statistics, *Results of Elections*, pp. 6–7 (appeared for the first time in 1981).

of the NRP. Tnuat Masoret Yisrael (the Movement for the Tradition of Israel—Tami), headed by Aharon Abu-Hatzeira—who broke away from the NRP a month before the elections and ran under the banner of ethnic discrimination—also drew votes from the Mafdal. Similarly, the internal struggle that haunted the party in the year preceding the elections and the accusations of corruption leveled against Abu-Hatzeira did not add to the NRP's attractiveness. Nevertheless, all these factors cannot explain how a party with such a record of stability, and which a year previously had even thought of increasing its power, lost half of its supporters.[2] A careful examination, however, reveals a set of broader factors which contributed to the NRP's sharp decline. Such an analysis will explain why the NRP lost many votes not only to Tami and Tehiya but also to the Likud.[3] This analysis will also try to explain the performance of the other religious parties.

To accomplish these goals we shall begin with a brief examination of the basic differences between the religious parties. On the basis of these distinctions we shall analyze their differing roles in the development of the Israeli political system. In the course of this analysis we shall identify three major elements that influenced the political behavior of the NRP but had little effect on the Agudah. The analysis of their political behavior will include an examination of their relations with Labor and the Likud. Finally, we shall concentrate on the 1981 elections, evaluate the contribution of the differing patterns of behavior on the election results, and examine briefly the role of the religious camp in the coalition that emerged from these elections.

The NRP and Agudat Yisrael: A Comparative Analysis

The common denominator of the various Israeli religious parties is their commitment to religious law (*halachah*). This commitment essentially differentiates them from the other parties, which emphasize social and national issues and approach Judaism from a more cultural and national perspective. The distinctive nature of the Jewish religion in its Orthodox interpretation is its comprehensive penetration into almost every aspect of life. Unlike most major religions, Judaism penetrates into questions of nationality, statehood, communal life, and the Land of Israel (Eretz Yisrael). There is thus a clear dividing line between the religious parties, whose ideologies are based on Orthodox principles, and the secular parties from the socialist and the civil camps, whose approach to the state is based on a mixture of universalistic and historical principles.[4]

Despite the common denominator, there are clear dividing lines between the two major movements in the religious camp: Mizrachi (the original movement which gave rise to the NRP) and Agudat Yisrael.[5] The main point of divergence between the two movements, formally established in the early years of this century, was their attitude toward Zionism. Whereas Mizrachi was prepared to participate in the Zionist organization, despite the latter's secular orientation, and to struggle from within to strengthen religion, the Agudah was in general opposed to it. While Agudah leaders could not see how redemption could be advanced by "sinners," many of the Mizrachi ideologists were even prepared to accept the State of Israel as the beginning of redemption. The Mizrachi movement consequently participated in the central organs of the Zionist movement and of the Jewish state, while the Agudah tended to abstain from participation. This tendency was manifested not only on the political but also on the social plane. The non-Zionist Orthodox community has been separated from the rest of the Jewish state by its educational system, which is run more or less independently from the state educational system, while the religious Zionist community cooperates with the state through its state-religious trend of education.

Another feature which distinguishes the two parties is their attitude toward modernization. The Agudah's position can be classified as more traditional and antimodern than that of the NRP. This distinction can be demonstrated in two distinct areas: higher education and political authority. The attitude of the Agudah toward secular higher education is generally negative, and it sees one of its main political tasks as mobilizing funds for *yeshivot* (rabbinical colleges) where the methods of learning closely resemble those formerly prevalent in Europe. The Mizrachi, by contrast, while establishing its own system of *yeshivot* where the scope of study differs in certain respects from the Agudah institutions,[6] also established a religious university, which is an integral part of the Israeli university system. In the area of political authority, while the NRP's political leadership is elected and consults with elected central party organs, ultimate political authority in the Agudah lies with the Council of Torah Sages—an unelected body whose legitimacy derives from the personal standing of each of its members in the Orthodox community. The Chief Rabbinate—the body with which the NRP leadership consults on occasion, and whose selection is influenced to some degree by the party—is totally different from the Council of Sages. It is a state organ, elected *inter alia* by public delegates, and the NRP leadership does not see itself as obligated to adhere automatically to its decisions in matters of religion and state. Thus the formal structure of the two parties reflects two different types of parties: Whereas the NRP resembles other Israeli parties in terms of structure and political decision making, Agudah differs in its nature as a clerically dominated party.

These distinctions between the movements have been translated into different modes of behavior in the political system as well as in society. Despite the deep cleavages between religious and nonreligious Jews, the two movements differed in their degree of integration into the Israeli polity and society. The limited participation of the Agudah has been primarily pragmatic,[7] whereas Mizrachi, and its descendant, NRP, have participated in Israeli political life not only because of pragmatic considerations but also as a matter of principle. While Mizrachi justified its religious demands as designed to influence public life and the character of the Jewish state, the Agudah's main concern was defending the ultraorthodox community. A parallel distinction can be made on the social level, where Agudah supporters are more distinctive in "their style of dress, way of life and residential exclusivity"[8] as well as in their attitude toward army service and secular Jews.

Although Agudah and Mizrachi represent the two main trends in the religious camp, there are other groups that influenced these two movements. To the right of the Agudah, in terms of religious separatism, are the Neturei Karta (Guardians of the Wall), which stand for total separation from the state, anti-Zionism, and the total boycott of the Israeli political process. To the left of Agudah stands Poalei Agudat Yisrael—the labor offshoot of Agudah—which has participated to a greater extent in the Zionist enterprise. It is interesting to note that despite the small size of PAY it did not totally merge with Agudah, partly because of the separatist position of the latter. In contrast, Mizrachi and its labor offshoot, Hapoel Hamizrachi—the larger of the two and the more integrationist—merged in 1956 and established the NRP.

In sum, despite the fact that the religious camp constitutes a distinctive force in the Israeli ideological-political map, it comprises two main movements that can be defined as an integration-oriented party (NRP) and a separatist party (Agudat Yisrael).

The Role of the NRP in the Israeli Political System

The basic differences between the NRP and the Agudah pointed out above gave rise to the two different roles which the parties played in the development of the Israeli political system. The more integrationist approach of the Mizrachi resulted in a central role for the NRP in Israeli political development, whereas the more separatist approach of Agudah limited its contribution. At the same time, the mere fact that the NRP represented a separate subculture within the Jewish polity provided it with a specific role, a phenomenon that can be found in other plural societies.

The dual character of the NRP—integration and segmentalism—has had an impact on both its electoral appeal and its behavior within the political system. It emerged as the largest party in the religious camp and at the same time became almost a permanent partner in Israeli coalition formation. Despite the relatively stable performance of the NRP, however, its role and behavior have changed over the years. In retrospect, it can be argued that the NRP's transformation was linked to that of the Israeli political system as a whole. Accordingly, we shall analyze the party's role in three major periods in Israel's political development: the formative years; the transitional period, in which the NRP became a partner in the Labor government; and the third period, in which it became a partner in the Likud government.

The NRP and Labor: The Origins and Development of the "Historical Partnership"

The Formative Years

The origins of the NRP's role in Israeli political development can be traced to the period of the Yishuv—the preindependence Jewish political community in Palestine. During that period a coalition between Mizrachi–Hapoel Hamizrachi and Mapai (Mifleget Poalei Eretz Yisrael—the Israeli Workers party), the largest faction in the Labor movement, came into being—a coalition that over the years came to be called the "historical partnership." Unlike Agudat Yisrael, which remained outside the central organs of the Yishuv, Mizrachi contributed to the consolidation of the Jewish political center in Palestine, which radiated authority both internally and externally.[9] This coalition was extended into the postindependence era and became a cornerstone in Israeli politics for almost thirty years, thus enabling the formation of relatively stable governments. What were the main factors that contributed to the emergence of this coalition and its maintenance for over four decades? Why did a secular party like Mapai choose to include the NRP in its governments and concede to its demands in religious affairs when it could form a ruling coalition without it?[10]

The Mapai-NRP relationship can be approached from three perspectives—conflict regulation, ideological proximity, and political strategy. The first approach[11] is influenced by the consociational politics theory, and it explains the relationship in terms of "accommodation politics."[12] The basis for the Mapai-NRP alliance was not their congruent ideological positions, but rather their conflicting interests in the area of religion and state. In the words of one student of religion and state, "both Labor and the NRP realized that the only alternative to a coalition was a Kulturkampf—a possibility which frightened them both."[13] Such coalitions, which are common in deeply divided societies, are based on accommodation and power-sharing arrangements among elites of opposing camps. Indeed, the Mapai-NRP partnership prevented a schism between the religious and anticlerical camps in the

Yishuv and later in the Jewish state. The consociational approach that characterized the Yishuv period, according to Dan Horowitz and Moshe Lissak,[14] was thus carried over to the Jewish state and was practiced with the religious party under different governments.

Although consociational arrangements are based on an agreement between elites representing different segments of society, there is a need for the existence of a strong overarching loyalty.[15] It was therefore only natural that this arrangement should be made with a party which supported the Zionist idea. In this sense the NRP was a more desirable partner than Agudat Yisrael—which was more separatist in nature. Nevethess, up to 1977, the Agudah parties, though not participating formally in the government, usually worked out tacit agreements through which they received recognition and financial support for their separate educational system in exchange for restraint on their part in the opposition. The NRP, despite strong criticism from the non-Zionist Orthodoxy, succeeded in reconciling its two main ideological principles—Zionism and religion. By sharing power with the ruling party it accomplished segmental autonomy in education, but as part of the state educational system it maintained veto power on religious legislation concerning personal law and the maintenance of the status quo in matters of public life—for example, Sabbath observance in public areas and kosher food in public institutions. Moreover, this arrangement provided the NRP with a substantial share of power in various ministries and in economic and political institutions.[16] In short, the consociational arrangement served the interests of both parties, thus avoiding an open conflict between the religious and anticlerical camps.

The second approach in explaining the Mapai-NRP relationship stresses the ideological proximity between the two parties.[17] According to this approach, what characterized the relationship between the Labor and Mizrachi camps was their partnership in the main tasks of the Zionist enterprise—settlement, defense, and immigration absorption. This partnership, which characterized both parties in the Yishuv period, was carried over to the state and, according to pro-Labor elements in the NRP, is still relevant today.[18] The proponents of this approach argue that while the Revisionists or the General Zionists (the main components of Likud) were never genuine partners in the Jewish state-building process, the Labor and Mizrachi movements—their youth and labor organizations, their kibbutzim and moshavim (agricultural settlements)—constituted the vanguard of the Zionist revolution. This sharing in the implementation of Zionism resulted in the political partnership that characterized the Israeli ruling coalitions throughout the formative years and beyond, transcending arithmetic considerations and disagreement on questions of religion and state. In contrast, such proximity did not exist between Labor and Agudat Yisrael, which separated itself from the Zionist enterprise and concentrated on religious institution-building rather than state-building. Poalei Agudat Yisrael, in this sense, did cooperate with Labor in settlement and other related enterprises.

Whereas the previous two approaches interpret the partnership as based on ideological differences and proximity, respectively, the third approach sees the partnership as originating from purely political interests. The thesis behind this approach is that the partnership served the particular interests of two elites and eventually broke down because they no longer perceived that alliance as serving their particular interests.[19]

Mapai-NRP cooperation originated in the mid-1930s, at a time when Mapai consolidated its dominant position both in the Labor camp and within the Yishuv. It was around that time that David Ben-Gurion emerged as the central figure in the Zionist organization—a role he fulfilled almost uninterruptedly until the early 1960s. Ben-Gurion, as a political realist par excellence, realized that power is relative and therefore maintained his dominant position by keeping his opposition divided. The secret to Mapai's dominant role in Israeli politics lay not so much in its electoral strength, which never exceeded forty-seven parliamentary seats (about 36 percent of the electorate), but rather in the fact that its opposition was divided between left and right, preventing them from forming an alternative coalition. One indication of this strategy is the fact that Ben-Gurion never formed a coalition with a party from either the Labor or the civil camp, that might eventually have endangered Mapai's dominant role.

Within this framework, the NRP did not threaten to become a majority party and thus an alternative to Mapai's dominant role. The relatively limited base of the religious party and its concurrent interests, limited mainly to religious issues, provided Mapai with both a safe partner in terms of power politics and a free hand in such areas as foreign policy, defense, and economic development, which it considered vital to both state and party interests. To accomplish these goals, Mapai, and especially its uncontested leader, was ready to provide its religious partner with autonomy in religious matters and to share power in areas pertinent to the religious party.

The NRP, for its part, had an inherent interest in cooperating with

Mapai in such a framework. First, this scheme provided the party with a monopoly over state religion, thus strengthening its position in the religious camp. In the competition between the NRP and the Agudah, the former could thus provide public benefits derived from its participation in the establishment and the state institutional framework. Second, the constant threat that Mapai would form a coalition with parties from the left wing of the Labor camp or the liberal camp, which were anticlerical in their outlook, also provided the religious party with an incentive to cooperate with the plurality party. Third, the main concern of the NRP in the early stages of statehood lay in religious matters, especially in light of the secular and even anti-religious climate prevailing during that period. Thus, the strategy of divide and rule practiced by Ben-Gurion and the exchange of a free hand in state government for concessions on religious matters were of little concern to the religious party as long as the religious community could protect its status and achievements. Moreover, the bargaining over religious issues that marked public life during that period provided the NRP with its main *raison d'être* in the eyes of a constituency that generally accepted the Zionist idea. In short, the Mapai-NRP partnership that characterized the first decade and a half of the Jewish state was based on the direct political interests of both parties.

In sum, the relationship between the NRP and the strongest party in the socialist camp, which was also the plurality party in the Israeli political system, can be interpreted from three different perspectives—conflict regulation, ideological partnership, and complementary political interests. To a certain extent all three elements are linked to the NRP's basically positive attitude toward other Zionist parties and its readiness to cooperate with them, in contrast to the Agudah's more reserved attitude. The validity of these elements can be tested by examining their impact during other periods of Israel's political development

The Transitional Period

Although the period immediately following Ben-Gurion's departure from Mapai leadership was marked in certain respects by greater tranquillity in questions of religion and state, *post factum* the seeds of change were planted during those years. These changes ultimately resulted in the breakdown of the "historical partnership." Since these changes were linked to transformations in the Israeli political system, we shall begin with an examination of the political strategy of Mapai that contributed to the transformation of the political system and then proceed to changes within the NRP.

Following Ben-Gurion's resignation in 1963, his heirs, Levi Eshkol and later Golda Meir, while appearing to continue his policies, actually instituted a basic shift in Ben-Gurion's political strategy. This shift was expressed in Mapai's drive to unify all the socialist-Zionist parties into one bloc. This process, which began with the alignment between Achdut Ha'avoda and Mapai, was completed on the eve of the 1969 elections when all the social democratic parties combined to form the Labor Alignment. At the same time, the right-wing parties initiated a process of merger, completed on the eve of the 1973 elections, when almost all of the nationalist and liberal parties were united into the Likud bloc under the leadership of Herut's leader, Menachem Begin. It was precisely this situation that Ben-Gurion had tried to prevent by avoiding mergers with other socialist parties and choosing coalition partners from all camps—civil, socialist and religious. Indeed, the appearance of two broad-based alliances provided the Israeli electorate for the first time in its history with an alternative to Labor domination—a fact that was ultimately translated into political reality in the May 1977 elections.

Although the veteran leadership tried to preserve the special relationship with the NRP, the transformation of the political map necessarily influenced this relationship. The new mergers of Mapai with parties to its left that were more strongly antireligious in character signaled a threat to the maintenance of the status quo in religious affairs. Similarly, the aggrandizement process on the left, carried out under the slogan of achieving a majority party that would not need to compromise with coalition partners, also worried the NRP with regard to its future role in the government. It was against this background that new voices criticizing the traditional relationships began to be heard within the NRP. But these new voices might have remained isolated were they not accompanied by another major occurrence in the Israeli political arena that had an important impact on the NRP's ideological position and its internal composition.

As indicated earlier, there was an ideological element in the Mapai-NRP relationship. One expression of this ideological affinity was the dominance of Hapoel Hamizrachi—the labor offshoot of Mizrachi—in the internal composition of the NRP. It was Hapoel Hamizrachi—and especially the leftist Lamifne faction in it—that aborted a proposed merger with Agudat Yisrael, thus allowing the NRP more flexibility in its relations with Mapai.[20] In addition, Hapoel Hamizrachi was linked to the Labor camp through an organizational bond between the Histadrut (the trade union federation) sick fund and Histadrut Hapoel Hamizrachi. The leader of Hapoel Hamizrachi, Moshe Haim Shapira, was recognized as the uncontested leader of the NRP. But in the mid-1960s a new faction was born within the NRP. This faction, led by Zevulun Hammer, which emerged out of the young guard of the party and was known as the youth circles, contested for power within the party. Its leadership and supporters, who came from basically urban and middle-class backgrounds,[21] were not sympathetic to the party's traditional cooperation with Labor, particularly when this alliance could serve as a vehicle for attacking the Hapoel Hamizrachi establishment. In criticizing this relationship, they concentrated on the tacit bargain by which the NRP confined itself to religious issues and conceded such areas as foreign policy, defense, and economics to the ruling party. This development coincided with the acquisition of land resulting from the Six-Day War. This occurrence was the second major change that affected Israeli politics in the 1960s.

The results of the Six-Day War had a major impact on the Israeli polity and especially on the national religious movement. Unlike Agudat Yisrael, religious Zionism could not help but be affected by the liberation of ancient Jewish territories where the kingdoms of Judea and Samaria had prospered, and which symbolized the historical and religious ties to the ancient past. In time, it resulted in the emergence of Gush Emunim—the bloc of the faithful—which drew its main support from the products of the national religious schools and the youth movement. The youth circles profited from these new feelings among the NRP's constituency and established their drive for power on an ideological basis, which in time promoted them to a major faction in the NRP.

The centrality of the territorial issue in the ideological and political transformation of the NRP, especially in light of the relative immunity of Agudat Yisrael to this issue, deserves further elaboration. The Mizrachi ideology of reconciling Zionism, which was mainly secular, and Orthodoxy, which was mainly non-Zionist or even anti-Zionist, placed the national religious individual in a peculiar position. The religious Zionists felt rejected by both worlds: The secular public viewed them as an antidemocratic element committed to imposing religious law on the state, while the ultraorthodox camp considered them to be Zionist reformists.[22] Similarly, while central institutions such as the foreign service and the military were secular-oriented, the more advanced rabbinical institutions in the country, headed by the leading

Talmudic scholars, were Agudah-oriented. One example of this dilemma were the *yeshivot hesder*, established by the NRP, which combined both military service and Talmudic studies. These institutions
were criticized by both sides—one criticizing the shorter military service, the other the diluted studies. The combination of the two principles—religion and Zionism—often resulted in compromises that
bothered the more fundamentalist element in the Mizrachi movement.
The acquisition of ancient territories of the land of Israel and the political questions regarding their future provided this camp with a cause
that combined both Zionism and religion—ideals on which the young
generation of the NRP were nurtured. Settlement of Judea and
Samaria provided them with the opportunity to become the vanguard
of the Zionist revolution within a religious framework. It justified
their religious upbringing vis-à-vis the nonreligious Zionists, whom
they could criticize for betraying the traditional ideals of Zionism such
as settlement and security. At the same time, they felt superior to the
non-Zionist Orthodox camp, which, despite its religious beliefs, did
not fulfill the commandment of settling the land of Israel. In short,
they could now become the forerunners of modern Zionism, not despite their religious outlook but because of it.

The implications of this ideological transformation on the national
political scene were far-reaching. First, it weakened one of the foundations of the traditional partnership between Labor and the NRP,
namely the implicit division of roles between the two parties. The national religious camp was no longer prepared to confine itself to narrow religious issues. Religion now encompassed questions of foreign
policy and national security. Moreover, the cleavage between Labor
and Mizrachi, which was once restricted to purely religious issues,
now extended to other areas, especially since the official position of
Labor favored territorial compromise. Second, the changing attitude
of the NRP brought it closer to Herut, which was traditionally opposed to the partition of the land of Israel and was also less secular on
questions of religion and state.[23] It was therefore only a matter of time
before the NRP would join a Begin-led coalition.

Turning now to the consociational element in Israeli politics, here
too we can identify a transition, although less marked than in the
areas of political strategy and ideology. Consociationalism, according
to Arend Lijphart, is based on "segmental cleavages typical of a plural
society and the political cooperation of the segmental elites."[24] The
emergence of the territorial issue and its transcendence of divisions
between the religious and secular camps created new cleavages, which

no longer overlapped the well-defined divisions over which the traditional leadership had control. Hence, the ability of each elite to deliver its constituency into the consociational arrangement was curtailed. Despite the participation of the NRP in the Rabin government from 1974 to 1977, the two Knesset members representing the youth circles, Zevulun Hammer and Yehuda Ben-Meir, actually behaved more like opposition members.[25] Moreover, during this period, the NRP leadership could not control the actions of Gush Emunim, despite the fact that most of its leaders and mass support came from the ranks of the national religious camp. Similarly, the extension of NRP ideology and activity into questions of national security intensified objections to the "historical partnership" within the Labor camp. To many within Labor, especially its dovish wing, this new development seemed to overstep the acceptable bounds of compromise and accommodation. Finally, if compromise seemed possible in religious affairs, it was much harder to achieve in such concrete questions as whether or where to establish settlements in the West Bank.

In sum, this period from the mid-1960s to 1977 can be defined as one in which major changes took place both on the national scene and especially in the role of the National Religious party. Because of its participation in the mainstream of Israeli politics, the NRP, unlike the Agudah, as we shall see later, was influenced by national events. As in the previous period, all three elements that constituted the "historical partnership" between the NRP and Labor continued to operate in the transitional period, though in a different direction. Thus when the Likud emerged as the plurality party following the May 1977 elections, the basis for a new partnership had already been laid.

The NRP and the Likud

The relationship between the NRP and the Likud, especially with the Herut leadership within the Likud, began to develop a decade before the 1977 elections. It was the NRP that played a major role in the formation of a national unity government on the eve of the Six-Day War and again following the 1969 elections. In retrospect, this move can be seen as a landmark in the ascendancy of the Likud, since it helped remove the stigma of irresponsibility and militancy that David Ben-Gurion had succeeded in placing on the right-wing parties and especially on their leader, Menachem Begin. In the following years, this relationship was intensified, especially between the growing force in the NRP—the youth circles—and the nationalist wing in the Likud.

The extent of this proximity can be demonstrated by the fact that on the eve of the 1977 elections Hammer and Ben-Meir committed themselves to preferring a Begin-led government over a Labor government in the event such a coalition should be possible.

This commitment on the part of the young leaders was of real weight, since on the eve of the 1977 elections they had succeeded in a quiet revolution that strengthened their position within the NRP. By joining forces with other factions in the party and forming the Movement for National Religious Revival, they succeeded in emerging as the largest faction in the party and ultimately in ousting the "strong man" of the NRP Yitzhak Raphael. Although the nominal leader of the party remained Yosef Burg, the head of the Lamifne faction, which was more moderate and closer to the Labor camp on social issues, the second and third slots on the list were given to the representative of Gush Emunim, Rabbi Haim Druckman, and to Zevulun Hammer. Number four on the list was Raphael's successor in his faction, Aharon Abu-Hatzeira, who represented not only the defeated faction but also a strong Sephardic constituency, which voted for the party that stood for Jewish tradition and values. The fact that the party gained two additional Knesset seats in the 1977 elections seemed to indicate that this revolution accorded with the desires of its constituency.

From a structural point of view there was no clear power concentration in any one camp, despite the fact that the Likud emerged from the 1977 elections as the plurality party, with forty-three seats, and Labor declined from fifty-one to thirty-two mandates. The Democratic Movement for Change, headed by former chief of staff Yigael Yadin and Amnon Rubenstein, was no doubt closer to labor on issues of national security. Labor and the DMC together controlled forty-seven seats in the Knesset, two more than the forty-five seats of the Likud and the two seats won by General Ariel Sharon's party. It was therefore the NRP which, with the help of Agudat Yisrael, enabled Menachem Begin to put together a majority coalition. This was considered a victory not only for the Likud, which could now dictate the conditions for the later addition of the DMC, but also for the more hawkish elements in the NRP as well as Gush Emunim.

The new partnership seemed from the outset an ideal alliance for the NRP from all three perspectives—consociationalism, ideology, and political strategy. From the perspective of the religious-secular cleavage, the NRP did not encounter any stiff resistance from the Likud. As a matter of fact, it was Agudat Yisrael rather than the NRP that demanded greater concessions on religious issues (for example, autopsies and abortions), most of which were met by the prime minister designate. The NRP, for its part, obtained the long desired Ministry of Education, which had always been denied to it by Labor. Education was one of the central areas in which the consociational arrangement had been practiced—resulting in two parallel educational trends, the state (nonreligious) and the state religious. Similarly, the ideological proximity between the Likud and the NRP leadership on the issue of settlements in the territories also seemed to provide a firm base for the partnership. Finally, as a result of the 1977 elections, the NRP emerged as a senior partner in the coalition, extending its responsibility beyond the confines of religious issues. The Ministry of Police, for instance, was abolished and annexed to the Interior Ministry, headed by Burg. Following the Camp David Accords, the leader of the NRP was nominated to head the Israeli negotiating team on Palestinian autonomy—a major foreign policy area.[26] During this period the voice of the NRP was heard on questions of national security, the economy, and the media.

But most of all, during the first three years the NRP emerged as a stable party, especially compared with other major parties. NRP stability was in sharp contrast to Labor, which became entangled in a power struggle; to the DMC, which in effect disintegrated; and to the Likud, which suffered from growing dissatisfaction with Begin's foreign policy, his performance as prime minister, and the Likud's economic policies, resulting in the resignation of his foreign, defense, and treasury ministers. It was only toward the end of the Likud's first administration that the NRP became involved in a series of internal crises originating in corruption charges against the minister of religious affairs, Aharon Abu-Hatzeira, and Rabbi Haim Druckman's threat to split the party unless Gush Emunim's representation on the party list to the Knesset was significantly increased.[27] Ultimately, it was Abu-Hatzeira who, following a controversial exoneration, left the party and formed a Sephardic-traditional party—Tami. These events, which occurred during the election campaign, cannot by themselves explain the sharp decline of the NRP in the 1981 elections. In view of the stability of the NRP in the preceding three years, its accomplishments in the last administration, and especially its record of stability in the previous nine elections, the reasons for its decline are clearly more profound.

Agudat Yisrael and the Israeli Political System

Agudat Yisrael, as a separatist party, played a much smaller role than did the NRP in the development of the Israeli political system. Following a short period during which it participated in government as part of the United Religious Front and for one year as a separate list, Agudat Yisrael remained outside the government from 1952 until 1977. As a result of its separatist ideology and behavior, it remained relatively immune to all three factors which influenced the NRP—consociational arrangements, and ideological and political changes in the political system. As a result, it preserved its political strength at a time when the other religious parties suffered major setbacks.

One of the reasons why the Agudah could afford to remain outside the political system was that the NRP did its "dirty work" for it. While the NRP was comprising and taking care of public religious life in the Jewish state, the Agudah achieved a modus vivendi with the ruling party regarding its separate educational system. In exchange for its nonactive opposition, the Agudah received from the ruling party concessions on the separatist content of its educational system and government subsidies for its schools.[28] Thus Agudah's separatism was expressed not only in its nonparticipation in government but also in its abstention from functioning as a full-fledged parliamentary opposition party. Similarly, even when it joined the Likud government in 1977 it did not become a full-fledged coalition partner; it refused to assume responsibility for government ministries, but rather concentrated on increased financial assistance for its educational system and additional religious legislation. The general consociational arrangement between the NRP and the ruling party provided the Agudah with a framework within which it could preserve its separate development without compromising its non-Zionist ideology or its traditional character.

The Agudah's separatist behavior also explains why it has not been influenced by ideological trends in the Israeli polity. Unlike Poalei Agudat Yisrael, with which it never merged and which participated in such Zionist settlement enterprises as kibbutzim and moshavim, the Agudah remained loyal to its Hassidic and rabbinical institutions, thus refusing to accept Zionist influence. It was therefore significant that while PAY adopted a hawkish line following the 1967 war, the Agudah refused to take a clear stand on foreign policy issues.

Agudah's separatism also made it immune to the changing structure of the Israeli political system. As long as the Labor camp dominated the Israeli political scene, the ruling party had no need of the Agudah for coalition building, especially when it included anticlerical parties.[29] The NRP was both more moderate in its demands on religious issues and larger in size. With the shift of power from Labor to the Likud in 1977, it was Agudah, together with the NRP, that made the difference. But despite its pivotal position in 1977, the Agudah, unlike the NRP, preferred to concentrate on religious issues and the direct concerns of its constituents rather than demanding a share in government power. By limiting its cooperation to parliamentary support, it was not only keeping in line with its separatist ideology, but also denying full legitimacy to Zionist parties that could potentially draw support from the Agudah's regular constituency.

The Religious Parties and the 1981 Elections

The 1981 election campaign was dominated to an unprecedented degree by the contest between the two large parties—the Labor Alignment and the Likud. This contest, which overshadowed even the previous election, finally established the fact that the Israeli political system had been transformed from a system dominated by one party to a two-party system. As we have demonstrated throughout this essay, the Israeli system has been moving in this direction since the mid-1960s. This trend, however, was not always apparent, since it was distinguished, and to a large extent accelerated, by mergers within the Labor camp. Labor's exceptional capacity for survival and the emergence of a strong center party—the Democratic Movement for Change—concealed the existence of the two-party contest during the 1977 elections. The situation on the eve of the 1981 elections was different. Labor's defeat for the first time in 1977, the absence of a strong force in the center, and the steady ascendancy of the Likud in the polls since February 1981, which resulted in a close race between Shimon Peres and Menachem Begin on election day, crystallized the fact that the choice with which the electorate was now faced was between the return of Labor and the continuation of the Likud.

Under such circumstances, the integrationist religious party was placed at a disadvantage to the separatist Agudah. Unlike the 1977 elections, in which the religious voter could not be sure whether his ballot would swing the election, this time the voter must have felt that his vote might well tip the scale. The national religious voter, accustomed to cooperation with secular Zionism and involved in national issues, was therefore prompted to cross party lines and help decide who should be the winner in the national contest. In contrast, the ultraorthodox voter, accustomed to seeing himself as separate from the secular camp, remained loyal to his overriding religious concerns.[30]

But the impact of the new political structure should also be viewed in the context of the NRP's ideological transformation. The close race between the two major parties affected the smaller parties that were identified in their foreign policy and in their preferences for prime minister with one of the great blocs. Thus the Civil Rights movement and Shinui (Change—a faction that had split from the DMC) scored below their expectations and lost votes to Labor. Shelli, the party that represented the most dovish sector in the Israeli Zionist left, and which was deserted on the eve of the election by many leading intellectuals who joined Labor in light of Begin's ascendancy in the polls, was totally eliminated in the 1981 elections. In the same manner, the NRP's identification with the Likud's foreign policy brought about comparable results. In this, the integration-oriented religious voter behaved like other ideological nonreligious voters who abandoned their traditional support for small parties in light of what they perceived as a decisive contest. The tense atmosphere of the campaign and the accusations that the two parties leveled against each other contributed to the voters' decision to vote for one of the major contenders according to their national preference. Because of prevailing beliefs in the national religious camp regarding the territories, it can be assumed that a larger portion of its votes went to the Likud. The only small party that was not affected by these realities was the party that had not taken a position on foreign policy issues and could not be identified with either of the two camps—Agudat Yisrael. PAY, which took a hawkish stand on foreign policy, was completely eliminated at the polls.[31]

At the same time, the bipolar structure and the nature of the 1981 campaign aided in the emergence of two newly established small parties, which also affected the NRP vote. The close race between the two major parties and the realization that neither would achieve a majority made it clear that small parties could obtain concessions from a party trying to establish a majority coalition. This logic appealed to one-issue constituencies, such as the group opposing the final withdrawal from the Sinai and the North Africans who identified with Abu-Hatzeira's claims that he was being discriminated against because of his origin. [32] There was a certain parallel between these two parties and the Agudah, in the sense that their constituencies felt separated in one major aspect from the rest of the electorate. Unlike the parties of the left and center, these parties did not perceive the continuation of the Likud as a disaster. Tehiya was also affected by the close race, however, ultimately receiving only three seats although the polls had earlier predicted that it would receive five. Tami's real potential is difficult to evaluate in light of the general campaign, in which the Sephardic-Ashkenazic issue reached unprecedented levels. It is hard to determine whether this election polarization helped Abu-Hatzeira or whether it drew to Begin voters who might otherwise have voted for him. In any event the emergence of the Sephardic issue did not help the NRP, which had a large Sephardic constituency,[33] and the Sinai withdrawal issue, which helped Tehiya, further slashed into the NRP's traditional territory.[34]

Finally, we have to evaluate the effect of the religious/secular division in Israeli society on the 1981 elections. As we have demonstrated, the NRP had benefited from this schism both by representing a well-defined subculture and by its role as mediator between the two camps. But this division was sharp when the ruling party was projected as anticlerical. Unlike Labor, however, the attitude toward religion of the majority in the Likud, especially the dominant Herut section, was more positive. Prime Minister Begin's public appearance, his personal identification with traditional Jewish values, strengthened these impressions. In the absence of a perceived threat to religious values, national religious voters could afford to vote according to other major issues that dominated the 1981 campaign. Voters who perceived the territorial issue as predominant and opposed Camp David could vote for Tehiya—a party that claimed loyalty to religious values. Religious Sephardic Jews who wanted to punish Labor for its presumed patronizing attitude toward "Oriental" Jews, an issue that dominated the campaign, could do so through Tami or the Likud. Those concerned primarily with the personality of Begin or Peres, another major issue, could vote according to their preference.

In contrast, Agudah supporters—impressed by their party's continued fight for religious legislation throughout the Ninth Knesset—could not perceive a substitute for the ultraorthodox party. The NRP, aware of the perceived reduced threat to religion and the existence of other parties trying to infringe on its territory, campaigned under the slogan "There is only one national religious party" and stressed the potential threat to the state religious educational system should the party be weakened by semireligious lists. In the prevailing atmo-

sphere of 1981, a major portion of its constituency was not prepared
to be intimidated into voting for the NRP.

The Religious Parties and the Likud Coalition

The coalition that emerged following the 1981 elections was composed of the Likud, the NRP, Agudat Yisrael, and Tami, totaling sixty-
one members of the Knesset. This coalition presented a "new majority" that has emerged in Israel, composed of three main elements:
hawks, religious voters, and Sephardic Jews—a coalition that not only
is reflected in the parties composing the government but also represents the main elements among Likud supporters. These three elements overlap to a large extent, as Sephardic Jews tend to be more
hawkish and traditional, and religious Jews are more committed to the
idea of Eretz Yisrael. Thus, the religious-traditional elements provided the Likud not merely with the necessary Knesset seats to form a
government but also with the strength to emerge as a plurality party.
The religious concessions demanded by the religious parties were
therefore more directed to the individual needs of each party than to
maintaining the status quo in religious affairs that was not challenged
by the Likud. On the surface, the religious parties should have been
satisfied with their achievements.

But the political configuration as it emerged following the 1981
elections presented the NRP with profound problems. Although the
party retained its main portfolios in the new government, the NRP
may have entered a critical stage with regard to its future. The decline
in the need for consociational politics (even if only perceived rather
than real), the similarity between its foreign policy and that of the
Likud, and the bipolar structure of the Israeli political system all
present an acute problem for a party whose strength stems from a
constituency that has to a great extent been integrated into the mainstream of Israeli society. It is ironic that what seemed to the NRP to be
its cardinal accomplishments may have turned out to be counterproductive. The relative integration of the religious Zionist camp into
Israeli society, the broadening of the NRP's interests and role, the
emergence of a plurality party with greater sympathy toward religion,
and the replacement of a dominant party structure by a competitive
party structure according the NRP the role of arbitrator—all these
factors combined resulted in the NRP's disastrous showing at the
polls. In addition to its decline, the NRP had to share its newly ac-

quired role of coalition-maker with the Agudah and Tami, which were running not far behind it. But what may be most distressing to the NRP is that by joining the new government it may be contributing to the strength of its main competitors—the Likud, Tami, and, to a certain extent, Agudat Yisrael.

In light of these considerations, the abstention of Agudat Yisrael from full partnership in the new government is not merely based on ideological grounds but is also prudent from a political perspective. By not sharing in government responsibility, and by limiting its cooperation to the parliament, it abstains from providing legitimacy to the religious-oriented Zionist parties, thus ensuring its continued separatism.

In sum, while the religious camp will continue to play a significant role in Israeli politics, its internal configuration and voting patterns, especially among its Zionist elements, may be changing. The 1981 elections may thus be perceived as an extension of the 1977 upheaval. If the 1977 elections presented a basic shift in the power relationship between Labor and the civil camps, the 1981 elections extended this transformation to the religious camp.

NOTES

1. Agudat Yisrael received 72,312 votes and Poalei Agudat Yisrael 17,090. Since the quota for one parliament seat in 1981 was 15,312, the Agudah was short about 4,000 votes to obtain a fifth seat. Had Poalei Agudat Yisrael passed the 1 percent threshold, it would probably have received this seat, since it had made a preelection agreement regarding surplus votes.

2. Daniel J. Elazar, "The 1981 Elections: Some Observations," *Jerusalem Letter*, VP 19, August 15, 1981, p. 4.

3. These estimates are based on an analysis made by the NRP; see *Maariv*, July 3, 1981; and Mizrachi–Hapoel Hamizrachi World Organization *Information Letter* [*Chozer Modeen*], August 1981; and *Hatzofe*, July 24, 1981.

4. On the basic differences between the socialist and the civil camps and their relation to the religious camp, see Daniel J. Elazar, "Israel's Compound Polity," in Howard R. Penniman, ed., *Israel at the Polls, The Knesset Elections of 1977* (Washington, D.C.: American Enterprise Institute, 1979), pp. 9–10.

5. The following analysis of the differences between the two movements is based on Eliezer Don-Yehiya, "Origins and Developments of the Agudah and Mafdal Parties," *The Jerusalem Quarterly*, Summer 1981, pp. 49–64; Gary S. Schiff, *Tradition and Politics, The Religious Parties of Israel* (Detroit: Wayne State University Press, 1977); and Ilan Greilsammer, "Les Groupes politiques marginaux en Israel: Caractéristiques et fonctions," *Revue Française de Science Politique*, vol. 31, no. 5/6 pp. 891–921. See especially their discussion of the differing attitudes toward Zionism and modernization.

6. Mizrachi *yeshivot*, for instance, emphasize Bible studies and Jewish philosophy in addition to Talmudic studies.

7. Don-Yehiya, "Origins and Development," p. 56.

8. Ibid., p 55.

9. See Dan Horowitz and Moshe Lissak, *Meyishuv Lemedina* [The Origins of the Israeli Polity], in Hebrew (Tel Aviv: Am Oved, 1977), especially chap. 7.

10. On Mapai's ability to form coalitions without the NRP see Don-Yehiya, "Religion and Coalition: The National Religious Party and Coalition Formation," in Asher Arian, ed., *The Elections in Israel–1973* (Jerusalem: Jerusalem Academic Press, 1975).

11. See, for example, Don-Yehiya, ibid., pp. 260–64; Horowitz and Lissak, *The Origins of the Israeli Polity*, p. 332; and Arend Lijphart, *Democracy in Plural Societies* (New Haven: Yale University Press, 1977), pp. 129–34.

12. For a comprehensive exploration of this theory see, for example, Lijphart, ibid., and Hans Daalader, "The Consociational Democracy Theme," *World Politics*, July 1974, pp. 604–21.

13. Don-Yehiya, "Religion and Coalition," p. 260.

14. Horowitz and Lissak, *The Origins of the Israeli Polity*, chap. 9.

15. Lijphart, *Democracy in Plural Societies*, p. 133.

16. Ministries that were traditionally in NRP hands were the ministries of religion and the interior. A third ministry was social welfare, which was exchanged in 1977 for education. Institutions in which the NRP plays a dominant role are the Chief Rabbinate and the religious councils that are power centers on the municipal level. In addition, there is a Mizrachi Bank, a construction company, and other economic enterprises that are connected to the NRP.

17. See, for example, Amatai Etzioni, "Alternative Ways to Democracy: The Example of Israel," *Political Science Quarterly*, vol. 74 (1959), pp. 196–214; Horowitz and Lissak, *The Origins of the Israeli Polity*, p. 313.

18. See, for example, remarks made by NRP leaders from the Lamifne faction, *The Jerusalem Post Magazine*, January 23, 1981, p. 4; and *The Jerusalem Post Magazine*, June 12, 1981, pp. 5–6.

19. Shmuel Sandler, "The Transformations of Israeli Policy," *Midstream*, February 1981, pp. 13–18; and Horowitz and Lissak, *The Origins of the Israeli Polity*, pp. 313–14.

20. Schiff, *Tradition and Politics*, pp. 54–56.

21. Ibid., p. 63.

22. See Eliezer Don-Yehiya, "Yetzivut u'Tmura b'Mifleget Macaneh: HaMafdal u'Mahapechat HaTzeirim" [Stability and Change in a 'Camp Party': The NRP and the Youth Revolution], in Hebrew, *Medina, Mimshal veYehsim Benleumiyim* [State, Government and International Relations], no. 14 (1979), pp. 37–38.

23. On this issue see Eliezer Don-Yehiya and Charles S. Liebman, "Zionist Ultranationalism and Its Attitude Toward Religion," *Journal of Church and State*, vol. 23, no. 2 (1971), pp. 259–73.

24. Lijphart, *Democracy in Plural Societies*, p. 5.

25. Elyakim Rubinstein, "The Lesser Parties in the Israeli Elections of 1977," in Penniman, ed., *Israel at the Polls, 1977*, p. 178.

26. This nomination contributed to Moshe Dayan's decision to resign from the foreign ministry; see *Maariv*, October 24, 1979, and *Yediot Aharonot*, November 16, 1979.

27. On the internal fighting in the NRP, see *Maariv*, August 29, 1980, and *Maariv*, May 29, 1981.

28. Schiff, *Tradition and Politics*, p. 185.

29. On the relationship between Agudah and Labor, see David Landau's analysis in *The Jerusalem Post*, July 3, 1981.

30. The different voting patterns of the two constituencies can be seen by comparing the size of their respective educational systems and their showing at the polls. While the percentage of the population attending the state religious school system was around three times the size of the NRP vote at its height (around 9 percent), the size of the population attending Agudah's separate educational system has been very close to its share in the electorate. Although it can be expected that children attending the former educational system do not necessarily come from religious homes, the large gap in the former and the correspondence in the latter indicate the differences between the two constituencies. Whereas the state religious system, in which the pupil is nurtured on religious and Zionist values, produced graduates who are involved in the major aspects of social and political life in the state, the Agudah's educational system produces graduates and caters to an audience that is segregation-oriented. On this theme see, Schiff, *Tradition and Politics*, pp. 192–93.

31. An illustration of this phenomenon can be found in the voting results in rural settlements (moshavim) that belong to Hapoel Hamizrachi and Poalei Agudat Yisrael (PAY):

    a. *Older moshavim of Hapoel Hamizrachi*: 1977 elections: NRP = 76.5 percent; Likud = 13.1 percent. 1981 elections: NRP = 62.5 percent; Likud = 18.7 percent; Tehiya = 5.9 percent; Tami = 1.4 percent.

    b. *Newly established moshavim of Hapoel Hamizrachi*: 1977 elections: NRP = 64.4 percent; Likud = 22.7 percent. 1981 elections: NRP = 46.1 percent; Likud = 31.3 percent; Tehiya = 5 percent; Tami = 7.1 percent.

    c. *Newly established moshavim of Poalei Agudat Yisrael*: 1977 elections: PAY = 54.6 percent; Agudat Yisrael = 16.8 percent; Likud = 10.4 percent. 1981 elections: PAY = 34.7 percent; Agudat Yisrael = 20.9 percent; Likud = 24.6 percent; Tehiya = 1.8 percent; Tami = 6.8 percent.

Source: The Central Bureau of Statistics, *Results of Elections*, pp. 50–51.

32. Aharon Abu-Hatzeira declared in an interview a month before the elections that his intention was that Tami should be a balancing force without which neither major party would be able to put together a government. See *Maariv*, May 29, 1981.

33. The extent to which the NRP lost Sephardic votes to the Likud and Tami can be seen in the election results of new towns and urban settlements where there are large concentrations of Oriental Jews.

    a. *New towns*: 1977 elections: NRP = 9.9 percent; Likud = 44 percent; 1981 elections: NRP = 2.8 percent; Likud = 49 percent; Tami = 6 percent; Tehiya = 1.5 percent.

    b. *Urban settlements*: 1977 elections: NRP = 13.1 percent; Likud = 43.1 percent. 1981 elections: NRP = 4.5 percent; Likud = 49.4 percent; Tami = 5.2 percent; Tehiya = 1.9 percent.

In older towns and urban settlements the NRP's decline was smaller and the gains of both the Likud and Tami were more moderate.

Source: The Central Bureau of Statistics, *Results of Elections*, p. 44.

34. In Judea and Samaria (the West Bank) the NRP declined from 48.2 percent in 1977 to 18.6 percent in 1981. Tehiya received 24.7 percent. The Likud lost 3 percent while Labor increased from 4 percent to 10.4 percent. Source: ibid., p. 38.

VI

POLITICAL IMAGES AND ETHNIC POLARIZATION

Asher Arian

Israel's most bitter, violent, and unsavory campaign ended on June 30, 1981, with the election of the Tenth Knesset. It settled very little, however. It created a virtual tie between the two largest political groupings in the country—the Likud with forty-eight of the one hundred twenty Knesset seats and the Labor-Mapam Alignment with forty-seven—and underscored the observation that the country was divided in an unprecedented manner.[1] The close elections retained for the religious parties the balance of political power that they had come to expect, although the National Religious party, the largest component among them, lost half its previous strength by falling from twelve to six seats.

Elections determine the division of power in a political community and as such have far-reaching influence on the body politic. But the election results themselves are conditioned by a series of political, social, and economic factors, some objective and others subjective. The most striking characteristic to emerge from the 1981 elections was evidence of polarization in Israel along ethnic, social, and political lines. Although these features were noted in the past, it was the degree of their intensity and the fact that these polarities tended to overlap one another that made the 1981 election campaign unique and its results disquieting.

Never before had the country divided so evenly and so massively for the two major parties. Never before had the electorate of the two parties been so homogeneous in its ethnic composition. Never before had ethnicity been exploited as a campaign theme in such a barely implicit manner. Never before had violence in the campaign seemed so threatening and immediate.

128

Ethnic Polarization

The 1981 elections witnessed an unprecedented crystallization of ethnic differences in Israeli politics. There had always been undercurrents of ethnic politics in Israel's cacophonic symphony, but rather than remaining the counterpoint, in 1981 they became the dominant melody.

Every group develops rules of selection and rejection of members. Often-used criteria include race, religion, sex, and—in the modern world—nationality. A group is partially defined by those who are excluded from its ranks. In the broadest sense, the most important ethnic difference in the Middle East as far as Israel is concerned is the difference between Jews and non-Jews. Jews are a small minority in the region, a majority in the state. Within the state, the non-Jewish groups (predominantly Arabs and Druse) are known in Israel as the "minorities"—a good example of a Hebrew concept with ideological loading. It is true that the Arabs and Druse are a numerical minority within the boundaries of the prewar Israel of 1967; referring to them as minorities carries the clear political message that a Jewish state means a Jewish majority. Sometimes, though, it appears that this usage restricts the ability of the language to portray adequately their religious and cultural affinity to Arabs and Druse in the territories and in the neighboring countries.

Today, however, the likely connotation of "ethnic differences" refers to differences among Jewish groups and not between Jews and non-Jews. The major distinction among Jews is between the Ashkenazim, who came to Israel from Europe and America, and the Sephardim, who immigrated from countries of Asia and Africa. Scholars, who would find this distinction too simplistic, would demand that finer distinctions be introduced. More appropriately three divisions should be used, consisting of an eastern community of Jews who never left the countries of Asia and Africa, the Sephardic whose language (Ladino) and ethnic culture originated in Spain before the expulsion of 1492, and the Ashkenazim (referring to Germany), whose hybrid language was Yiddish. Relative size, influence, affluence, and cultural attainments have shifted during the Jews' two-thousand-year diaspora, but for the last four hundred years Ashkenazim have been the largest and most important group in Jewish history. They have appeared dominantly in the histories of western and eastern European nations during that period, and later they were prominent in the history of the

United States and formed the nucleus of the founding generation in Israel.

Today, language is no longer an appropriate indicator for ethnic differences in Israel, since both Yiddish and Ladino are vanishing languages and, even at their height, they did not penetrate everywhere. Yemenites spoke neither, and many southern European communities were exposed to both. In this century and especially since the creation of Israel, Hebrew is increasingly taught to Jews as the earlier language distinction fails.

For our purposes, the basic distinction between Sephardim and Ashkenazim will suffice. Using a related measure, the Central Bureau of Statistics reports data based on place of birth and father's place of birth. There is a very high correlation between the European- or American-born Ashkenazim and the Asian- or African-born Sephardim.[2]

Demographics

As our concern is with politics in Israel today and not with a definitive delineation of the various ethnic groups in Israel, we will not delve into the fascinating topic of intraethnic differences within the Jewish community. Suffice it to say that the differences between Iraqi and Moroccan Jews (both Sephardim) are as great or greater than the differences between Russian and German Jews (both Ashkenazim). The more recent interactions of these Jews with their host country enlarged their common heritage as Sephardim or Ashkenazim just as a more distant history enlarged the common heritage shared by all Jews as they were developing the rituals, traditions, and language shared only by Ashkenazim or Sephardim.

For our topic, these basic data are needed:

1. Jews comprise about 84 percent of Israel's population; Arabs and Druse living in the pre-1967 borders and in Jerusalem—but excluding those living in areas under Israeli military jurisdiction—make up the other 16 percent.[3]

2. Of the 14.5 million Jews in the world, some 22 percent live in Israel.[4] About 85 percent of the world's Jews are Ashkenazim; the other 15 percent, Sephardim.[5] About 10 percent of the world's Ashkenazim live in Israel compared with about two-thirds of the Sephardim. The Sephardim, however, make up about 55 percent of Israel's Jewish population and the Ashkenazim about 45 percent.

3. The two ethnic groups differ from each other in terms of place of birth. Of Israel's 3,200,000 Jews at the beginning of 1981, more than

800,000 were born in Europe and the United States; almost 650,000 were born in Asia and Africa. The number of Israeli-born whose fathers were born in Europe and America was a little over 525,000, whereas the Israeli-born whose fathers were born in Africa or Asia numbered more than 800,000.[6] An additional half million were born in Israel of fathers who were also born in Israel. At this stage of Israel's development—but not in fifteen or twenty years—it is safe to conclude that most of the last group are Ashkenazim, reflecting their earlier arrival in the country.

4. The reproduction rates of the various ethnic groups are also different, although less so over time. The gross reproduction rate of Jewish mothers born in Asia and Africa was 1.48 in 1979 compared with 2.04 in 1969; for European- and American-born Jewish mothers it was 1.30 in 1979 compared with 1.32 in 1969. Part of this change is attributable to the fact that the foreign-born population of both ethnic groups is aging and the largest fertile group now tends to be the Israeli-born. That group's rate has fallen too, from 1.43 in 1969 and 1.33 in 1979.[7]

The gross reproduction rates of the non-Jews is much higher, but it too is falling. For Moslem mothers it was 4.36 in 1969 and 3.22 in 1979; for Druse it was 3.59 in 1969 and 3.14 in 1979.

5. Because the age structure and the growth rates of the groups differ, the impact on the political system through the composition of the electorate is not identical (see table 6–1). European- or American-born voters and their Israeli-born children comprised a majority of the electorate in 1981 as they did in past elections, but it is clear that they will soon be smaller in number than the Asian- or African-born voters and their Israeli-born voting children. We have seen that the latter group is already a majority of the Jewish population and that their growth rates are higher than the Europeans'. In the 1981 elections the Ashkenazim had a voting potential of fifty-two Knesset seats; the Sephardim, forty-eight. The shrinking of the Ashkenazic base is evident when compared with their potential in the 1969 elections: fifty-nine for the Ashkenazim, forty-three for the Sephardim. The potential of the Sephardim will be more fully realized when their children who are under voting age (53.7 percent for the children of Asian or African descent, 35.8 percent for the children of European or American descent) begin voting and when the Ashkenazim, who tend to be older and who have fewer children, make up an increasingly smaller percentage of the electorate. Arabs and Druse constitute ten percent of the electorate.

TABLE 6-1

Voting Potential of the Jewish Population in Israel, 1969 and 1981

	Percentage in Population		Percentage under Voting Age		Knesset Seats	
	1967	1980	1969	1981	1969	1981
Israeli-born; father Israeli-born	6.5	13.2	62.3	70.7	4	6
Israeli-born; father Asian- or African-born	18.7	25.3	81.6	53.7	5	18
Israeli-born; father European- or American-born	16.4	16.4	49.1	35.8	13	16
Asian- or African-born	27.8	20.0	11.5	1.7	38	30
European- or American-born	30.6	25.1	3.6	5.1	46	36
Total Population	2,344,877	3,218,400			106	106
Total Percentage of Population under Voting Age			31.6	30.5		
Total number of Knesset Seats is 120					120	120

Note: Assuming 80 percent participation; 12,000 votes per seat in 1969, 17,000 votes per seat in 1981.
SOURCES: *Statistical Abstract of Israel 1967*, pp. 40–41; *Statistical Abstract of Israel 1980*, pp. 57–58.

6. Projecting these figures into the future and thereby calculating the composition of the electorate is risky since the population of Israel has known great fluctuations in the past and is likely to do so in the future. Israel is a country whose past was largely determined by immigrants and whose ideology is still based on the central concept of gathering in the exiled Jews of the world. The Jewish population in 1948 was made up of a little more than a third Israeli-born; in 1980, 55 percent. Population change in Israel is not simply a matter of fertility rates and life expectancies but is also determined by immigration—and of course by emigration.

7. Although we have stressed the importance of ethnic polarization in the 1981 elections, the impression that this will be an important factor in future elections must be avoided. Much of Israel's future political life will turn on this very point. At this point in the analysis we must observe that deterministic forces are not at work making it inevitable that ethnic differences will again be as salient in the future as they were in the 1981 elections. Things may be very different when the "desert generation" of Jews who immigrated to the country will no longer be dominant numerically, culturally, and politically and a new Israeli-born generation emerges. The language gauge used before probably allows us a glimpse of the future: The young Israeli-born generation speaks neither Yiddish nor Ladino—it speaks Hebrew.

Measures of ethnic integration abound, but one will suffice for illustration. The rates at which Jews marry across ethnic lines rose from 12 percent in 1955 to 20 percent in 1978.[8] In addition, the social acceptability of the behavior increased in the sense that the rates of inter-ethnic marriage of both grooms and brides became more nearly equal. In 1955 a little over a third of the marriages were between a groom from Asia or Africa and a European or American bride, with two-thirds of such marriages following the reverse pattern. In 1978 the Asian or African groom and the European or American bride combination accounted for almost half of the marriages; the reverse combination, the other half. That the two types of marriages are equally prevalent points to the increasing social acceptability of inter-ethnic Jewish marriage in Israel, since, while both types of marriages are on the rise, it is the marriage of the high-status bride (European or American) with the lower-status groom (Asian or African) that is increasing faster.

The Political Dimension

The 1981 elections witnessed a clear identification of the two major parties with ethnic groups—the Alignment with the Ashkenazim, and the Likud with the Sephardim. The correlation of ethnic group with electoral behavior became more pronounced than in the past, although the general pattern was not a new one.

The Alignment had enjoyed the role of dominant party in the political system that it had founded and shaped. It was the major political force in the 1920s, in those early formative years of the British Mandate when the major political institutions of the country, such as the Histadrut (the General Federation of Labor), were developed. Its leadership spoke for the young pioneers, newly arrived from Eastern Europe, anxious to fulfill the Zionist dream under very difficult economic and physical conditions. By the time the larger waves of immigration began coming in, during the period before World War II and immediately after the declaration of independence, the forebears of the Labor party were firmly in position as leaders of the state soon to be proclaimed.

During this period, Mapai (later Labor) and the Histadrut, which it controlled, filled many functions and provided many services generally provided by the modern state. Defense, educaton, housing, employment, culture, health, manufacturing, and sport, among others, were activities that the party sponsored or controlled. It is no wonder then that new immigrants were often caught up in the web of the party. There may be no similar experience in a normal adult's life parallel to the dependency encountered after immigration to a foreign country. Certain features may ameliorate that dependency: for example, if the same language is spoken as in the home country or if one intermingles exclusively with compatriots from the county of origin. To be sure, some immigrants to Israel continued to speak German, Yiddish, English, or Arabic and avoided some of the culture shock of the new society. But for those who were forced to deal with the new reality, some special footing in the system was always helpful. Being affiliated with one of the parties was often such a footing, and as the biggest and most powerful of the parties, Mapai was successful in recruiting the largest number of immigrants.

Recruiting meant winning voters, for the leaders of the labor movement realized that the ultimate test of their appeal was at the polls. The legitimacy provided them by independence and sovereignty aided them mightily, and some new immigrants could not easily distinguish between the state, the army, the party, and David Ben-Gurion.

The Irgun Zva Leumi, the militia headed by Menachem Begin that later formed the core of the Herut movement, was stigmatized as being an underground organization, outside the structure of the national institutions headed by Mapai. This was ironic, since the activities of the Hagana and Palmach were equally illegal from the British point of view, but the power to define legitimate and illegitimate was held by the leaders of Mapai. Ben-Gurion placed the Irgun in the company of the other ostracized group (the Communists) when he declared that all parties were candidates for his coalition government except the Communists and Herut.

Mapai proved itself a model "party of democratic integration" by being flexible enough to attract large groups of voters and their leaders through changes in government and party policy and by revising ideological planks in its platform.[9] It carried a large number of European votes, since many of them had been oriented in youth groups abroad to the leadership and institutional arrangements that Mapai developed. Many of the new immigrant groups from non-European countries also supported Mapai, for organizational, ideological, and pragmatic reasons.

The important point to stress is that while an increasingly large share of the electorate was of Sephardic origin, Mapai maintained its dominant role as the largest plurality party and the leader of every government coalition. More frequently now than then, attempts to appeal to the Sephardic population at election time by lists set up by Sephardim themselves largely failed. It was only before the mass immigration of the early 1950s that representation in the Knesset was achieved by lists manifestly linking themselves with the Sephardim and Yemenites.[10] Even the three seats won by Aharon Abu-Hatzeira's Tami represented only a small fraction of the Sephardic vote.

The point that must be clearly made was that neither of Israel's major political parties in 1981 was ethnic, in the sense that neither had organized politically to further specific ethnic ends. The electoral support of both parties was largely ethnic related, but that is another matter entirely. Both the Alignment and the Likud were run by Ashkenazim, as had always been the case with most parties in Israel. While the appeal to the ethnic vote characterized the 1981 elections and the social bases of political support were more closely related to ethnicity than ever, the parties themselves were not ethnic.

In fact, the Alignment tried to deal with its lack of appeal among Sephardic voters by placing Sephardim in places assured of election on its lists. By any mechanical measure of representation, the Alignment did this more successfully than did the Likud. Of the members of the Knesset elected by the two parties, the Alignment had fourteen Sephardim; the Likud, nine. Both parties were led by men born in

Poland, but both put Sephardim in the number two slot. The Alignment had a Sephardic woman, Shoshana Arbeli-Almoslino, as its second candidate. Born in Iraq, she had been a very effective parliamentarian in the out-going Knesset. The Likud put David Levy as number two. Minister of housing and immigration absorption and the Likud's candidate to head the Histadrut, Levy was born in Morocco and lived in Beit Shean, a development town in northern Israel that manifested many of the social and economic problems with which the underprivileged population must contend.

The Alignment may have been helped by having Arbeli-Almoslino in second place; the Likud was certainly not harmed by making Levy prominent. Everyone knew that the second place on the list had symbolic value only and no one thought that it held any promise of power or succession. In general, representation was not the issue. When asked what group people wanted to see better represented in the party list for which they intended to vote, only 11 percent mentioned an ethnic group while 34 percent wanted younger people, fresh faces.[11] The Likud enjoyed the more appropriate image; the number of its Sephardic candidates was irrelevant to the issue.

In the 1981 elections the term "ethnic party" was often used. It was supposed to portray the support of the Jews from Asian and African countries and their children for the Likud. The Alignment, however, was closer to being an "ethnic party" than was the Likud. The larger concentration of voters by ethnicity was to be found in the Alignment, with some 70 percent of its voters Ashkenazim. The percentage of Likud voters who were Sephardim was sixty-five. This had not always been the case. When dominant, the Alignment was heavily supported by the Ashkenazim, but the Sephardim also often voted for the Alignment. The bulk of the Likud's support had also come from the Ashkenazim in the past; after all, the Ashkenazim comprised a majority of the electorate. The Likud was set up in the 1970s; in the 1950s and 1960s its constituent parties, the Herut movement and the Liberal party, drew from either end of the social and ethnic spectrum. Herut was heavily supported by lower-class Sephardim; the Liberals, by upper-class Ashkenazim.

Polls going back to the late 1960s indicate that then, too, about 70 percent of the Alignment vote was from Ashkenazim. What had been changing on the political map of Israel was the ethnic composition of the Likud vote and the relative size of the two parties. In the late 1960s both parties were predominantly Ashkenazic; by 1981 the Likud had become predominantly Sephardic while the Alignment

TABLE 6-2

Alignment Percentage of Two-party Vote by Continent of Birth, 1969–1981 [a]

Date of Poll	Birthplace of fathers of Israeli-born voters			Birthplace of non-Israeli born voters		Percent of total two-party vote preference	Number in sample preferring two parties[b]	Total sample size
	Israel	Asia Africa	Europe America	Asia Africa	Europe America			
Sept 1969	70	77	83	79	90	84	698	1,315
Oct-Nov 1969	40	62	73	68	81	74	1,026	1,825
May 1973	60	51	57	66	79	70	1,066	1,939
Sept 1973	57	22	42	62	75	63	287	548
Dec 1973	41	24	41	43	77	52	274	530
March 1977	37	26	50	41	71	52	639	1,372
April 1977	39	31	42	43	68	49	180	497
May 1977	53	32	38	35	61	49	198	485
June 1977	29	10	30	33	56	37	255	465
March 1981	46	47	68	48	71	57	765	1,249
April 1981	46	31	68	33	71	52	585	1,088
June 1981	43	27	55	35	64	46	797	1,237

[a] Surveys were conducted by the Israel Institute of Applied Social Research, except for March and June 1981, which were conducted by the Dahaf Research Institute.
[b] Respondents giving "Alignment" or "Likud" answer to vote intention question.

had retained its Ashkenazic predominance. The turnabout seemed to be in 1977 when a majority of the Likud vote was Sephardic for the first time. If we couple this fact with the growth of the Sephardic electorate and the abandonment of the Alignment by many Ashkenazim in favor of the Democratic Movement for Change (DMC) in 1977, the enormity of the Alignment's problem becomes clearer. The period of incubation of the bitterness and frustrations felt against the ruling Alignment ended before the 1977 elections, and the bitterness and frustration emerged full-blown in the vote. In 1981 the Sephardim continued their disaffection from the Alignment while many Ashkenazim who had deserted in 1977 returned.

We have described the contribution of each ethnic group to the two parties and have found that the portion of Ashkenazim in the Alignment electorate has been high and consistent, regardless of the fluctuations in the size of the Alignment vote, and that the Sephardim as a portion of the Likud vote has been growing and was, in 1981, slightly lower than the Ashkenazic portion of the Alignment vote. By turning the question around and asking how members of the two ethnic groups divided their votes in 1981 between the two large parties, we get a mirror-image answer. About 60 percent of the Ashkenazim voted Alignment; about 30 percent voted Likud. About 60 percent of the Sephardim voted Likud; about 30 percent voted Alignment.

The fortunes of the Likud and the misfortunes of the Alignment were evident along generational lines as well as along the ethnic and demographic ones. The Likud did even better among the second generation of Sephardim than it did among the first. The Alignment's support was greater among Ashkenazim who immigrated than among their children who were born in Israel (see table 6–2). The Likud gained most in those groups that were youngest and growing fastest; the Alignment—losing support within all groups over time—did best in the group that was oldest and shrinking most rapidly.

Neither the Likud nor the Alignment was an "ethnic party" in 1981. Neither of them organized along ethnic lines nor carried an overt ethnic message. Almost a third of the "wrong" ethnic group voted for the party.

Images and Ideology

Images played a central role in the 1981 elections: the Likud was viewed as an antiestablishment party representing the underprivileged in Israeli society, willing to use the "big lie" in portraying its policies in order to be reelected; the Alignment was seen as the party of the bosses anxious to return to the government to which their establishment status seemed to entitle them; Begin was looked upon as a self-confident leader expressing some of the deepest doubts of the Jewish people regarding the degree to which non-Jews could be trusted and representing the Israeli penchant for self-assertiveness even if cooler minds thought it dangerous at best, suicidal at worst; Peres was seen as an indecisive politician who would do almost anything to further his own career, whose smooth tongue sometimes appeared slick, and who was set on seizing the opportunity to be prime minister. Ideological differences between the parties were much less crucial in determining the election results. In a basic sense, this was a non-ideological election.

Although emotions ran high and many found fault with both of the major contestants, this was not an "anti" election. Many voted for the party of their choice because they thought it was better, not only because the other was worse. There was no evidence of alienation from the political system or withdrawal from the election. The participation rate was 78.5 percent, as high as usual in Israeli elections.

Despite the complaints frequently heard in Israel about the country and its quality of life, the country was generally perceived in a very favorable light by the electorate (see table 6–3). There was no evidence of disillusion or despair. The electorate seemed to believe in the basic justice of its country and its country's course, a peace-loving country anxious to live in peace with its neighbors. The country was faulted for being—relatively—lower on its score for pursuing social justice (hinting, of course, at the ethnic issue), although here too more than half the sample gave the country a high score on the issue and fewer than a quarter gave it a low score. But this ratio is considerably worse than other dimensions in which the symbols of good and righteousness were stressed by the population.

The election campaign itself was a different matter (see table 6–3). While the country was held in high regard, the campaign was less universally revered. The campaign was divisive—and was perceived as such. It was expensive, bitter, and widely perceived as such rather than as educational, edifying, or helpful to the electorate in making up its mind. The politicians saw the elections as crucial—as well they were for many careers and ambitions—but the electorate tended to take a more relaxed view of the situation, perceiving the elections as important, but not fateful.

TABLE 6-3

Voters' Perceptions[a]
(Percent)

Of Israel		Of the Election Campaign	
Strong/weak	75/9	Positive/negative	46/33
Generates hope/despair	74/10	Short/long	39/30
Just/unjust	75/7	Educational/not educational	30/47
Place I want/don't want to live	88/3	Helps/does not help making up mind	33/47
Place where all Jews should/should not live	72/13	Helps/does not help the country's problems	36/46
Democratic/ undemocratic	87/4	Helps/does not help to see the differences among the parties	47/35
Is/is not characterized by social justice	53/23	Unites/does not unite the people	26/48
Is/is not ready to be good neighbors with Arab states	81/6	Helps/does not help to know the leaders	48/32
Seeks/does not seek peace	87/3	Gives/does not give a feeling of belonging to the country	46/31
Is/is not the realization of the Zionist dream	65/16	Wasteful/worth the expense	66/18
		Crucial/not crucial	43/33
		Important/unimportant	55/24

[a] Based on a seven-point semantic differential battery administered to a representative sample of Israel's Jewish adult urban population (N = 1,237) by the Dahaf Research Institute. The numbers in the table are the sum of the percentage of the sample identifying the subject with a given characteristic, with the three categories left of the center point being summed and presented left of the slash and the three categories right of the center point summed and presented right of the slash. The size of the middle category is the difference between 100 and the sum of the two reported figures. For example, on the seven-point scale, 87 percent reported that Israel was in the first, second, or third category on the democratic side of the continuum, 4 percent were in the three categories on the undemocratic end, and 9 percent (100−91) were in the fourth, or middle, category.

The Campaign

The campaign strategies of the two largest parties differed considerably. The governing Likud was intent on keeping the campaign focused on security and foreign affairs; the opposition was keen on centering on economic and social matters. The Likud wanted to stress its popular leader, Menachem Begin, and attack the less popular head of the Alignment list, Shimon Peres. The Likud attempted to project the image of a party that had only begun its important work in restructuring the economy and the society after years of Alignment abuse; the Alignment argued that the policies of the Likud were disastrous and that only an experienced, responsible party such as the Alignment could regain for Israel the respect of the international community, a record of sustained economic growth, and a renewed belief in itself.

The highlight of the period before the campaign began in earnest was the runoff between Shimon Peres and Yitzhak Rabin for the top spot on the Labor list. Rabin had been prime minister between 1974 and 1977 with Peres as his defense minister.

Before the elections in 1977 Rabin had narrowly defeated Peres for first place on the list, but then before the elections he had relinquished it to Peres after Rabin's wife had been found to have violated foreign currency regulations. The fight at the beginning of 1981 had been brewing a long time and had turned ugly upon the publication of Rabin's book, in which he described Peres in most abusive terms. Even after the victory of Peres over Rabin in the Labor party's convention by 70 to 30 percent, the animosity between the two did not lessen. It plagued the entire campaign and especially the organization of the campaign staff and the party list for the election. Only a few days before the election did the atmosphere change when Peres agreed to dump Haim Bar-Lev as shadow cabinet defense minister and give the position to Rabin. The Likud, and especially Begin, exploited the situation by attacking Peres but speaking neutrally about, and occasionally even praising, Rabin.

In this same period, the Likud was plagued with a rift-stricken government and with a world-record annual inflation of more than 130 percent. The members of its government had proved cantankerous, often bickering in public. The inflation rate seemed to stem from the liberalization policies initiated by the new Likud government soon after its 1977 victory in an attempt to relieve some of the undesirable effects of the economic controls that the Alignment had instituted over the years.

The polls at the beginning of the year 1981 showed the Alignment on its way to an unprecedented absolute majority; the Likud, to a disastrous defeat. When Yigal Hurvitz resigned as minister of finance over a dispute in the government regarding a pay increase for the nation's teachers, which he considered inflationary, the government faltered, and new elections were set for June 30. In Israel, only the Knesset can disband itself; no act of the government or the president can bring about new elections. But since the government coalition also controlled the Knesset, its will was heeded, and the elections were set for the summer, scrapping Begin's hope to last until the constitutionally set date of the third Tuesday of the Hebrew month of Heshvan that would have put the 1981 elections on November 17.[12]

Until this point, the campaign was in effect a one-party race. The Alignment was far ahead in the polls because the Likud was not yet running. The Alignment enjoyed the excitement and exposure of the Peres-Rabin race, and the poor showing of the governing Likud in the polls only made them more self-confident. The liability of the polls is the best proof of the proposition that ideology played only a minor role in the 1981 elections, since no parallel ideological shift occurred to correspond with the steady growth of the Likud in the polls and the deterioration of the Alignment strength. We witnessed the shift in the three polls reported in table 6–2. What is significant for our purposes is that the weakening of the Alignment and the strengthening of the Likud occurred in all ethnic categories but most forcefully among those born in Asia and Africa (a drop for the Alignment from 48 percent to 35 percent in the period between March to June) and even more so among their Israeli-born children (a drop from 47 to 27 percent). The atrophy was general, but it was more pronounced among the Sephardim.

The new minister of finance, Yoram Aridor, effected an abrupt about-face of the economic policy and began lowering excise taxes on items such as color television sets in spite of the bitter criticism of the academic world and much of the press that when an economy is faced with a staggering inflation rate of more than 130 percent one should cut government expenditures and encourage economic growth rather than bring about additional expenditures on private consumption. Whatever his policy was worth in economic terms, it was a brilliant stroke of electoral politics. From a group in disarray, the government suddenly seemed united; it seemed that an audible sigh of relief was heard among the citizenry after a year of dire warnings by Hurvitz that the economy was at the edge of disaster. The government had lost three of its most visible members—Moshe Dayan as foreign minister, Ezer Weizman as defense minister, and Hurvitz as finance minister. Those who remained tended to be meeker in the face of Begin's leadership of the government and the Likud; plans were being made for the elections and the uphill battle to be fought against the Alignment.

One of the first major skirmishes was the election of the Histadrut—Labor Federation—council. Held on April 7, these elections were billed as a kind of preliminary to the main event—the Knesset elections. About two-thirds of Israelis are Histadrut members and entitled to vote for the council. The Alignment list was headed by lackluster Yeroham Meshel, a longtime Histadrut leader. Peres did not intervene in the setting up of the Alignment list or the election campaign for the Histadrut, preferring to win the support of the leaders of one of the party's strongholds without opening new fronts. A tacit division of Labor prevailed: The head of the Histadrut, Meshel, who was also the head of the Alignment list to the Histadrut elections, ran his own campaign. Both he and Peres ignored the fact that the Knesset elections were less than three months away.

The Histadrut is a major power center in Israel's political, social, and economic life. Most Israelis are members; most receive their medical care from the Histadrut's sick funds (*kupat holim*). Workers are organized and represented by the Histadrut, and it employs tens of thousands of workers in its industrial and manufacturing plants. The Likud, not unaware of the Histadrut's power, had been competing in Histadrut elections since 1965. In 1981 the Likud put Minister David Levy at the head of its list and ran a campaign centered on him, ignoring matters of policy or performance.

The Alignment won almost two-thirds of the vote, but the Likud did as well as it had in the 1977 Histadrut elections, gaining more than a quarter of the vote. Although the Alignment's performance was better than it was in 1977, the participation rate was low by Israeli standards, with only about 55 percent voting. The low voter turnout gave an advantage to the Alignment since many lower-class voters, who would have tended to vote Likud, stayed at home.

Both parties claimed victory. Most important, the results of the Histadrut elections indicated that Aridor's economic policies could work electoral miracles (economic ones remained to be seen), and the spirits of the leaders of the Likud rose accordingly.

The Likud realized that its major achievement was the peace treaty signed with Egypt and the process of normalization that was under way. Less than a month before election day Begin arranged for a summit meeting with President Sadat of Egypt in Sharm-el-Sheikh. The Alignment for its part suffered from a more dovelike image compared with Begin's tough line. Peres's Jordanian option was portrayed by the opposition as the road to a Palestinian state; the Alignment's countercontention was that Begin's handling of the autonomy talks would lead to the disappearance of the Jewish state since a majority of the country's citizens would soon be Arabs. The handling of the economy and the availability of a team of managers of renown were the strong points that the Alignment planned to stress.

There was much irony in the presentation of the foreign policy positions. Begin, who had been outlawed by the British and lacked legitimacy among the Zionist establishment in the prestate period because of his unyielding stand, became the bearer of peace. After all the wars brought on by the Alignment, the Likud promoters told the Israeli electorate, it was Begin and the Likud who had brought peace with Israel's largest and most important neighbor. Not only was the Alignment widely perceived as responsible for Israel's past wars, it was also perceived as more dovish than the Likud. This characterization fits in well with the popular Israeli belief that Arabs respect and respond only to force and that, therefore, the mighty can best deal with them.

These appeals were expressed in the slogans used in the campaign. The Alignment chose "Together for a Strong Israel," trying to capitalize on the positive symbolic value of unity and strength. The Likud chose "Peace and Security," emphasizing that it was the party of both. The significance of this slogan can be properly undertood only if we remember that soon after the Six-Day War an ultradovish list ran for the Knesset under the banner "Peace and Security" while other groups stressed that their priorities were security and peace. Now the Likud had adopted the dovish slogan and fitted it to the tough line of the Likud and Begin.

Peres argued that control of the West Bank with its more than one million Arab inhabitants would ultimately mean a majority of Arabs in the Knesset and hence an effective end to the Jewish state. A political solution to the problem must be sought implementing sage military precautions, but, finally, the solution to preserving the Jewish nature of the state must be found by reaching an agreement with Jordan. As noted, the Jordanian option backfired when the Likud argued that it meant giving the land to King Hussein and ultimately to Arafat. But even the rhetoric of the Alignment appeal proved unsuccessful. When asked, more respondents thought that the Likud would be more likely to retain the Jewish nature of the state than the Alignment. The dangers of continued occupation of the territories were not effectively conveyed to the public. For many, the "Jewish nature of the state" evidently meant close ideological and coalition ties with the religious parties, and at that the Likud seemed to be better. No ideological debate was joined. Begin's image was one of toughness, even though it was his government that had agreed to return Sinai; Peres's image was soft and indecisive.

On economic issues no clear ideological debate developed either. Haim Ben-Shahar, president of Tel Aviv University and Peres's candi-

date for minister of finance, argued against Aridor's give-away electoral economics and in favor of curtailing inflation and unemploy-
ment and promoting growth. Aridor said his way was better and
promised to continue his policies after the elections as well. While
most people perceived Aridor's policies as an election gimmick, they
also admitted that they had never been better off economically. The
Likud warned of the drastic measures that the Alignment would impose if brought back to office; the Alignment, of the terrible consequences of continuing the irresponsible policies of Aridor. By the end
of the campaign, Ben-Shahar, a little-known figure before his appointment to the shadow cabinet, was about even with Aridor in
popularity, but neither seemed to recruit voters on his own. Supporters of the Likud tended to prefer Aridor; supporters of the Alignment, Ben-Shahar. There is no evidence that either Ben-Shahar or
Aridor, as candidates, swung voters to his party. Aridor's policies were
favored by Likud voters; Ben-Shahar's, by Alignment voters. The
Alignment failed to center the campaign on the economy; the Likud
succeeded in neutralizing the issue.

The most popular campaigner was Prime Minister Begin. He consistently out-polled Peres in popularity polls. Rabin retained his popularity in the polls even though he was not a front-running candidate.
It may be true that Rabin would have run better than Peres, but the
point to remember is that against Begin, in the conditions of the 1981
elections, any Alignment opponent would have had a very hard race
to run.

The bases of support for Begin and the Likud overlapped: The
young, Israeli-born, especially those of Asian and African origin,
lower-income and lower-education groups supported Begin over-
whelmingly. Peres and Alignment support was centered in older, European, higher-education, and higher-status groups. And so was
Rabin's. There was no important difference in the patterns of support
between Peres and Rabin when running against Begin.

Begin's appeal to the crowd—some called it demagogy—was as
great as it had been during his fighting days in the opposition during
the late 1940s and 1950s. Calls of "Begin, King of Israel" were widespread during the campaign, his supporters edging toward the frenzy
of mass hysteria frequent in other Middle Eastern settings. Peres's
crowds were more polite, subdued—and smaller. Peres lacked the
personal appeal that Begin enjoyed; an extraparty organization named
Alef (citizens for Peres) was set up to assure his nomination and election by trying to improve his public image.

The tomatoes thrown at Peres during a Passover folk festival of Moroccan Jews in Jerusalem was the first sign of violence in the campaign. It became fashionable among certain groups to bait Peres, almost like a seasonal sport. Whether the Likud actually had a hand in organizing the anti-Peres demonstrations (as the Alignment asserted) is beside the point; what is important is that the expression of anti-Peres feeling fed on deeply held animosities and could easily be expanded much beyond the scope of the original group that began interfering at his rallies.

The reaction to the violence was immediate. It accelerated the verbal violence between the two parties, which had already escalated in the campaign, and it polarized the electorate along ethnic lines as never before. It made support of the small parties a luxury that many felt they could not afford—the elections were between two large forces. The stigmatization of the supporters of the Likud by the Alignment as unruly antidemocrats forced many—especially Sephardim—who had voted Likud in 1977 but were disappointed with its performance to reconsider their decision. They saw in the invective a manifestation of the lengths to which the Alignment would go to regain (and by implication, to retain) power. They were offended by Peres's reference to "two cultures" (a phrase he repeated in his stillborn victory speech on election night), which they took in an ethnic sense while he meant it in a political one.

The fear of being an embattled minority losing to the Sephardic hordes undoubtedly worked in the Alignment's favor. If the issue lost it some Sephardic votes, it won the Alignment many more Ashkenazic ones. It was also the first time in the long campaign that the Likud's momentum was broken. Everything had worked in the Likud's favor, from Aridor's economics to foreign policy crises such as the Syrian missiles in Lebanon, Begin's verbal attacks on West Germany's Helmut Schmidt, and the Israeli attack on the nuclear power installation in Baghdad. The Alignment floundered: Its economic attacks were impotent, and it was forced to play to Begin's strengths in the fields of foreign and security affairs. When the violent nature of the campaign became an issue working for the Alignment, its leaders played it to the full.

Israel had known violent political campaigns in the past, and those familiar with Israel's educational system, with the cases tried in the courts, or even with Israel's soccer fans, know that violence is not unknown in the society. But instead of being an unpleasant feature of everyday life, in the 1981 campaign it became a focus and an issue. Partially because television is prohibited from showing candidates on

the screen for the month before the election, the television crews began covering the crowds. June was a hot month—and not only because it was summer.

Political Ideology

The heat of the campaign produced more noise than light. Although
policy questions were raised, the dominant themes of the elections
were the emotionally charged issues of Begin versus Peres, democracy
versus fascism, political violence versus political tolerance, continued
progress with the Likud as opposed to returning to the old ways of the
Alignment, the growers of tomatoes against the throwers of tomatoes.

Because the positive pull of one party and the negative push of the
other were so central to the 1981 elections, ideological differences between the parties were relegated to a secondary role. Of course, there
is a basic sense in which all politics in Israel are ideological. Messages
are packaged in ideological containers; code words are frequently attached. The generation of political leadership active in the 1981 election campaign had grown up during the period when issues and
phrases such as *fascism, socialism,* and *revisionism* and the basic values
of the labor movement had intellectual content and emotional impact.
For many of the voters in 1981, however, the ability of these words to
call up images of great events, men, or battles or to arouse feelings of
deep admiration or hatred was limited. Yet the leadership persisted
in its patterns of communications, talking of these things, which
meant little to most, as well as of the Holocaust and Zionism, which
meant more to many.

The Israeli political system has the reputation of being ideological
in character, and indeed political communication is often presented
in ideological terms. Policies are seen to flow from an overview of
society and the nature of the Jewish state, and it is important for political communicators to show how this action-oriented program fits in
a general pattern of behavior and governing. Upon closer examination, however, it is clear that the style of political communication has
overshadowed the importance of the substance. The public is conditioned to hear politicians explain, attack, plead, or defend in ideological terms. One does not try to extend military control over parts of
Lebanon or destroy Iraqi nuclear capacity: One prevents Holocaust,
for the Christians of Lebanon and for the Jews of Israel. One does not
merely oppose the Likud or try to win the election for prime minister:
One tries to save the country from revisionism and Beginism (a Peres
phrase that seemed to be a cross between Khomeiniism and fascism).

If ideology means a master plan, a system of ideas based on social goals and phrased in terms of social and political action, then the campaign was nonideological. In a campaign that saw the parties more competitive than ever before and ethnic groups more polarized than in the past, it was not easy to mistake the elections as an ideological struggle over the nation's future. The 1981 elections centered on images and candidates, the frustrations of one ethnic group and the fears of the other.

In 1981 there was no great debate in Israel over the future of the country or its policies. There was broad agreement—"national consensus," in the language of Israeli politics—regarding the continued existence of Israel as a Jewish state and with borders reaching from the Mediterranean Sea to the Jordan River. Only marginal groups considered pulling back to the pre-1967 borders or annexing all of the territory outright. In practical politics, where the subtle variations between policies make all the difference, it is basically on the tactics of holding on that the parties are divided. The Likud is now committed to the Camp David Accords, which provide for autonomy for the West Bank and Gaza Arab populations; the Alignment, to territorial concessions with the Jordan River retained as a "defense border." Reality has forced the leaders of both parties to concentrate less on ideology and more on the tactics of continued security and existence.

Without doubt, the country is moving to the right. When asked "With which political tendency do you identify?" more than a third said "right" in 1981, compared with 16 percent in 1969 and 8 percent in 1962. The "right" has become the largest single response category (see table 6-4). But we must be careful not to mistake this identification with political ideology. While the "left/right" distinction is meaningful to most of the sample and widely used within the system, it is not a measure of ideology. What has happened in Israel is that the cues generated by the parties have become central in determining the left/right distribution, quite unrelated to attitudes or political ideology.

The literature on the subject would lead us to expect that as a society's ideological orientation shifts, so too should its positions on political issues.[13] The fascinating finding about Israel is that, although the country has moved to the right politically, the distribution of attitudes on important matters has remained constant. We see this clearly in table 6-4, in which hard-line stands on returning the territories were about as prevalent in 1981 as they were in 1969.

The picture is less static than it appears, since changes have been taking place in the political context in which the question was asked.

TABLE 6-4

Left/Right Tendency and Issues, 1962–1981 [a]
(Percent)

	1962	1969	1973	1977	1981
Left/Right tendency					
Left	31	6	3	4	4
Moderate left		19	19	14	13
Center	23	26	33	29	27
Right	8	16	23	28	35
Religious	5	6	7	6	6
No interest in politics					
No answer	33	27	15	19	15
Return the territories					
None		38 [b]	31	41	50
A small part		52	52	53	42
Most		5	10	7	4
All		1	2	7	3
No answer		4	5	2	1
Economy					
Capitalist	7	10	—	11	10 [c]
More capitalist	19	24	—	18	25
More socialist	39	38	—	31	40
Socialist	15	19	—	25	20
No answer	20	9	—	15	5
Sample size	1,170	1,314	1,939	1,372	1,088

Note: Question not asked.
[a] Surveys conducted by the Israel Institute of Applied Social Research.
[b] N = 380 for data in this column.
[c] Data in this column from Dahaf Survey, see note 11.

The 1973 question was asked before the Yom Kippur War; the 1981 question, after most of Sinai had been returned. The samples are different, and the distribution of responses is not identical. Still, what is striking is the relative stability of the attitude over time in the society. Ninety percent or more in both 1969 and 1981 favored returning none of the territories or only a small part.

This attitudinal stability even as the political continuum is moving to the right is more confounding since the population has not become more capitalist in economic matters, as might be expected from the "right" label. Almost 60 percent favored socialism throughout the period. Government intervention is often decried, and the economy has

150   Political Images and Ethnic Polarization

been liberalized; yet the movement to the right is not reflected in this important attitude. The stability of these attitudes over time forces us to consider the sense in which the system has changed.

What we have witnessed in Israel over the past few decades is a process of political change, not ideological change. The stability of attitudes and the shift to the right of political power has been made possible because ideology is not central to Israeli political life. The growth of the Likud and the growth of the right must be understood as a reaction to the years of dominance of the Alignment and the left. The terms are important as labels but not necessarily as indicators of ideological content. The Likud means not only right, it also means non-Alignment and hence nonleft. High levels of response to the left/right questions are artifacts of the passing of dominance and the emergence of competitiveness. The right and the Likud are increasing in strength over time, and the left and the Alliance are in decline. But when we look at the responses of only those who reported that they intend to vote for one of the two parties, the picture changes. Then the right and the Likud increase, but only the percentage of those who report that they will vote for the Alignment is in decline. The portion of the Alignment voters who identify themselves as left is constant. The shrinkage of the left is a result of the decline of the Alignment; the growth of the right stems from the greater legitimacy and increasing political power of the Likud.

The fact that political labels should fill a function of veto by pointing out whom we want to avoid is not surprising to observers who know the nature of political communication in Israel. This function was filled by the left in the prestate and early state era—the period of dominance—when the left was widely considered the appropriate legitimate authority in the system. Now as that basic understanding is being overturned, the term *right* fills the role of identifying the "bad guys" (that is, the *left*) as much as it does of identifying the group with which one might wish to identify (the *right*). The prime motivator is the identification with one of the political parties; from that flows identification with one of the political labels. This in turn has been facilitated by the fact that the party system has become more competitive and less dominated by one party.

The explanation for this topsy-turvy phenomenon lies in Israel's political and social history. It was the parties of the left, predominantly Achdut Ha'avoda, and later Mapai, that developed the political institutions of the country and were instrumental in absorbing the immigrants who came later. If in Europe the leaders of socialism had to struggle to unite the workers to battle with the rightist establishment, in Israel the pattern was reversed. The establishment was of the left— and operated in the name of the workers. The newcomers were to be absorbed in existing socialist organizations; those who balked and tried to express their opposition to the establishment found a ready ally in the rightist Herut movement and the more centrist Liberal party. The real proletariat of Israel was increasingly rejected by the establishment socialists, and as their frustrations grew, so too did their search for political outlets for their perceived deprivation.

That the growth of the right is a reaction to the left can be understood by contrasting the Israeli experience to that of Europe. In Europe, since the beginning of the century, the left worked and organized to replace the forces of the right—the establishment—in power. Now suppose that it is the left that is in power, that has privileged positions, and that is associated with the faults of the existing system. The focus of identification for the out-group in this case would be the right and not the left. If we recall that these terms are relative, Israeli politics makes much more sense. On May 5, 1789, the left emerged in France because the nobility took the place of honor to the king's right at the first joint meeting of the States-General, and the representatives of the third estate were on the king's left. On July 20, 1981, the Likud was on the left of the Knesset's chairman because that spot provided better exposure to the television cameras covering the opening session of the Tenth Knesset. The Alignment, although members of the Socialist International, sat on the chairman's right because the Likud had the majority in the committee that decided on such arrangements. Left and right in Israel are an artifact of the political party system and achieve their meaning by virtue of the parties and not from the ideological direction that they might provide.

Two factors closely related to the rise of the right are the political and demographic changes that have occurred in Israel since independence. Until 1967, Herut and Begin were ostracized by the Mapai establishment as being outside the system of consensus prior to the formation of the state. In 1967, in the period before the Six-Day War, Gahal (a combination of the Herut government and Liberal party) joined the National Unity government, and Begin became a minister in the government of Israel. Gahal's leaving the Unity government well before the 1973 Yom Kippur War, highlighting the decline of Alignment dominance, enhanced the legitimacy of Gahal and Begin. Not only were the political fortunes of the Likud and Begin rising because the political fortunes of the Alignment were declining, but time was working in the Likud's favor. Twenty-five years after independence, a sizable portion of the electorate did not know of the stigma that Begin carried, let alone why. The intergroup fights of the past generation busied older people and scholars but not the man in the street. His conceptual world of politics was different as was his view of the roles of the right and the Likud.

The ascent of the right could be seen in the organizations of *both* parties. The Herut dominated the Likud as Rafi dominated the Alignment. The Liberal party and the other components of the Likud were hardly visible and certainly unimportant ideologically. In the Alignment, the dominant role of Mapai crumbled, and the younger Rafi leaders (Peres, Dayan, and Navon) became relatively more influential. The ideological differences within the parties were often greater than those between parties.

Party Images

A social myth is a convenient way of ordering reality. While reality is usually complex, myths have a simplifying quality about them. They are easily grasped, widely accepted, and able to convert masses of detail into an understandable whole.

Similarly, the image that a party or a leader has is no less important than his real opinion or personality. If Peres, for example, was thought of as insincere or Begin as unstable, conflicting evidence could easily be put aside in favor of the popular image that allows one to grasp the essence of the man more easily.

In the 1981 campaign the Alignment was perceived as the establishment party even though it had been in opposition to government for four years (see table 6–5). The Alignment's negative image was also evidenced in that it was perceived to be the party more concerned about its own interests than those of the citizens' and not very honest. The Likud was closer to the ideal party image and was perceived as a slightly stronger party, as honest, as one that could be believed, and as a party more concerned about the citizens than about itself.

In politics, perceptions are as important as reality, or more so. Perhaps the sample's perceptions reflected reality, but it is certainly noteworthy that a party in opposition for four years still retained in the public mind many characteristics of an established, governing party. The Likud still benefited from its image of newness, of innocence, and was given credit for its efforts in undoing many of the difficult legacies it had inherited from the Alignment. In fact, 41 percent of a

TABLE 6-5

Party Images[a]
(Percent)

	Ideal	Alignment	Likud
Strong/weak	93/2	44/33	50/33
Right/left	55/13	28/40	77/7
Old fashioned/progressive	15/61	48/26	42/31
Middle class/working class	28/32	27/42	55/14
Young/old	52/10	17/51	28/35
Sephardic/Ashkenazic	11/11	6/47	18/25
Worries about itself/the citizens	3/89	43/37	31/45
Inexperienced/experienced	4/86	4/79	45/38
Honest/corrupt	—	35/39	57/18
Cannot/can be believed	—	36/42	32/48

[a] Based on a seven-point semantic differential battery administered to a representative sample of Israel's Jewish adult urban population in April 1981 (N = 1,088) by the Israel Institute of Applied Social Research. See note a, table 3.

national sample reported that the argument "Four years are not suffi-cient for the Likud to undo what the Alignment had destroyed in thirty years" was a convincing reason to vote for the Likud.[14]

On other dimensions there were differences in the parties' images as well. For example, the Alignment was the opposite of the ideal on the young/old dimension: the ideal being young, the Alignment per-ceived as old. The Likud also had an older image, but much less ex-treme than that of the Alignment. While the ideal called for a pro-gressive party, both parties were perceived as old-fashioned, but the Alignment more so than the Likud. A strong party was called for, and the Likud was perceived as slightly stronger than the Alignment. In fact, on almost every dimension the Likud was closer to the ideal than the Alignment.

On class and ethnic dimensions the differences between the parties and their images were striking. The ideal party was almost evenly di-vided among those who preferred a middle-class party, those who preferred a working-class party, and those in between. The Align-ment was perceived as close to that ideal, although more working-class, while the Likud was very far from the ideal with a high prepon-derance of middle-class responses. As we have seen, the workers tended to support the Likud and not the Alignment even though the Alignment was the Labor party associated with the socialist movement.

The ethnic dimension also fitted the pattern. The socialist label gave the Alignment claim to being the worker's party, but the Alignment was also overwhelmingly Ashkenazic, or European. As such, the Alignment had negative appeal for the Sephardim, who tended to have less education and lower-status occupations. Both the Likud and the Alignment were led by Ashkenazic politicians, but the public perception of the Alignment as overwhelmingly Ashkenazic, when in fact its leadership was no more Ashkenazic than the Likud's, indicated the rejection of the Alignment.

In the 1981 campaign, the Alignment was broadly perceived as the party of the European, upper-middle-class bosses and the Likud as the party of the Sephardic, lower-class workers. This image was heightened by a campaign that featured expressions of violence and political intolerance, especially at Alignment rallies by individuals popularly portrayed as young Sephardic toughs inspired by Likud rhetoric. The ethnic tension was brought to a head during a huge Alignment rally held in Tel Aviv three days before the election when a popular entertainer indulged in ethnic slurs against the Likud electorate, even evoking their relatively low army ranks in the supposedly egalitarian Israel Defense Forces. The polarization of the two parties and their respective ethnic supporters fortified the images already prevalent: the Alignment as the party of the bosses, running the Histadrut, the kibbutzim, and other economic institutions that oversaw the dependency relations with which many of these individuals had lived since arriving in Israel in the early 1950s.

The image of the kibbutz had undergone a radical change since the years of independence when kibbutz membership was an ideal and the kibbutz member a folk hero. The image of the kibbutz was not bifurcated: For the Alignment supporter, the kibbutz was a preserve of socialist and idealist values and an example of economic success and social equality as well. The kibbutz member was seen as the Israeli landed gentry, loyal, affluent, and entitled to rule. For the Likud supporter, the kibbutz epitomized values perverted: in the name of non-exploitation, exploitation; in the name of equality, inequality. How else to explain the kibbutz factories in outlying regions in which the kibbutz members were bosses and the workers Jews (and Arabs) from surrounding settlements? The most successful workers could never reach manager level since that was preserved for kibbutz members. The explanation was basic: Since it was kibbutz capital that built the factory, it was only right for kibbutz members to manage the collective's property. Along with the disregard of socialist values, the tensions also reflected the basic social fact that the kibbutz members tended to be Ashkenazim, that they supported the Alignment over-whelmingly and had achieved positions of power and leadership in the Alignment, and hence in the country, above their proportion in the population, and that the workers in kibbutz factories were often Sephardim and Likud supporters.

The Likud was perceived as the party of Second Israel, the Jews from more primitive cultures with exotic music and sharp foods. They had been given so much by the state—education, housing, jobs—and yet they were basically ungrateful and, more than that, pre-sented a serious threat to the continued strength of the state. Efforts at integration meant lower levels of schooling for the whole popula-tion. The Sephardim brought about the popularization of mass cul-ture and the weakening of the more ideological values of the past. Their social problems were associated with unruly behavior in the schools, on the buses, and in the movie theaters, and now this lack of discipline and respect for Israeli tradition was being expressed in the election campaign.

As in most social myths, there was some truth to these perceptions. Social problems were growing in Israel; the introduction of Sephardim at the highest levels of social and economic elite groups was proceed-ing more slowly than full integration would require. The almost ex-plicit expression of the connection between myth and party acceler-ated the identification of the Ashkenazim with the Alignment and of the Sephardim with the Likud. The implication on the one hand was that Sephardim are violent, undemocratic, unsuited for governing and must be defeated. On the other, it was: No! The Alignment have not learned the lesson, they have not changed. There they are decid-ing who should be in which ministry, taking us for granted again. They'll use and exploit us as they always have. Besides, they can't even get along with each other.

Conclusion

The 1981 election results reflected deeper social processes. One of the most important of these was the clear emergence of social class politics in Israel. Ethnic polarization was the outward expression of the un-realized expectations of many Sephardim who had aspired to and reached the middle class but were stymied in their mobility and the reaction of the Ashkenazim who were fearful that their privileged status was in jeopardy. It is fashionable to discuss the ethnic problem as if its focus was in the development towns of Israel and the under-privileged neighborhoods of the big cities, but the statistical fact is that the Jews living in these places constitute a minority of the Sephardic community. Their problems are more acute and therefore most visible, but the bulk of the Sephardic voters have achieved middle to high lev-els of education and income to an extent greater than the stereotype of the slum-dweller permits. The feeling that the Alignment's vision of society meant the continued domination of Ashkenazim and the con-tinued relegation of Sephardim to second levels of management, status, and power was as important a reason as any other for the mas-sive support of the Likud by the Sephardim.

Another festering issue barely mentioned in the campaign was the fundamental justification and goal of the State of Israel. Many Ashkenazim tend to accept the vision of Israel as a modern, liberal, Western state. The continued domination over a vast Arab population in the territories presents a problem for holders of this view. Another way of conceiving the Jewish state is that its legitimacy stems from ba-sically religious sources. Whether God-given or not, the ties between the people, its history, and the land are ultimately a matter of belief and therefore differ basically from the rationalist model of the mod-ern state. Many Sephardim, who tend to be more traditional, respond to the logic of the religion-sanctioned state. Menachem Begin used the symbols and language of religion masterfully; the Alignment, while attacking the religious parties and their disproportionate gains through coalition bargaining, appeared at times to be antireligious.

Ethnicity is an extremely important factor in Israeli political life to-day, but its centrality over time is likely to be transitory. Much more crucial over the long run are social cleavages based on class differ-ences and divisions concerned with religion and religiosity. One of the reasons that the 1981 elections were so violent and polarized was that these cleavages overlapped. The upper-class secularist—who also tended to be Ashkenazic—voted Alignment. The lower-class tradi-tionalist—who also tended to be Sephardic—voted Likud. The fact that these dimensions laced together acceleratd the effect of each of them. Ethnicity will remain a central issue as long as the overlap exists. But if the Alignment's practices and image change and significant groups of the Sephardic community perceive the Alignment to be open to Sephardic leaders, aspirations, and demands, the tension of the ethnic element will lessen in Israeli politics. But if the growing Sephardic population does not perceive such a change on the part of the Alignment, the Likud's fortunes are likely to continue to grow. It is useless to speculate here what effects that changes of leadership in either party, international crises, or massive immigration—to name a few—might have on the equation. What is important to stress is that ethnic polarization is the symptom of a more fundamental cleavage within the Israeli society and polity.

An ideological consensus within the society clearly establishes the norm of equality for all Jews as a direct extension of the notion of "gathering in of the exiles." Ethnic political organization does not conform to this norm. There is, of course, no similar consensus regarding religion. The political organization of the religious groups and their success in gaining at least some of their demands by partnership in the government coalitions have narrowed the religious cleavage through participation in the legitimized struggle for power through the electoral and coalition processes. Organizing politically over ethnic differences, in contrast, has never been legitimized in the sense that most efforts have been unsuccessful. The norm being unity, the evidence of ethnic polarization in the 1981 elections was shocking. The unsettling—even dangerous—feature of the emergence of ethnicity is that it correlates so strongly with other indicators of social mobility. As long as the Alignment is perceived as denying opportunities for continued social advancement, the growing Sephardic community is unlikely to vote for it.

The Alignment did not use the power bases in its control—the Histadrut, the kibbutzim, the sick fund, the workers' councils—to restore its image as a worker's party. On the contrary, its elitist, Ashkenazic image was augmented through the years. The Likud benefited from the Alignment's stagnation—in part because of its popular policies, in part because of Begin's appeal.

The Likud capitalized on the Alignment's internal divisions and establishment image. As the Likud becomes more comfortable with government power, the demands made on it are likely to grow. Simply castigating the Alignment's failures will no longer be enough. It must develop policies and a second generation of leadership equal to the expectations of the growing Sephardic electorate without alienating the large number of Ashkenazim who support it. The Likud will enjoy many of the advantages—and be exposed to the political dangers—which they won at the polls.

NOTES

1. Soon after the elections, Shulamit Aloni joined the Alignment, making the size of the Knesset delegations of the two largest groups equal.

2. See s.v. *Encyclopedia Judaica*, "Demography." For a broader analysis see Sammy Smooha, *Israel: Pluralism and Conflict* (Berkeley: University of California Press, 1978).

3. *Statistical Abstract of Israel—1980*, p. 57.

4. Ibid., p. 33.

5. *Encyclopedia Judaica*.

6. *Statistical Abstract of Israel—1980*, p. 57.

7. Ibid., p. 89.

8. Ibid., p. 83.

9. See for example Peter Medding, *Mapai in Israel: Political Organization and Government in a New Society* (Cambridge: Cambridge University Press, 1972).

10. Hanna Herzog, "The Ethnic Lists to the Delegates' Assembly and the Knesset (1920–1977)—Ethnic Political Identity?" (Ph.D. diss., Tel Aviv University, 1981).

11. From a national sample of 1,249 conducted for me by the Dahaf Research Institute in March 1981.

12. Basic Law: The Knesset, *Article* 9.

13. See, for example, David Butler and Donald Stokes, *Political Change in Britain* (New York: Macmillan, 1969).

14. See footnote 11.

VII

MUTUAL INTERVENTION IN DOMESTIC POLITICS
ISRAEL AND THE UNITED STATES

Samuel Krislov

General Principles

The conventional wisdom on whether nations should intervene in one another's internal politics is as stark as it is pietistic, as drab as it is old: It isn't done; it is frowned upon; it is obvious to the host government, leading to expulsion (as with Citizen Genet); and, in any event, it is likely to be ineffectual. Complex democratic societies react in unpredictable ways to political events, and efforts to influence politics can boomerang. Still, governments have been caught in embarrassing efforts to influence public opinion of other countries often enough and have been found to engage in immoral and illegal (not merely risky) ventures often enough to throw into doubt those comprehensive disclaimers.

Israeli-U.S. relations are a good test of these propositions. For quite different reasons those relations are of great concern to each country. They are well publicized and regularly analyzed. Since American public opinion is seen as a crucial testing ground for issues in the Middle East, most of the major events occur with a maximum of publicity. (It is extraordinary and symptomatic that both Menachem Begin and Anwar Sadat called virtually all major American television interviewers by their first names.) Leaks of information abound, used both as tactical maneuvers and as forms of personal aggrandizement. Revelations are in short order succeeded by analysis of tactics and diagnosis of strategies. Short-order history is the pattern in this crucial area of events. Both the visibility and the pace of events and analysis are extraordinary.

The dimensions are quite different for the two countries. The asymmetries are pronounced in both foreign policy and internal aspects.

For Israel the United States is a shield and support and virtually the only source of economic and military aid. This dependency is a product of neither Israeli nor U.S. planning. Rather it has emerged as a consequence of contraction of other support. First the countries of the Eastern bloc, originally firm allies and the major source of arms during the Israeli War of Independence, moved toward implacable hostility, starting with the imprisonment and use of Mapam leader Mordechai Oren in the Slansky show trial of 1952. The Communist countries have completely shunned Israel since the Yom Kippur War; Romania has been the only Eastern bloc country to maintain foreign relations. The decline in the warm collaboration with France—a collaboration at its peak in the Suez invasion of 1956—was roughly contemporaneous with these developments and in many ways more traumatic for Israel. It presaged the slow evaporation of Western liberal support for Israel as the Palestinian refugee problem undermined any perception of its moral superiority, as the Holocaust receded in historical consciousness, and as the Organization of Petroleum Exporting Countries (OPEC) made clear the high costs of overt support for Israel. This trend made David Ben-Gurion's early efforts to steer a somewhat middle course in world affairs impractical and made the country dependent on those few countries that remained friendly. In recent years Israel's own stridency and impatience with anything but 100 percent support has left it with a corporal's guard of allies, many of them, like South Africa and South Korea, also shunned by other countries. Concomitantly, the United States has been freed from any need to doubt Israel's loyalty or its reliability in the Western alliance. As the Reagan administration has openly acknowledged, this reliability is an asset for the United States in the Middle East, a sure card paid for by U.S. support in the face of regional hostilities and suspicions engendered by the partnership.

In their respective domestic situations, the asymmetry is quite opposite. The identification of a substantial portion of the American Jewish community with the fate of Israel lends a substantial advantage in the rough-and-tumble of policy discussion. That identification appears to have grown steadily and dramatically since the Yom Kippur War. Although the number of Jews in the American public is small enough, their participation in elections is relatively high, especially in primary elections; in fact, Jewish participation in active politics—by contributions, candidacy, and advocacy—is disproportionately high. With the Israeli apparatus to provide some cohering influence, the Jewish and non-Jewish Zionists constitute a formidable political force throughout the American political arena. Indeed, this power has itself been at issue, especially during 1981. Such traditional sympathizers as Senator Charles McC. Mathias (Republican-Maryland), and former Representative Paul McCloskey (Republican-California) have expressed misgivings, suggesting that Israel's supporters are overzealous to the point of neglecting American interests.[1] The U.S.-Israeli partnership itself is not questioned, but the tactics of its U.S. defenders are challenged. Particularly criticized were the 1980–1982 efforts to drive a wedge into the U.S.-Saudi alliance. In many ways the most interesting (and questionable) complaint was George Ball and Representative McCloskey's claim that discussions could not be held within the executive branch without Israeli knowledge; in effect, then, Israel was part and parcel of all American policy discussions before any U.S. position was arrived at and well before any nation-to-nation bargaining.

No comparable lobby exists in Israel. The American residents in Israel retain strong connections—friends, family, even citizenship—in the United States. They tend to "think like Americans" and are generally part of the dovish Ashkenazi upper stratum. (A small group of ultrareligious hawks, however, is also drawn from American emigration. Virtually all recent American immigration into Israel has been religious, even ultrareligious. There is still no isomorphism of religious and territorialist views, although a trend in that direction has been evident for perhaps a decade.) The American immigrants, like most Israelis, recognize and cherish the crucial importance of the United States to Israel's survival. Unlike Israelis in the United States who defend their homeland against criticism, Americans in Israel do not feel obligated to defend American policy against Israeli criticism.

It is believed important in Israeli politics that the incumbent government deal effectively with the United States. Although this includes a good measure of rapport and cordiality, it implies above all else that the government be able to secure from the United States the best deal possible. Side payments—increases in aid or trade and arms concessions—are extremely significant for Israeli survival, but they are for image-building purposes and not of primary importance. Tensions preceding agreements can be an asset if they culminate in a reassurance that the government is diligently pressing Israel's just case.

(Israel's public opinion is characterized by an almost legendary belief in Israel's fundamental moral rectitude in all matters, even as its day-to-day politics are characterized by an incredible range of minute ideological differences on every conceivable issue.)

Continuous tension with a U.S. administration has been a source of weakness for any Israeli government, particularly one about to stand for election. Prime Minister Menachem Begin was not alone in believing that the rift that became evident between the governments of Jimmy Carter and Yitzhak Rabin after their White House conference in 1977 and after Carter's speech in Clinton, New York, played a major role in Begin's victory, in spite of Rabin's efforts publicly to minimize the disagreements.[2] And much of Begin's effort during the period before the Israeli election was devoted to forestalling any visible U.S. reaction or at least containing any adverse comment.[3] Indeed, Begin always emphasized the warmth and cordiality of his U.S. relationships, even seeing extravagant praise and backing in the very mildest of polite comments.[4] (This is good politics for Israel, but those who have worked with him suggest that this view stems from a need so internalized that Begin actually misperceives reality to be what he wishes it to be.) In any event, tension is more likely to be damaging to a government seen as dovish or accommodating than to one with firm views. If accommodation is not perceived as succeeding in achieving good relations, then firmness, at least, is its own reward; intransigence must be met by perceptibly sterner rebukes, since some rough edges are to be expected, and some tension is discounted in advance by hard-line voters.

Since the situations of the two countries are, then, obviously not interchangeable, they have developed practices to meet their needs and to exercise their potential. The United States can be confident of its capacity to persuade, if it uses its influence decisively. In this respect, it has little reason to influence leadership choices. A pliable negotiator or docile foreign policy ally has more difficulty selling a program at home once it is hammered out in negotiation. And for the United States details are relatively insignificant. It is the bold major strokes—the Sinai withdrawals, the Palestinian issue, the problem of Jerusalem—that are at stake for the United States and for its prestige and position in the region. When conflict arises, the United States directly addresses its views to Israeli elite opinion, but in diplomatic, gentlemanly fashion. It does not expect to campaign for the truly vital goals, only to argue in private about the particulars.

For Israel almost the opposite is true. All matters are of serious concern, and casual details may be crucial. A few kilometers are the essence of concrete security. It is of considerable importance who makes the decisions for the United States, and involvement in policy arguments is the real weapon. The awareness that access is a necessary road to persuasion makes the Israeli public and media almost paranoid in their personalistic dissection of the character and motives of foreign decision makers. Overreaction to praise or blame on Israeli matters and preoccupation with personal propensities are everywhere. Analysis in terms of national interests and commitments is rare, as though Israelis fear that such arguments are only their own propaganda coming back to confuse them. Denunciation of decision makers who act upon a country's need for oil as opportunists or lackeys is merely an exaggerated form of mistrust of any statesman's considered policies. Human sentiment, not national interests, is what Israeli public opinion relies on—and then mistrusts.

Israeli Involvement in U.S. Politics

In one sense, Israel's birth was given a send-off by President Harry Truman's endorsement, an action taken on Truman's initiative and based in part on what was perceived to be political advantage in his desperate come-from-behind victory in 1948. Projected as a wise move in Clark Clifford's famous reelection memo to his chief, it was apparently successful: Truman held the New Deal coalition more or less together, as history shows.

But certainly no new pattern of American politics ensued. Adlai Stevenson did reasonably well among Jewish voters; his control of language is said to have had special appeal. Nonetheless, Dwight Eisenhower courted and received considerable votes from that community, a defection roughly comparable to erosion in the Democratic vote generally. There is no evidence that Eisenhower's harsh reaction to the Suez incursion and his successful insistence on immediate return of all the seized territories hurt him in the election. His commanding lead from the beginning of the campaign of 1956 would have made evident the foolhardiness of testing the decision in public, and his diplomatic triumphs over the British and French made Israeli acquiescence inevitable.[5]

Similarly, mounting the barricades for either John Kennedy or Richard Nixon in 1960 would not have occurred to anyone whose interests were in the Middle East. Neither was sufficiently committed,

although both made the correct noises. Kennedy emerged as the re-
cipient of the floating Jewish vote by effective use of the bigotry issue,
while holding on to the liberal Democrats through an increasingly
strong stand on improving social ills. Lyndon Johnson triumphed
over an opponent of Jewish descent in an election determined for
Jews, as for other voters, by the domestic issues, the "reckless" image
of Barry Goldwater, and problems of the Far East, not the Middle
East. Hubert Humphrey's standing with Jewish community leaders
was close and intense, and he needed no Israeli influence or aid to
open up such channels. Rather, it was Israel that needed his aid.

It was George McGovern's campaign that brought to the fore the
potential of mobilizing a "Jewish vote"; the issue was presented by
Rabin, then ambassador to the United States, acting in a flat-footed,
not uncharacteristic way that was inappropriate to his mission. Without a sense of the delicacy of his role, Rabin openly indicated support
for President Nixon's reelection, though in an interview in Hebrew
that took place in Israel. This provoked harsh reaction from a number of prominent Jewish leaders, both those who were McGovern supporters and those who resented the appearance of Israeli intrusion.[6]
The incident has remained a sore point in the American Jewish community; it is safe to predict that Israeli ambassadors, at least, will not
soon repeat the performance, if for no other reason than the fierce
reaction of community leaders. The incident had no electoral efficacy
either. Nixon, to be sure, improved his vote over 1960, but Jewish
voters were probably the voting group most loyal (or, at worst, second
to black voters) to the decaying coalition supporting McGovern.[7]

Some background is appropriate to understanding the entire incident. Rabin's views were in fact generally shared by the Israeli leaders;
Prime Minister Golda Meir privately expressed the same sentiments.[8]
Their motives were both positive and negative. Meir and Rabin had
achieved considerable rapport with Nixon and the Department of Defense and received solid diplomatic backing and access to defense
technology that allowed Israel to develop an autonomous arms industry. This freed Israel from dependence on the United States for all
but the most advanced and most expensive armaments, and even in
this area Israel was sometimes in a position to reciprocate. After a
shaky start, the State department drew closer to the Israeli position,
and Henry Kissinger (despite his own and the White House's reluctance to involve him—a Jew and a refugee) was drawn more into
Middle East affairs, where he was to be unusually effective.[9] (The
technique of using Semites as mediators in the Middle East—Sol

Linowitz, Robert Strauss, Philip Habib—has proved especially effective; perhaps because it invokes America's pluralism, it becomes an overt token of mutual respect and accommodation.) Kissinger, like Nixon, had a special relationship with the prime minister, so that from the standpoint both of policy and of personal interaction the Israelis felt most positive about Nixon in 1972.

Their negative feelings about McGovern were not about his attitudes toward Israel per se. On the contrary, McGovern was generally one of that group of Senate stalwarts, like Frank Church of Idaho and Gaylord Nelson of Wisconsin, who were pro-Israel (and, like them, he was defeated for reelection in 1980). It was, rather, his general foreign policy of retraction of commitments and his defense policy of reducing outlays that caused Israeli concern. As Ben Wattenberg, a founder of the Coalition for a Democratic Majority, put it: "McGovern will want to react to protect Israel. But where Johnson committed the Fifth Fleet in a crisis, McGovern will have to send a rowboat." [10]

These considerations were crucial for the Israeli elite, but not for American Zionist leaders or Jewish community leaders who did not already have the same orientation. Conservative Jewish spokesmen did work more vigorously for Nixon, but no new Republican voice emerged from the Jewish leaders. And, with negligible exceptions, the later conservative trend in American Jewish political orientation has been motivated much more by reevaluation of the Soviets or by domestic concerns than by the Israeli connection.

Certainly no clear preference emerged among Israelis in the Gerald Ford–Jimmy Carter election of 1976. Both figures were relatively untried and the Middle East did not emerge as a salient issue.

The Carter administration was a period of activist attention to the Middle East. The Camp David Accords, achieved through Carter's active intervention, were a triumph of American diplomacy, demonstrating the value of broad American influence. Yet the aftermath proved again Joseph J. Sisco's law: "Nothing in the Middle East is as good or as bad as it appears at first glance." The first drawback was Egypt's isolation and the failure to involve other Arab states; the second was the Israeli disenchantment and withdrawal from the spirit of Camp David. As its chief architect, Moshe Dayan, and the minister most effective in implementation, Ezer Weizman, were isolated from influence (leading to their resignations), the country moved toward a more militant stance. As the Carter administration prepared to bring pressure to implement the sections of the accords on autonomy, Begin began to resist.

From an Israeli government standpoint then, the U.S. election of 1980 presented some hard choices. Camp David had removed the threat of war with Egypt for a long time to come. Sadat's recognition of Israel was a departure from Israel's status of pariah in the region. A good deal of this was a product of Carter's influence, not merely of U.S. policy.

But from Begin's viewpoint the Carter administration was less attractive than a Reagan government. Time was clearly a consideration. The time required for a new administration to find itself would offer some easing of U.S. pressure for a considerable period. The signs of a weakening U.S. commitment against direct contact with the Palestine Liberation Organization (PLO)—a commitment made when Israel agreed to forgo the triumph of wiping out Sadat's trapped army in the Sinai—were clear. Reagan's attitude toward the PLO was as starkly rejectionist as Begin's own. The differences on the West Bank settlements were also pronounced. The Carter administration, in regarding such settlements as a provocation and as an illegal act, shared what is substantially the dominant world opinion; Reagan's comments sounded sympathetic to Israeli policies. Finally, by his actions in 1977 Carter had suggested dissatisfaction with the Rabin government at election time.[11] The prospect of a similar performance—this time to Begin's detriment—could hardly have been attractive.

Neutrality in word and deed was the logical conclusion of all these considerations. Begin was caught between his obligations to an American president who had staked his reputation to achieve peace and his hope of a Reagan victory. The election was a difficult one to predict. A stickler for legal niceties anyway, Begin must have hoped his neutrality would prove contagious when his campaign for reelection occurred, within months after the American election.

Begin's announced strategy was strictly enforced among those under his control, but there was consternation when Weizman showed up in the Carter campaign entourage. After a period of merely speaking warmly of Carter, he formally endorsed him. Again, American Jewish leaders were dismayed, only to feel reassured when the announcement was received as an anticlimax in a dull campaign. But reaction from Israel was more pronounced; the cabinet rebuked Weizman and went to great pains to emphasize that since he no longer was a member of the government, he spoke only for himself.[12]

Carter had the endorsement of an Israeli military hero, an engaging political figure, and a nephew of the first Israeli president. Within his cabinet were Philip Klutznick (a longtime Zionist leader and Jewish community stalwart) and two other Jews, and his immediate staff and administration contained record numbers of Jews. The instinct that led him to attempt to bolster his standing with the Jewish community proved perceptive. He polled poorly in Jewish areas, with Jewish defections apparently far exceeding the considerable erosion of support from other Democratic voters. This was true especially in New York, where Senator Edward Kennedy had campaigned vigorously against Carter's turn to the right on budgetary issues and had scored his one impressive primary win.

It is generally believed that what cost Carter most heavily was suspicions among Jewish voters about his plans for Israel. That suspicion fed upon Zbigniew Brzezinski's aristocratic Polish origins, which opened him to suspicions of anti-Semitism (a spurious issue, since his family was noted for its liberal views), his association with a Brookings Institution report outlining a comprehensive solution of Middle East conflict, and his published views on settlement with the Palestinians. But the doubt became significant with two very dramatic events, whose impact went beyond mere words or gestures.

The first was the revelation in August 1979 by Israeli intelligence sources that Andrew Young, the American ambassador to the United Nations, had met with the PLO representative to the United Nations on a procedural matter of no great moment, in violation of the Kissinger agreement and the instructions of Secretary of State Cyrus Vance. Such meetings were in fact countenanced at low levels, and, as Yasser Arafat later triumphantly pointed out, the Lebanese cease-fire of July 1981 implicitly involved the Israelis in such a tacit recognition. But Young's meeting was both an act representing his own opposition to the policy and a possible signal for the future. By publicizing it, the Israelis forced attention on the matter. As they must have hoped, Vance had to insist on Young's firing, and a not-too-friendly figure was removed from power. The Carter people pleaded with the Israelis to let it be handled sub rosa, presumably with only a behind-the-scenes rebuke. By going public the Israelis unleashed a strong negative reaction from the black community against American Jews, who were seen as haughtily using power. In fact the American Jewish community was not involved at all. The highly emotional situation brought into focus the question of ultimate recognition of the PLO and reinforced the notion that Young was punished for being found doing what the Carter people were secretly aiming at.[13]

The second incident was equally dramatic but quite inexcusable. In response to Israeli persistence in establishing settlements on the West

Bank, the United States joined in a U.N. resolution condemning Israeli action and obduracy. Traditionally the United States vetoed such resolutions in the Security Council or, at worst, abstained. It was therefore quite a dramatic step when the United States voted for the resolution.

The resolution also referred to a previous U.N. resolution on Jerusalem. On its face the U.S. vote was a gratuitous shift in policy, casually and indirectly—almost deviously—announced. It seemed to confirm all the worst fears about the Carter administration's ultimate purposes and the suspicion that the White House could act precipitately, without discussing the interests of its allies, for transitory or illusory advantage.

Incredibly, this action was taken on the eve of the New York presidential primary. There President Carter faced the formidable challenge of Senator Kennedy. The Iranian crisis, which had aborted Kennedy's efforts in other key states, was becoming stale, and the rally-to-the-president tide was beginning to ebb. With this new issue, Kennedy was to score a strong victory in New York, adding some life and luster to his challenge and allowing him to bring his campaign with dignity to the convention hall.

But worse was yet to come. In a strange salvage effort, the Carter administration repudiated its vote and claimed error on the part of Secretary Vance. The original draft resolution, it was explained, had two references to Jerusalem. President Carter had instructed Vance and U.S. Ambassador Donald F. McHenry to vote for the resolution if the Jerusalem clause and other language were adjusted. The excision of the first reference to Jerusalem was agreed to, but there was misunderstanding about the second.[14]

It was generally assumed that Vance was taking gentlemanly responsibility for a presidential boner. In truth, the matter makes no sense and reflects badly on the Carter administration's competence, regardless of what assumption is made. If an error in fact occurred, it was a disastrous one; any gain in warmth from the Arabs was offset by the contempt engendered among them and America's European allies. Furthermore, it is difficult to understand why the error was not caught at some level of policy implementation.

If no error was made and a clumsy lie was resorted to, that itself was hardly reassuring. In any event, sheer political incompetence was clearly involved. Some months later Clark Clifford, in a television appearance with Bill Moyers, suggested that Carter had no feel for first-term and second-term issues. Clifford thought the Panama Canal matter should have been resolved in the last years of an administration, not before an election. Perhaps there was urgency there.[15] But the time to shift a stance on a sensitive policy issue is hardly in the heat of a campaign. If Camp David was Carter's finest achievement, the U.N. vote was his nadir. And that event, more than any other, colored perceptions of his fundamental orientation on the Middle East.

If the election had been a close one, this might emerge in the reckoning of historians as a decisive blunder, comparable to Ford's Polish faux pas in his television debate with Carter. But the issue of the economy and the president's negative and narrow campaign gave Reagan a landslide victory, eclipsing any small-group influence.

The Israelis clearly and correctly avoided any direct involvement in the American political campaign. On key events that "provided a context" for indicating an orientation, the Israelis' role was somewhat mischievous from the standpoint of the incumbent, creating image problems for the president. Since, as their friends often complain, Israeli politicians tend to play each event by itself, oblivious of long-range consequences, these events were probably treated as questions of short-run advantage.

If the Israelis intentionally undermined Carter, however, they miscalculated in other ways, since the effect of the Reagan sweep was to defeat a large number of (chiefly Democratic) senators who had been ardent defenders of Israel. Where the constituency was politically strong, positive support was still to be expected, although Senator Paula Hawkins of Florida will never bring to the issue the concern that Senator Richard Stone did. But where the support was an accident of the heart—as for Church or Senator Gale McGee of Wyoming—the loss was both long range and significant.

U.S. Involvement in Israeli Politics

Trying to alter Israeli electoral politics was once seen as a Herculean task. Even before the establishment of the state, elections in the Jewish community resulted in a considerable plurality for Mapai, the moderate socialist labor party led by Ben-Gurion. Although it was nominally anticlerical, Mapai had a good working relationship with its religious counterpart, the National Religious party (NRP). Dominated by the worker faction of the party, the latter was mildly favorable to a welfare state, had a vague but centrist defense and foreign policy, and was willing to give its backing to a Mapai-dominated government in return for concessions in the area of its special concern, religion. These two parties formed the nucleus of every government of Israel until 1977, and since that time Begin has found Mafdal (the NRP) a necessary partner in his coalitions. Yosef Burg, the nominal leader of Mafdal, has served in the cabinet continuously since 1952; he currently holds three portfolios (Religion, Interior, Police) and, as head of the autonomy team, performs a major task that would normally fall to the foreign office.

Efforts to break from the system have been continuous. The process of cabinet formation, however predictable in the rough, is time-consuming and enervating. Parties have perfected tactics of bargaining that approach blackmail. After a time in office, governments have hung together only with great difficulty. Political loyalty, not efficiency, has necessarily evolved as the primary requisite for office. Ministries are, in Brian Chapman's term, "colonized," seen as party resources rather than governmental enterprise. Coordination becomes a major diplomatic task.

Ben-Gurion's attempted solution was to alter the electoral arrangements. He was fondest of a single-member-district solution. His advocacy here proved quixotic, as did the effort of the Democratic Movement for Change (DMC) to adopt the same solution as its major goal. Pragmatically, Ben-Gurion and his successors have sought to create megaparties, to secure aggregation before the election and—the "Garden of Eden" of Israeli parties—even a majority. In the early years such consolidations resulted in a drop-off of the parties' expected combined vote, perhaps because of the formerly crucial nature of apparat operations in Israeli politics, or because of the diminution of ideological uniqueness, or because of voters' fears of a majority party, or some combination of those. The balancing of the Mapai-led megaparty (the Labor Alignment) with the Herut-dominated Likud has changed this configuration. The Alignment's absorption of neighbors on the immediate left and the Likud's absorption of rightist groups have destroyed the centrist position of the Alignment and have magnified the crucial role of the religious parties.

A second impetus for change has been the persistent call for ethnic parties to replace ideological parties, which were, after all, largely based on turn-of-the-century eastern European politics. Ethnicity, however, has not proved an acceptable focus for Israelis. The sole real exception to this—Aharon Abu-Hatzeira's Tami party, which in the 1981 election won three seats—had a special ethnic appeal for Moroccan emigres but added a religious orientation that to Israeli sensibilities qualified it as "ideological."

The third effort to induce change in the Israeli system has centered on techniques to influence the voters. This has meant Americanization of the process in a number of ways: (1) Television is used as a major vehicle for presenting views. Israel by law allocates free television time to the parties in accordance with their current Knesset membership. Production costs, however, remain a major expense. (2) As the old-style apparat organizations have been sharply diminished in their effectiveness, media and publicity techniques are increasingly used to fill the vacuum. David Garth, for the Likud, and David Sawyer, for the Alignment, served as imported American campaign experts, backed up by numerous public relations experts. (Dahaf, a public relations firm, worked for Begin in 1977 and for Shimon Peres in 1981.) These costs cannot be hidden by diversion of communal personnel or organizational funding. Election costs must be more clearly accounted for, therefore, than in the past. The major parties, especially the Alignment, had American sources of funds. Tami and another Sephardic minor party were funded by Nissim Gaon, a West European tycoon of Tunisian origin. (Gaon paid for advertisements to justify his contributions.)[16]

The system was, however, really altered by two sharp shocks and three long-range developments, culminating in the unprecedented election of 1977. The long-range developments included the following: (1) With the passage of time, the state's founders have died, oddly leaving only Begin, the classic oppositionist, to represent historical and personal continuity. (2) Demographic changes have occurred in the population, causing the Sephardic vote to become an increasing proportion of the total. It is most probable that 1981 may have been the last or penultimate election with a plurality of voters of Ashkenazi extraction. The proportions of these communities' votes for the Alignment and the Likud have remained roughly constant, so that this shift in the voting base has important implications for their relative strength, strongly favoring the Likud. (3) The NRP has become more militant on the territorial issue. Latent tendencies in this direction were galvanized by an internal struggle within the party. The "youth circles" not only employed biblical and other religious arguments on the West Bank but also argued that seeking patronage was not a proper objective of the party and even beneath the dignity of their religious aspirations. The new generation of Alignment leaders, sabras raised in the anticlerical faith of their fathers, had no sense of tolerance or affinity for the religious. That Begin spoke with religious overtones and was, though not "observant," still a traditionalist made

reassessment of the alliance between the NRP and the Labor Alignment that much easier.

The first shock wave included a series of events that led to a general
decline of Alignment leadership in the wake of the Yom Kippur War
debacle. Prime Minister Meir attempted to maintain the government
without political retribution, leaving the former chief of staff, David
Elazar, as scapegoat. Meir's resignation was, however, apparently a result of her illness and caused a crisis of leadership. Leadership passed
to the untried Rabin, a product not of Mapai but of Achdut Ha'avoda,
one of the parties absorbed in the Alignment. A series of revelations
of corruption by prominent party leaders, culminating in the revelation that Rabin had violated the prohibition against unauthorized foreign bank accounts, conveyed a feeling of a disintegrating, decaying,
and incompetent political structure. It was in reaction that the DMC,
essentially a centrist Mapai breakaway, emerged as a potent electoral
force in 1977.

The second shock wave to party loyalists, more subtle but even
more disturbing in its implications, related to the U.S.-Israeli connection and the growing strains on that partnership. Indeed, 1977
seemed to suggest an imminent collision no matter which administration exercised power in Washington.

After the Six-Day War, the Israelis more than half-expected pressure to return to the old borders and were prepared to resist full restoration. To their amazement little pressure was exerted. Washington
felt that President Gamal Abdel Nasser had misread the Suez restoration as a license to be grandiose with an insurance policy against failure. Rational settlement would come, as Abba Eban once suggested,
when all other efforts were perceived as exhausted.

Washington, however, made several efforts to get Israel into a mood
for concessions. It found that some of the old Arab intransigency was
rubbing off on Israel. This was exasperating but not of monumental
importance to American decision makers. It became more urgent
when the Yom Kippur War required a massive American airlift to res-
cue Israel's failing military power. Unfortunately, the action also galvanized OPEC. Cost of the support was high but not unbearably high
even for a country intent on recouping from the Vietnam disaster by
minimizing its foreign and defense expenditures.

The U.S. leverage on Israel yielded a high return, however. The
Israel Defense Force was restrained from humiliating Sadat through
liquidation of the trapped Third Army in the desert, which might well
have provoked a Soviet reply. This underscored the U.S. advantage in

maintaining communications with all sides. And in September 1975 Kissinger, using a carrot-and-stick approach, persuaded the Israelis to cede a substantial portion of the Sinai. (The reluctance of Israel had been underscored by the collapse of Kissinger's efforts to negotiate substantially the same agreement only months earlier, climaxed by his leaving the region in tears.)

Internally the costs to the Israeli leadership were much greater than appreciated abroad. Used to leadership that bobbed and weaved, that gave ground to advance, and that was alternately conciliatory or aggressive in the light of external conditions, Israelis on the surface accepted the retreat. Ben-Gurion's acumen in such situations had set the model for such acceptance. But underneath, the feeling remained that they had been outsmarted in an international game and had given up a great deal for nothing. Rabin, the basically unproven leader, had agreed to Sadat's acquiescence in a one-sided gift of land— including the Abu Rudeis oil fields—for nothing tangible in return. Kissinger's perception that this was a major step forward was yet to be confirmed; Sadat's flight to Tel Aviv to offer peace was still a pipe dream. Begin and other hard-liners were ruthless in deriding the withdrawals and the hapless leaders who implemented them. There was more than a hint in the criticism that the withdrawals reflected moral cowardice in the face of American pressure rather than the realities of global policies. (Had the fiasco of 1974 not occurred, it is conceivable that the reception would have been worse. The government, after all, had demonstrated resistance to pressure in the abortive negotiations.)

But abroad these steps were seen as long overdue and as tiny steps. Problems of implementation were seen as marks of weakness of the government rather than a fact of political life. (To be sure, the Rabin government was "weak," but the "strong" Meir regime had taken no comparable courageous actions. In political realities, as opposed to intellectual criticism, the government also was nonetheless challenged as too conciliatory rather than too rigid.) The failure of foreigners to understand Israeli public opinion has led to mishandling of demands made upon the elite and sometimes the miscalculations of alternative policies likely to ensue if they were defeated and replaced.

Signs of difficulties between the Israeli government and the Ford administration abounded. The first half of 1976 witnessed a continuous battle over the amount and nature of aid to Israel, with the White House persisting in a threat to veto aid over the $2.2 billion figure backed by the Office of Management and Budget. Rabin traveled to the United States and secured what he thought was a commitment from Kissinger, but the secretary of state was overriden in this matter. (This was finally admitted by Kissinger after several months of political doubletalk.) [17] Rabin's failure to resolve the conflict or to increase the flow of vital materials hurt him at a crucial point, since his ace in the hole politically had always been his Pentagon contacts. That the foreign aid bill ultimately moved toward Israel's figures through various devices months later or that Ford in the last weeks of the campaign (October 9) announced the sale of key weapons did not help much in restoring Rabin's image.[18] Neither did Ambassador Malcolm Toon's public criticism of Israeli lobbying tactics in Congress over the appropriations bill.

All of this became history when Ford was defeated for reelection. Only a few weeks later, on December 19, Prime Minister Rabin chose to dismiss the ministers of the NRP because of that party's abstention on an ultrareligious motion of censure over a ceremony welcoming the arrival of F-15 planes, which had trickled on past the hour for the beginning of the Sabbath. Although the vote of confidence was a comfortable 55–48, Rabin apparently assumed he could gain in image by a more positive move to elections. Perhaps he hoped to preempt diplomatic moves in early 1977, maintaining the normal pseudo-honeymoon with a new administration. To further implement this logical but ill-fated strategy, Rabin scheduled a March meeting with the new president in spite of opposition leader Begin's vigorously pietistic argument that it was unseemly for a prime minister to appear to play politics with foreign affairs. Rabin, it turned out, was instead to be played with; Carter was to indulge himself in one of his curious foreign policy sermons, a maneuver almost as mysterious and mischievous as his effort to negotiate a SALT agreement through a public statement of terms.

Rabin was greeted with a warm sentiment endorsing "defensible" borders—making Carter the first U.S. president to go beyond the U.N.'s "secure and recognized" borders. Arab criticism quickly brought a statement that nothing new was intended, however. The Carter-Rabin discussion was, by all accounts, a disaster; the chemistry was bad, and the two were at cross-purposes. Rabin sought a little cachet for his reelection campaign and wanted little done; Carter was anxious to get moving. He found Rabin rigid and inflexible. At the conclusion of the visit Carter unilaterally outlined a solution for the Middle East that was built around minimal adjustment of the pre-1969 border but was a recognition of Israeli spheres of influence and strategic placement familiar to those aware of the Allon plan or the Brookings approach. More pointedly, a week later in Clinton, New York, Carter was to speak of a "Palestinian homeland" but to insist again that this did not constitute a departure in U.S. policy.[19]

From Rabin's point of view this was all disastrous, and the Alignment had to explain quickly that the conflict was no greater than in the past. Instead of glowing in a political gain, the prime minister was trying to cut his losses. James Reston commented sardonically on Carter's "open mouth" policy and pointedly noted that neither Rabin nor Vance had known of the pronouncements.[20] The obvious point that governments fighting for reelection are not good prospects for accepting self-abnegating plans was also made.

The peculiarity is that all agree Carter had not intended to pull any carpets from under the prime minister. The conflict, including Rabin's prompt rejection of the approach, all came from the policy disagreement, which, by all logic, should never even have occurred.[21] The disregard of Rabin's domestic situation may have come about from assumptions of the Alignment's invincibility. But the suspicion lingers that it was simply a product of carelessness, the lack of any sense of political timing.

Rabin's downfall, however, was swift and sure and unrelated to these incidents. The revelation of his wife's illegal bank account and concomitant perjuries coming in a season of Alignment scandals made his position untenable. He withdrew as candidate for prime minister and was replaced by the man he had narrowly defeated in an intra-party election, Peres. But this too could not stem the tide, and the Likud gained a 4-to-3 plurality, helped mightily by the unprecedented surge of the Democratic Movement for Change, which gained fifteen Knesset votes. Begin now faced Israel's mighty problems and a few of his own. For he had to overcome the foreign image of a former terrorist and persistent demagogue.

The choice of Moshe Dayan as foreign minister was brilliantly conceived to bolster Begin where he was weak, possibly including his standing in Washington. Dayan was a perennial favorite with the State Department because of his flexible and creative approach to problems. Although the choice may have been a concession by Begin to Washington, its purpose seems to have been broader, and it was effective.

Camp David was a triumph of American leverage, with Dayan and Ezer Weizman providing excellent assistance. Begin, as a matter of Israeli politics, found the Labor Alignment effectively fighting for his treaty. Still later, with Weizman in opposition, Begin could claim the treaty where it was advantageous and blame others for its costs. In 1981 the Likud used the slogan "Better the hardships of peace than the suffering of war" and tried to project the image of a hard, but not inflexible, bargainer. ("Peace *and* security" was its other banner line.)

The point at which Begin moved into a collision course with the Carter administration was, as noted earlier, over the settlements. This could have created a situation for Begin analogous to Rabin's problems in 1977. Reagan's election must have been a great source of relief to a politician already far behind in the public opinion polls. Begin received subtle aid from Reagan's articulation of a strong anti-PLO position and his indication that the settlements were perhaps detrimental but not illegal. By standing firm, Begin suggested, he had ultimately helped bring about a change in U.S. attitudes. Although the shift in U.S. tone over the PLO was not really a change in policy, the threat inferred from Carter's hints of a potential change was worrisome enough to Israelis that Begin was seen as having won a significant victory. Much the same was true of the settlement policy; he had brazened through in spite of overt U.S. displeasure, and now it was seemingly no longer an issue.

The Reagan administration was most cooperative in providing an interlude of smooth relations that clearly bolstered Begin. On the one hand, it was recognized that new, risky policies are not salable at election time. (Sadat indicated this most emphatically by calling off autonomy talks explicitly because he recognized that no breakthroughs were possible in those "dog-eat-dog" days.) But the Reagan administration was also having its own foreign policy difficulties, both in shaping up a working relationship between the State Department and the White House and in formulating programs to implement its firmly held principles. In the Middle East, in particular, it was concerned with expanding potential deterrence to Soviet expansion rather than resolving the region's problems or shifting priorities among claims of its allies.

An early exception was the administration proposal to sell Airborne Warning and Control System (AWACS) planes to Saudi Arabia. Although they were ultimately to oppose the decision in public, the Israelis tried several times to settle the matter through negotiations for offsetting equipment. The issue was joined by pro-Israeli groups on assurances by military experts of danger to Israel and the absence of a visible advantage to the United States. Once the battle was evident, the Begin government had no choice but to join in. American Jewish groups were visibly angry at the hesitation and most critical of negotiations over side payments, which could not, after all, eliminate the danger if it was a reality. The Begin administration indicated it was reluctant to battle a new administration in its first months. It was not only a bad way to start a partnership but also a time (the early honeymoon period) of maximum political influence for an American president. These explanations have validity, but it was also highly probable that avoiding any conflict with the United States was a basic cornerstone of Begin's election strategy and that departing from that position—as in the raid on the Iraqi atomic reactor—was carefully weighed, with a public explanation prepared in advance.

Throughout the campaign Begin insisted on his effective rapport with the United States and, for that matter, with Egypt and Sadat. Contrary suggestions were greeted with sarcastic questions about the critic's authority to speak for the other country and its leaders. Even Reagan's refusal to meet with Begin during the preinaugural period was treated positively; although the official explanation was that Reagan did not wish to complicate U.S. policy or embarrass President Carter by meeting foreign leaders, he did meet with Chancellor Schmidt. As the election in Israel was a long way off, this was interpreted as Reagan's wish to have more time to tackle the Mideast rather than a personal rebuff or a left-handed endorsement of the opposition.

Although Sadat was clearly irritated by the lack of progress on the autonomy issue, he cooperated by at least not creating any crises. Egypt's stake in the outcome was hardly clear-cut in any event. The Alignment was more flexible on the West Bank but not notably so on the PLO issue, and an Alignment regime might well be more effective in dealing with U.S. opinion. But Sadat's main objective was to complete the final transfer of the Sinai territories scheduled for April 1982. Begin could easily be seen as the one who politically could still deliver and, as the signer, was still the one most obligated. (Mrs. Sadat in a lecture at the University of Minnesota in May 1983 confirmed that her late husband had preferred a Begin victory.) Sadat therefore played things carefully. When the Alignment seemed a sure winner, he carefully and rather quietly expressed his dissatisfaction with the stalemated talks and sent observers to the party convention. When Begin surged back, comments were indirectly attributed to Sadat to the effect that Sadat preferred keeping the old relationship. When Begin requested a conference late in the campaign, Sadat obliged. What appeared to be mainly a public relations ploy for campaign purposes (a meeting to enhance Begin's image) would emerge as a cover for the Iraqi raid.

The attack on the Baghdad reactor occurred with three weeks remaining in the campaign and left Peres at a distinct disadvantage. Inevitably Begin gained in domestic support. The opposition leader's criticism opened him to charges of undermining not Begin but Israel abroad. Peres equivocated and finally arrived at a policy of criticizing only in Hebrew and only for domestic purposes. He also adopted the stance of criticizing not the attack, which he mildly endorsed, but its timing.

The U.S. government, however, emphatically condemned the raid. Begin was ready for this and explained in various sotto voce formats that Washington would publicly condemn but privately praise the raid. This provoked Washington to stronger statements and, most important, to refutation of virtually every statement advanced by Begin about the urgency of the raid. (Especially devastating was the U.S. denial that an active reactor could not be attacked without dire consequences for the surrounding population.) This day-to-day condemnation by the U.S. government was not responded to in depth by the Begin administration, which also accepted the U.S. action of joining in the U.N. vote of censure. However, this was made easier to accept because U.N. Ambassador Jeane J. Kirkpatrick, in explaining the U.S. vote, said that America's reason for supporting the resolution was "Israel's failure to exhaust peaceful means for resolving this dispute." She also said that "nothing in this resolution will affect my government's commitment to Israel's security." Having discounted such moves in advance, Begin must have realized that these actions were relatively mild and, if given attention, would hurt him all the more.

Throughout the campaign, too, Begin had emphasized his open door to negotiator Philip Habib. Now he claimed that his earlier bellicose rhetoric on the Lebanese crisis had been a necessary cover for the Iraqi incursion.

The sticking point was, however, the use of U.S. planes in the attack in spite of Israel's pledge to use them only defensively. American protests were dismissed by a spokesman who suggested that Israel alone had the right to determine its defense needs, a matter not really at issue. The lack of interest in U.S. concerns expressed was salt in the wounds; as editorialists pointed out, Israel could not expect the United States to continue to subsidize damage to its standing in the region. The minimalist U.S. response was to suspend F-16 shipments to Israel; Begin quickly protested this "unjust" action. Since the United States was anxious to strengthen Western forces in the region, it was obviously also a temporary punishment.

The alarming, almost contemptuous, attitude expressed by Begin toward all allies and external opinion finally provoked U.S. response, particularly by the press. Flora Lewis urged U.S. pressure in the election, suggesting that Begin's defeat was vital.[22] George Will, the conservative analyst known to be influential in the White House, viewed possible reelection as a disaster. A few unidentified voices in the administration expressed the hope that Begin would be defeated. The prime minister personally complained to Ambassador Samuel Lewis about Washington's tilt against him.[23] With the arrival of election eve, these matters had received a few lines in the press, but the voters had paid much less notice than Begin had. Although an element in the decision of those who rejected Begin was his effectiveness, or lack of it, in dealing with the West, it was a more general doubt. Conflict with the Reagan administration was not perceived as a problem or an issue.

The Straining of the Rules

In 1982–1983 U.S.-Israeli difficulties were to be exacerbated by events even more than such difficulties had been in the past. A change in the balance of relations in the Middle East occurred with the neutralization of Egypt. Israel now had a clear surplus of security and was not in the short term militarily dependent on the United States. That had been more or less true for a long time, though imperfectly perceived. Ultimately the dependency is as real as ever, both for the economy and for military reequipment if all-out war should break out. But that becomes less likely as the threat of war recedes. Readjustment to this new military dominance has been difficult, particularly when Israel began to use its power not only against the Iraqi reactor but also against the PLO in Lebanon. The tragic massacres by Phalangist troops who were permitted into Palestinian refugee camps by the Israel Defense Force created emotional, ethical, and diplomatic problems with ramifications not yet fully played out. These events sorely tried the partnership between the United States and Israel as well as their mode of dealing with each other. It is now doubtful that these events will reverberate at election time, although for a dramatic period they looked as if they might.

An unprecedented event was the scrambling of both countries' political party lines over Reagan's peace initiative in the Middle East. When Secretary George Shultz formulated his plan in 1982, he talked with opposition leader Peres and many others. These talks exploded into an issue both in Israel and in the United States. Shultz and Peres were accused of conspiring to sacrifice the independence of Israel by involving a party leader in framing a policy statement of another power. Peres denied that he had participated in the drafting or had had anything more than a normal exchange of views with Shultz. The formal denial underlined the degree to which Israelis are critical of alleged attempts to manipulate Israeli politics. William Safire echoed the criticism in a very sharp attack on the administration for such collusion.[24]

The outcry, charges, and countercharges of partisan manipulation were the most novel part of the affair. Israel has long taken advantage of American political divisions, as Rabin has noted. Indeed, Ambassador Moshe Arens spoke during the Lebanon crisis of the "family" nature of U.S.-Israeli relations and the desirability of political involvement and frankness.[25]

The issue faded mainly because Israel, adroitly rebounding from the debacle of the massacres, accepted much of the Shultz initiative and reached agreement with Lebanon. This left President Assad of Syria to demonstrate intransigence and wreck Reagan's effort. The reasoned report of the Kahan Commission, accepting limited responsibility for the misdeeds of Israel's allies, also contrasted with Arab insistence that the actual perpetrators not be condemned. But the insistence on the limited punishments prescribed and the deftness of policy were probably also a product of the replacement of the scalpel of Arens for the meat ax of Ariel Sharon. At any rate, the policy respite has eased strains on the process as well as the day-to-day relations between the countries.

Another incident, however, confirmed the rules. Secretary of the Interior James Watt suggested in a letter to Ambassador Arens that American Jews supporting ecological and conservation policies opposed to atomic energy were endangering support of Israel.

Such an argument is not unprecedented. President Johnson used to argue that Jews opposing the Vietnam War put into doubt the U.S. habit of keeping its commitments. Henry Kissinger argued that the Jackson amendment endangered Israel by upsetting détente and Soviet restraint on the Syrians and others. Kissinger apparently even used the Yom Kippur War crisis to browbeat American Jewish leaders to go to Senator Henry Jackson to seek withdrawal of the proposal—which he refused. Kissinger succeeded in securing a pledge from the Israelis that they would be neutral—as propriety suggested—but he wanted them to join him in urging the American Jewish community to oppose the measure. (Apparently he did not, however, link aid to

Israel with such action in dealing with Israel as he tried to do with panicky Zionist leaders.) [26]

In any event, the outcry over the Watt letter underscored the impropriety of linking purely domestic issues with Israel and assuming the ambassador had influence over an issue totally out of his domain. Watt at first announced that he was proud of his argument. A month later he announced that he had erred and that it was an unfortunate incident. Arens quickly indicated that Watt was a friend of Israel, whose motives at least were good. Clearly Arens wished to avoid any echoes with the Andrew Young affair. [27]

Conclusion

So far as we know, both Israel and the United States have avoided official intervention, except in trivial instances, in each other's politics. It is evident, however, that considerable consequences flow from their ordinary transactions. The effects do not come from endorsements or expressions of opinion but from events and reactions to them. Rabin's or Weizman's endorsement has no more and probably less influence than Max Fisher's or Arthur Hertzbert's would have, especially if either of the latter were to abandon his traditional affiliations. But the specter of Carter casually redrawing (or, if you will, restoring) boundaries suggested to Israelis that conciliation had lost any influence in Washington—a message loud and clear though opposite to that intended. The Young incident more effectively substantiated Israel's argument that the United States was, sub rosa, doing what it had solemnly promised not to do.

Not surprisingly, U.S. actions have had much greater influence on Israel than vice versa. This is not because of U.S. wisdom or manipulation. It is a product of greater U.S. leverage and the responsiveness of the Israeli public to U.S. stances. But U.S. power sometimes has been poorly used. The Israelis are adept at fending off outside pressure and arousing guilt in those who use it. The skill was learned as early as the 1920s, when the small Jewish community of Palestine succeeded in facing down Anglo-American Zionist representatives, led by Justice Louis Brandeis, who demanded an accounting of funds raised. The principle under which the Yishuv (the Palestinian Jewish protoofficial community) won was that those on the firing line, who bear the risk, must be free to make the vital decisions. Echoes of this persist in Israel's attitude toward Diaspora Jews and toward the United States.

But ultimately power is where power rests, especially if it is employed with skill and discretion. The lessons of the past indicate that Flora Lewis's suggestion that the United States intervene in Israeli electoral politics would have been much too little, too late, and too crudely direct. But to create an image, an atmosphere, and even a reality at strategic and early moments is feasible. In any event, the difficulty of projecting the effects on a volatile electorate and complex party coalition discourages tampering much more than ethical injunctions do. Past efforts, like Carter's poorly defined maneuvers, suggest that greater care and perspicacity are needed to be effective. At least the lessons of avoiding inept involvement seem to have been learned.

For the Israelis, the risks of American electoral politics are normally even greater. The advantages of having a friend in the White House are great, but under most conceivable circumstances, the choice concerns the intensity of the friendship, in ways not easily calculable. The quiet in the Humphrey-Nixon campaign paid off most handsomely— with Nixon's strong support, for example. In any event, criticism appealing to fewer than one in thirty in an electorate is not a good bet. Longer-range advantage inheres in broad coalitions and bipartisan support. Overt neutrality at election time, access to all camps, and graduated response to support or coolness are components of the optimal strategy. Criticism of policies, not individuals, parties, or even administrations, is the straight and narrow path from which one veers at some risk. Tepid support in the White House leaves intact the basic support present in the traditional Pentagon ties; dramatic confrontation threatens to end low-level, day-to-day cordiality. A challenged president may forbid or prevent relationships with those who pursue him.

In spite of the crucial nature of their reactions, then, these disparate partners are not much different from other countries in their situations or in the strategies they use. Overt interference is almost certainly a mistake, and subtle interference is difficult and unpredictable. Both nations have resources more direct and effective than electoral manipulation. How these resources are employed may have electoral consequences, however; taking account of such consequences and minimizing them should be (but have probably not been) major elements in assessing tactics.

It has been suggested by Philip Geyelin that Begin thinks Reagan worked against him politically, although Begin helped Reagan. (Peres, however, is convinced that the unnecessarily frequent "Dear Menachem" letters from the president helped the prime minister.)[28] Israel's tactics on the autonomy talks diminished Carter's major achievement, the Camp David agreement. It will not have escaped Reagan's or anyone else's attention that Begin's West Bank policy was developed not to influence American politics but to demonstrate his conviction in the face of world opinion. Whether Geyelin is well informed about Begin's views or not, the matter does serve as an illustration of political reality. Political maneuvers do not generally determine policy but are an aspect of a policy that is predetermined. As a calculation in close options or in the matter of presentation of a stand, anticipated reactions may be an aspect of a decision, but rarely its essence.

While Israeli-American relations conform to most patterns of interactions between large and small countries, there are some striking differences. Statesmen of the world generally see one another as members of a club and wish one another well. But, since the Nixon-Meir era, Israeli and U.S. leaders have sometimes been discontented with one another.

It is striking how leaders of the world band together. Familiarity clearly breeds acceptance. Even changes of Soviet and U.S. leadership are viewed apprehensively in the other country. The known devil takes on angelic attributes. But the warmth is generally more genuine and more positive. Perhaps leaders fear that overthrowing leaders might be contagious; they tend to be sympathetic to those who are under fire. Sometimes there is an attempt to give support, although that is easier said than done. Carter instructed his Commerce Department officials a few months before the British general election to do what they could for his friend James Callaghan.[29] Given the time available and the complex economic problems involved, it is unlikely that even Carter thought this was more than a gesture.

It is widely assumed, however, that Chancellor Helmut Schmidt agreed to a common agricultural program for the European Economic Community (EEC) that was considerably less than optimal for West Germany to produce a highly visible diplomatic victory for his hard-pressed friend Valery Giscard d'Estaing.[30] (In both instances, of course, the electoral results were negative.) Schmidt also broke ranks by taking an even more deviant step, that is, by openly hoping for Carter's electoral defeat. Given the anti-Americanism rife in his own party and the great importance of West Germany to NATO, Schmidt could expect little loss and perhaps even some net gain from such a step, even if Carter lost, especially since the prime minister had been visibly preening himself as one of the more perspicacious leaders of the West.

The tensions that led Carter to want to be relieved of the personal burdens of Rabin and Begin, that probably led Reagan to look forward to the defeat of a conservative in Israel, and made Begin eager to see his "friend" Jimmy Carter defeated in 1980 are almost certain to persist. Like procedural rules in an assembly, best enforced during crucial debates, the rules of diplomatic nicety are most useful at times of tension. Neutrality in another nation's electoral politics is clearly the best policy. But there is, underneath this simple homily, a greater reality. In each country there is the problem of mutual understanding and perception. Neither can afford to abandon that arena of opinion formation in the other country; therefore each participates in electoral politics willy-nilly. There are forces that cause countries to come closer or to veer away from what is perceived as another country's interests. Actions that are neither crude nor offensive can strengthen or weaken those forces. Wisdom as well as cleverness is needed to play such a complex game to advantage and without offense to the other partner. Israel has proved adept at short-range image building in the United States, often at a cost of its long-range effectiveness. The United States has not yet found a consistent or constructive style for successfully intervening in Israeli politics, although by a painful process of learning it seems to have reached the point of not blundering into counterproductive actions.

NOTES

1. Paul McCloskey, "To Attain Peace in the Middle East," *Los Angeles Times*, August 2, 1981; George Ball, "The Coming Crisis in American-Israeli Relations," *Foreign Affairs*, Winter 1979–80; and Charles McC. Mathias, "Ethnic Groups and Foreign Policy," *Foreign Affairs*, Summer 1981, pp. 185–90.

2. See Yitzhak Rabin, *The Rabin Memoirs* (Boston: Little, Brown, 1979), pp. 299–300. Similar views were expressed in interviews with Shlomo Avineri (Washington, D.C., May 1981) and Simcha Dinitz (Jerusalem, July 19, 1981).

3. See, for example, Wolf Blitzer, "Steady As She Goes," *Jerusalem Post*, July 3, 1981; and Philip Geyelin, "Begin Visit Promises to Be Interesting," *Washington Post*, September 8, 1981.

4. Simcha Dinitz noted this trait in early relations with Begin. It has since become a standing joke of Israeli politics. For some examples, see Ezer Weizman, *The Battle for Peace* (New York: Bantam, 1981), pp. 120, 373.

5. See, for example, Herman Finer, *Dulles over Suez* (Chicago: Quadrangle Books, 1964).

6. See *Washington Post*, June 11, 1972, and editorial, June 15, 1972. For Rabin's version, see his *Memoirs*, pp. 232–33.

7. Compare Robert Cantor, *Voting Behavior and Presidential Elections* (Itasca, Ill.: Peacock, 1975), p. 55; and Gerald Pomper, "The Presidential Election," in Marlene Pomper, ed., *The Election of 1976* (New York: McKay, 1977), table 3.2 and p. 63.

8. Interview with Simcha Dinitz.

9. For Kissinger's difficulties, see his *Years of Upheaval*, excerpted in *Time*, March 7, 1982, pp. 19ff.

10. Ben Wattenberg, speech, Minnesota Academy of Sciences, April 1972.

11. See notes 2 and 19.

12. *New York Times*, October 29, 1980; and Wolf Blitzer, *American Jewish World*, November 14, 1980. Weizman's book does not refer to his performance on this matter but vigorously defends Carter (*Battle for Peace*, pp. 288–89).

13. See *New York Times*, August 16, 1979. Young noted Israeli unwillingness to minimize the damage (*New York Times*, October 17, 1979).

14. On the U.N. vote and the "extraordinary" Carter repudiation, see *New York Times*, March 2, March 4, March 5, and March 15, 1980.

15. "Bill Moyers' Journal," March 16, 1981.

16. See *Jerusalem Post*, June 26, 1981. Similar full-page advertisements appeared the same day in Hebrew in leading papers, noting the frequency of previous foreign contributions and suggesting that ethnicity was an issue created by the dominant Ashkenazi attitudes.

17. See *New York Times*, January 28, 1977; March 10, 1977; and October 12, 1977.

18. Kissinger's testimony before the Senate Appropriations subcommittee, as reported in *New York Times*, April 25, 1977.

19. See Rabin, *Memoirs*, pp. 299–300; and *New York Times*, March 8 and March 10, 1977. On the Clinton speech, see *New York Times* of March 17, 1977; on Rabin's minimizing the rift, see *New York Times*, March 14, 1977. Recent memoirs by Vance and Brzezinski reinforce the impression of complacency. They suggest that Rabin was invulnerable until the bank account scandal. In the light of growing domestic discontent in Israel, this seems a doubtful judgment.

20. See the column of James Reston, *New York Times*, March 16, 1977. See also the March 19, 1977, story (*New York Times*), in which Brzezinski too disclaims advance notice of the Clinton statement.

21. Interviews with Stuart Eizenstat and Philip Klutznick (Washington, D.C., April 1981) and Simcha Dinitz.

22. Flora Lewis, *International Herald Tribune*, June 25, 1981.

23. *Jerusalem Post*, June 29, 1981. Interviews with U.S. consulate and ambassadorial officials, June 1981.

24. See *New York Times* in late August and early September 1982, especially September 15, 1982; for Safire, see *New York Times*, September 2, 1982, and September 15, 1982.

25. Rabin, *Memoirs*, p. 142; and *Boston Globe*, September 19, 1982.

26. Mattei Golan, *The Secret Conversations of Henry Kissinger* (New York: Quadrangle, 1976), pp. 53–56, 172–73.

27. On Watt, see *New York Times*, June 25, 1982, and July 29, 1982.

28. See Geyelin, "Begin Visit," and *Jerusalem Post*, May 16–20, 1982.

29. Interview with anonymous White House decision maker, April 1981.

30. Lewis, *International Herald Tribune*, June 25, 1981.

VIII

THE ROLE OF THE MEDIA IN THE 1981 KNESSET ELECTIONS

Judith N. Elizur

When the 1981 parliamentary election campaign began, the Labor Alignment was the popular favorite to oust an ailing, brooding Menachem Begin from power. Halfway between January and June, the polls began to show a definite slide in support for the Alignment. By the end of May, the parties were neck-and-neck; and by mid-June it looked as though Begin's Likud party (the coalition of Begin's Herut party and the Liberals) would have a runaway victory. But somehow the Likud trend was stopped, and the elections were a draw. What role did the media play in this drama?

Far more than in other recent elections, the 1981 race in Israel was waged at open-air mass meetings, in contrast to political campaigns in other democratic countries, where television has the greatest impact. Menachem Begin did what few politicians have been able to do since the days of David Ben-Gurion and Golda Meir: get out the crowds. What influence did the media have on Begin's supporters, who were responding with all their hearts to this charismatic orator? And what influence did the media have on his opponents, who were at first derisive and then more and more alarmed by what seemed to them old-fashioned demagoguery?

To find the answers to these questions, one should begin by going

Research for this paper was supported by a grant from the Central Research Fund of the Research and Development Authority at the Hebrew University. I wish to thank the staff of the Advertisers' Association, Tel Aviv, for their assistance in preparing tables 8–2 and 8–3. The research assistance of Devoran Malveh is also acknowledged with thanks. Professor Elihu Katz and Dr. Haim Eyal made helpful comments.

186

back to the elections to the Histadrut (general federation of labor) on April 7, 1981. That contest, considered a test of the strength of the two leading contenders in the parliamentary elections, held the key to the campaign strategy used in the following months. The results of the elections to the Histadrut should have lit a warning light in the Labor camp instead of being interpreted as the guarantee of a shoo-in victory; they also could have indicated to the Likud where the seeds of its setback would lie. Although the Labor Alignment held a substantial lead in January public opinion polls, the Likud held its strength in the April elections to the Histadrut, surprising most observers. Two explanations are usually given: the new economic policy of the government, leading to a change in the voters' perception of their well-being; and the ethnic appeal of the top Likud candidate. The Alignment should have noted these factors in preparing its media strategy for the elections to the Knesset but it did not do so. The Likud ran its campaign accordingly.

Two themes used in the Histadrut election advertisements provide insight into the subsequent Knesset campaign. The Alignment ad stated, "As in the past, so also in the future—leadership that is forceful, balanced and responsible." The Likud slogan promoting its candidate for the top office was "David Levy—the strong man for the Histadrut." These themes emerged over and over again in the parliamentary race: the team versus the dominating leader; rationality versus the charisma of strength; nostalgia for the past versus life in the here and now.

Table 8–1 indicates the climate of opinion within which the election campaign took place. Public approval of the Begin government's performance had declined in 1979 and 1980 and reached a low point in January 1981. Because of this vast dissatisfaction, Prime Minister Begin agreed to call for elections in June, four months before the latest date stipulated by law. But by March the Likud had regained the public's favor, and by May the cabinet had reached its highest level of approval in two years.

The change in public opinion came about despite the editorial opposition of all the major newspapers in Israel and in the absence of support from television. (The Election Law [Propaganda] of 1959 enjoins the state-owned television from playing any role in election campaigns other than providing free time for party election propaganda.)[1] The torrent of anti-Begin editorial comment and analysis apparently did not register with the Likud's supporters, who formed their own judgment of the changed economic situation and of the

TABLE 8-1

Public Opinion of the Begin Government

Question: In your opinion is the government successful or unsucessful in the
following fields? (Numbers indicate the percent who responded
"successful" and "mostly successful")

	Sept. 1979	Sept. 1980	Jan. 1981	Mar. 1981	May 1981
Economic affairs	11	14	9	15	23
Social affairs	18	18	16	21	30
Security matters	69	56	56	67	56
Foreign affairs	44	20	30	37	41
Overall performance	25	17	14	20	34

SOURCE: Hancoch Smith survey results as reported in *Ma'ariv,* June 5, 1981.

stormy international environment. It appears that Begin, the consum-
mate politician, was far more effective in helping the electorate make
up its mind than were the media.

Image Problem of the Parties

Interestingly, at the start of the 1981 campaign all the political parties,
large and small, had image problems of considerable magnitude. The
Likud was far behind in the opinion polls; its economic policy, as exe-
cuted under one Liberal finance minister, Simcha Ehrlich, and one
La'am faction member, Yigal Hurvitz, was generally considered to
have been a failure. The prime minister, despite the achievement of
the Camp David agreement, was seen as an ill, despondent figure and
as unable to control his feuding cabinet, which had lost both Moshe
Dayan and Ezer Weizman, its two most popular figures.

   In the 1981 elections Weizman withdrew from politics altogether.
Dayan decided to run on his own ticket, Telem. The Likud was further challenged on the extreme right by ultranationalist Geula Cohen,
who formed a new party, Tehiya, with other secular and religious
allies.

   The Alignment was riven by internal conflict. The Peres-Rabin rivalry was barely papered over for the Histadrut elections. Formation
of the list of Knesset candidates in the party convention set bloc
against bloc in acrimonious debate. Labor unity in April was still more
a hope than a reality despite its favorable standing in the polls. Shimon
Peres had to contend with his negative image as a machine politician

lacking the credibility or the authority to control his party's feuding factions.

Other parties were in trouble too. Yigael Yadin's Democratic Movement for Change (DMC), which had come from nowhere in 1977 to become the third largest party, had splintered in the intervening four years to such an extent that it dissolved before the 1981 elections. Yadin himself decided to retire from politics altogether. Only one of the DMC's factions, Shinui, survived, but it had limited appeal as a moderate center party.

The National Religious party (NRP), badly hurt by scandals involving two of its cabinet ministers, was also torn by factional rivalries. It was further damaged by a split at the end of May caused by rising demands by ethnic constituents for representation. The resulting new party, Tami, led by Aharon Abu-Hatzeira, was able to run its own ticket in the elections, thanks to financing from supporters abroad.

The many small first-time and veteran party lists lacked the funds necessary to pay for press and television advertising and were not eligible for the free television time that would have enabled them to become known to the public. It is not surprising, therefore, that of the thirty-one lists presented to the voters only ten received more than the minimum number of votes necessary to put a candidate into the Knesset.

Change in Election Law

The Election Law [Propaganda] of 1959 was changed in order to give the established parties a greater amount of free television time than they had previously been allowed. The old provision in the law granted ten minutes to every party list, plus four minutes for every member each party had in the outgoing parliament.[2] Suggestions for altering this formula were made but objected to by small or new parties, which felt that changes would give further undue advantage to the larger, established parties. The amendment, which was adopted on June 15 in the midst of the television campaign, left the uniform ten-minute allocation untouched but increased the allocation per member to six minutes.

The old formula would have given the Likud ten minutes plus another four minutes for each of its forty-two Knesset members, for a total of 178 minutes of television election propaganda; the Alignment would have received ten plus four times thirty-two, or 138 minutes.

The new formula gave the Likud 262 minutes and the Alignment 202, thus increasing their share of the free time allocated to all the lists. The one-sidedness of both the old and the new formulas was protested during the Knesset debate and appealed to the Supreme Court, but the protest had no effect on the Knesset's ultimate vote.

Although the law provides the parties with free television time, they must bear all production costs. This presents a problem to parties without large financial resources; in 1981 the cost of mounting an extensive television campaign was estimated at 3,000 shekels per minute. The cost of newspaper advertising also limited the ability of many of the smaller parties to present themselves extensively to the public. (Many news stories during the campaign dealt with the financial straits of the various parties, including the Likud.)

Pattern of Media Use

Unlike in the United States, where virtually all paid election campaigning is conducted on television and at hours negotiated by the candidate and the station, in Israel the candidates spend a considerable amount of their resources on newspaper advertising. This pattern, already established in the 1977 elections, continued in 1981.[3] The high level of newspaper readership and the legal strictures on allocation of television time (party propaganda can be presented only at the time set aside by the Central Elections Committee, rather than at any point during the broadcast schedule) are two factors working in favor of a continuation of this pattern of media use. A third factor, which might have been expected to work in the opposite direction, is the difficulty of covering continually mounting expenses. New parties that are granted the minimum amount of time for their television presentations have no choice, however, but to utilize the press to make themselves and their candidates known to the public. This was most dramatically illustrated in the 1977 elections by the Democratic Movement for Change, which began its press advertising campaign months ahead of the two major parties. In the 1981 campaign, Dayan's Telem, Abu-Hatzeira's Tami, and Tehiya were the most prominent of the new parties confronted with the same dilemma, lack of recognition. Telem and Tami had funds for frequent and conspicuous ads, as did Tehiya, which ran many ads with the identical text, hoping to make its impact through repetition. (See table 8–2.)

Smaller parties, including even those represented in the Ninth

Knesset, such as Shulamit Aloni's Citizens' Rights movement, and
Shelli, ran out of funds before the end of the campaign. Even though
the small parties tried to conserve their meager resources for television advertisements (in one case resorting to black-and-white film
rather than color to save money), financial constraints were severe.
And today's mounting advertising and production costs in both media
do not augur well for the participation of new or small groupings in
future political campaigns.

Newspaper Advertisements

As in the 1977 campaign, newspaper advertising by all parties was divided among the four largest dailies without much attempt to aim
specific advertisements at specific audiences. That is, the same advertisements appeared in almost all papers, as though their readerships
were identical. There was one exception: the Likud "punished" the
independent morning daily *Ha'aretz* for its criticism of the Begin government by placing almost no advertisements in the paper during the
campaign. (See table 8–3.) The Likud's decision was no doubt based
on the nature of the paper's readership, which was assumed to be
largely anti-Begin. The overwhelming predominance of the two largest parties in the newspaper advertising campaign is evident from the
total inches printed by each party. The NRP, Telem, Tehiya, and Tami
bought the next largest amount of advertising space, with all other
parties trailing far behind.

A review of 1,170 advertisements placed by the Alignment and the
Likud shows that the Alignment purchased three advertisements for
every two purchased by the Likud. Of the total, 648 (59 percent) were
placed by the Labor Alignment, 486 (41 percent) by the Likud (see figure 8–1). An analysis of the scheduling of their newspaper ads reveals
a difference in strategy between the two parties: the Likud clearly
built to a climax, whereas the Alignment effort was much more dif-
fused. During April and May, the Likud printed only 28 percent of its
ads; the Alignment printed 43 percent. In the month of June, however, the Likud ran 72 percent of its total, compared with the Alignment's 57 percent. Furthermore, the Likud conducted a veritable blitz
in the closing days of the campaign. This high level of visibility at the
end of the race was most marked on election day itself, when the
Likud ran 95 ads, compared with 59 by the Alignment.

The campaigns of the two largest parties made very different impressions. The Alignment effort was Hydra-headed, with little appar-

TABLE 8-2

Advertising Expenditures of Political Parties in the Daily Press, 1981 Campaign

(in shekels)

Parties with representation in the 10th Knesset	April[a]	May	June	Total
Agudat Israel[b]	—	—	6,340	6,340
Citizens' Rights Movement	—	159,969	309,930	469,899
Labor Alignment[c]				
Labor Party	3,456,388	5,432,845	8,890,504	17,779,737
Citizens for Peres	366,533	1,015,294	620,581	2,002,408
Histadrut	775,196	120,107	560,289	1,455,592
Mapam	43,256	43,060	33,441	119,757
Likud	977,735	2,867,463	7,488,620	11,333,818
National Religious Party	122,780	99,099	1,688,361	1,910,240
Shinui	369,039	135,160	536,292	1,040,491
Tami[d]	—	—	(see Others)	—
Tehiyah	—	339,799	1,261,341	1,601,140
	—	476,936	1,215,227	1,692,163

in the 10th Knesset (partial list)

Flatto-Sharon	—	20,792	548,683	569,475
Independent Liberals	75,488	77,038	385,689	538,215
Shelli	38,426	16,325	134,263	189,014
Others[e]	68,178	336,473	3,564,618	3,969,269
Gush Emunim[f]	—	—	13,248	13,248
Rafi[g]	255,970	—	—	255,970
TOTAL	6,548,989	11,140,360	27,257,427	44,946,776

[a] April figures also include outlay on advertising for the Histadrut (General Labor Federation) elections, which took place on April 7. But since these were a trial run for the parliamentary elections in June, the total effort may legitimately be kept in mind, especially since the parties' treasuries must pay for both.

[b] Figures may also include Poalei Agudah advertisements, which were not coded separately because the sums involved were so small.

[c] Four groups placed ads for Alignment candidates, all part of the same electoral effort.

[d] Tami split off from the NRP at the end of May and placed ads from that time forward. However, these were included in "others" for June.

[e] A rough estimate is that between one-third and one-half of the June figure represents Tami's advertising expenditure.

[f] An extra-parliamentary grouping.

[g] Merged later with Telem.

SOURCE: Advertisers' Association, Tel Aviv.

TABLE 8-3

Advertising Inches in Hebrew Daily Press
April–June 1981
(by party)

Newspaper (political affiliation)	Alignment[a]	Likud	NRP	Tehiya[b]	Telem[b]	Shinui	CRM
Ma'ariv (indep.)	29,266	25,659	4,348	3,781	2,939	1,318	336
Yediot Aharonot (indep.)	23,938	18,858	2,295	2,300	2,272	1,308	459
Ha'aretz (indep.)	13,632	1,601	126	—	1,079	474	612
Davar (Histadrut)	10,863	656	148	11	437	177	221
TOTAL	77,699	46,774	6,917	6,092	6,727	3,277	1,628

[a] Includes advertisements placed by three bodies: Labor Party: 27,264 in *Ma'ariv*, 17,697 in *Yediot*, 10,053 in *Ha'aretz*, and 9,417 in *Davar*; Citizens for Peres: 158 in *Ma'ariv*, 4,939 in *Yediot*, 3,162 in *Ha'aretz*; Histadrut: 1,844 in *Ma'ariv*, 1,302 in *Yediot*, 417 in *Ha'aretz*, and 1,446 in *Davar*.
[b] May and June only. No separate figures are available for Tami, which split from NRP at the end of May and thereafter ran its own campaign.
SOURCE: Advertisers' Association, Tel Aviv.

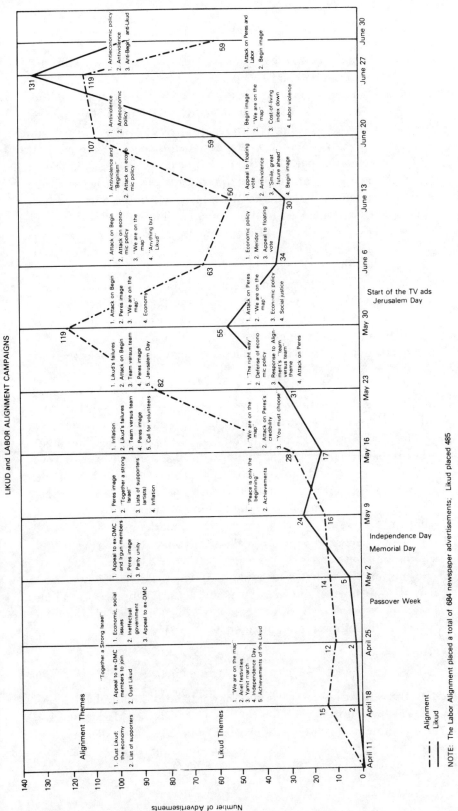

SCHEDULING OF NEWSPAPER ADVERTISEMENTS and SEQUENCE OF THEMES, APRIL - JUNE 1981

LIKUD and LABOR ALIGNMENT CAMPAIGNS

Number of Advertisements

Alignment Themes

"Together a Strong Israel"
1. Appeal to ex DMC and Irgun members to join
2. Peres image
3. Oust Likud

1. Economic, social issues
2. Ineffectual government
3. Appeal to ex DMC

1. Appeal to ex DMC and Irgun members
2. Peres image
3. Party unity

1. Peres image
2. "Together a strong Israel"
3. Lists of supporters (artists)
4. Inflation

1. Inflation
2. Likud's failures
3. Team versus team
4. Peres image
5. Call for volunteers

1. Likud's failures
2. Attack on Begin
3. Team versus team
4. Peres image
5. Jerusalem Day

1. Attack on Begin
2. Peres image
3. "We are on the map"
4. Economy

1. Attack on Begin
2. Attack on economic policy
3. "We are on the map"
4. "Anything but Likud"

1. Antiviolence and "Beginism"
2. Attack on economic policy

1. Antieconomic policy
2. Antiviolence
3. Anti-Begin, anti-Likud

Likud Themes

1. "We are on the map"
2. Ariel festivities
3. Yamit march
4. Independence Day
5. Achievements of the Likud

1. "Peace is only the beginning"
2. Achievements

1. "We are on the map"
2. Attack on Peres's credibility
3. "You must choose"

1. "The right way"
2. Defense of economic policy
3. Response to Alignment's "team versus team" theme
4. Attack on Peres

1. Attack on Peres
2. "We are on the map"
3. Economic justice
4. Social justice

1. Economic policy
2. Meridor
3. Appeal to floating vote

1. Appeal to floating vote
2. Antiviolence
3. "Smile, great future ahead"
4. Begin image

1. Begin image
2. "We are on the map"
3. Cost-of-living index down
4. Labor violence

1. Attack on Peres and Labor
2. Begin image

Start of the TV ads
Jerusalem Day

Independence Day
Memorial Day

Passover Week

Alignment
Likud

NOTE: The Labor Alignment placed a total of 684 newspaper advertisements; Likud placed 485

Figure 8-1. Scheduling of Newspaper Advertisements and Sequence of Themes, April–June 1981 Likud and Labor Alignment Campaigns

ent coordination among the groups placing ads in its behalf. Citizens for Peres, for example, had a separate budget and worked out of its own headquarters. Its party messages were variously presented in the name of the Alignment, of the young guard, and of the kibbutz movement. A series of anti-Likud cartoons appeared without any clear sponsor; some advertisements were designed by individual members of the committee supervising the party's election propaganda (Yossi Sarid), some by the advertising man hired for the campaign (Eliezer Zurabin, who had run the Likud effort in 1977!), and others by other advertising firms involved in the campaign. The overall impression was one of extravagant use of funds (sometimes for page after page of full-page ads), lack of coordination, undistinguished graphics, and texts that lacked impact.

The Likud, by contrast, ran a tight ship. One advertising firm handled all of its ads, with clear authority coming from one key man on the party committee. Its material was cleaner graphically and gave evidence of unity of planning throughout. (The only exception was the personally financed series of candidate Ya'acov Meridor near the end of the campaign.)

A detail that emerges in figure 8–1 is the drop in volume of newspaper ads at the beginning of June, when the parties began advertising on television. Both parties made the judgment that voter attention was focused on the electronic medium at that point in the campaign. After mid-June, however, the volume of newspaper advertising rose again, with the Likud building to a higher and later peak than the Alignment. To the extent that their finances permitted, the other parties attempted to compete with the two dominant ones by taking out full-page ads. Tami's were the most professional graphically; most of the small parties, however, were all but invisible. New parties representing pensioners, deprived social strata, young couples in need of housing, and even individuals like ex-pugilist Rafael Halpern and maverick member of the Knesset Assaf Yagouri competed for attention, but their efforts were wasted. Only Meir Kahane's ads caused a stir with their offensive and inflammatory texts.

Television Advertisements

The 1981 campaign on television followed almost identically the pattern established in 1977. The two major parties used their extensive time allotments as they had four years before, dividing their nightly programs into separate segments, interspersing spots of a serious nature with lighter entertainment. Each party hired an attractive woman to act as anchor. The Likud also used a well-known entertainer to deliver a nightly satirical attack on Alignment personalities. Very little cartoon material was used.

As in 1977, both parties allocated television time for a debate between their two top candidates. The debate itself was fairly pedestrian and lacked spontaneity because of the stringent ground rules laid down by representatives of the two sides. The results were generally felt to favor Peres, more because of his aggressive style (and Begin's unusual tenseness) than because of any new message brought by him.

The Likud's level of professionalism in the television campaign surpassed that of all other parties. Coordination of press and television material was much more marked in the Likud campaign than in the Alignment's. The smaller parties, hampered by constraints of time and money, had to forgo gimmicks and were forced to present their messages directly. Moshe Dayan, for example, appeared in almost all of his party spots, thus strengthening the impression that Telem was to be his personal vehicle rather than a broad-based party. The National Religious party had a unique dilemma; thrown badly off-balance by the May 26 decamping of Aharon Abu-Hatzeira to form his own party, it lost about ten days in redefining its identity. Meanwhile, the television campaign had begun, and the party needed to appear. The NRP opted for a rerun of its 1977 television presentation, deliberately ignoring its internal power struggle and the ethnic revolt that was uppermost in its constituents' minds. The pastoral image thus presented was unconvincing and, in retrospect, may have had a part in the party's poor showing at the polls.[4]

Tehiya, the ultranationalist extreme right-wing party, presented an image akin to that of an enthusiastic youth group, with many scenes of hiking in the heart of nature, flag waving, and earnest exhortation. Interestingly, the television spots played down Geula Cohen, the female founder of the party, in favor of male leaders such as Hanan Porat and Yuval Ne'eman who appealed to religious and secular voters alike. The other small parties, both old and new, generally made poor appearances on television, mainly using the "talking head" format because they lacked the money for more expensive advertising. Their inability to make proper use of the medium raises doubts as to the equity of existing time and funding provisions in the election laws. The laws may, however, prevent ad hoc groups and individuals with limited appeal from distracting the public's attention from the more stable and established political parties in the future.

Setting an Agenda

Current research in communications stresses the agenda-setting function of the media; that is, more than they tell the public what to think,
the media suggest what they should think about. If this is correct, then
there should be a high correlation between the subjects of news and
editorial comment and the issues that the public identifies as important.[5] A political party conducting an election campaign would be expected to treat those issues in its campaign propaganda in order to
respond to public concerns.

Media Agenda

Of the political stories in two leading independent Israeli dailies during the election campaign, a majority dealt with foreign and security-
related issues and a minority with domestic issues. The period under
analysis was replete with dramatic events such as Begin's quarrels with
Germany's Chancellor Helmut Schmidt, with France's Giscard d'Estaing, and with other European leaders; the Syrian missile crisis; Philip
Habib's mission in Lebanon; and Israel's bombing of an Iraqi nuclear
reactor. Journalistic values, irrespective of party interest, dictated reporting these stories at the top of the news. Begin's role was central in
all of the stories. He was not absent from the media; he dominated
them. It cannot be said, therefore, that Begin won without the aid of
the media, for he was always at center stage in the news stories, even
if editorial comment was critical. His presence was felt even more
strongly on television, where there is only news reporting and no political discussion programs in the 150-day period before elections.

As table 8–4 indicates, April headlines were dominated by foreign
and security issues in at least two newspapers. Newspaper stories
dealt with Israel Air Force activity in southern Lebanon and with
Israel's opposition to the Reagan administration's plans to sell AWACS
planes to Saudi Arabia. The subject of strikes was prominent among
the domestic issues covered by the press. The difference in orientation between the two newspapers was greater in May, when *Ha'aretz*
devoted twenty-two of twenty-four headlines to foreign and security-
related issues; *Ma'ariv* had seventeen of twenty-four in this category.
Domestic matters, including inflation and strikes, were secondary.
May, therefore, was Begin's month to dominate the news, which dealt
mostly with the missile crisis in Lebanon and with the Habib mission.

TABLE 8-4

Newspaper Headlines, April 30–June 30 by Issue

	Ma'ariv			Ha'aretz		
	Domestic[a]	Foreign[b]	Security[c]	Domestic	Foreign	Security
April	3	6	5	1	7	6
May	7	6	11	2	11	11
June	7	9	9	7	11	6
TOTAL	17	21	25	10	29	23
Percent of total ads placed	27	33.3	39.7	16	47	37

[a] Domestic issues: the economy, strikes, election news
[b] Foreign issues: peace with Egypt, Anwar Sadat, the United Nations, the French elections (Mitterrand's victory), U.S. foreign policy
[c] Security issues: all items relating to Israeli military activity in Lebanon, the missile crisis, the Habib mission, the Iraqi nuclear reactor
SOURCE: Content analysis of main headlines in *Ma'ariv* and *Ha'aretz*, April 14–June 30, 1981.

Both newspapers devoted more headlines to internal matters in June, especially after the middle of the month. The conduct of the election campaign (including concern about violence) and predictions as to the election's outcome were the top stories at the close of the campaign.

Public Agenda

Two polls published in June give an indication of the issues that were foremost in the public's mind at the time. One, which appeared in *Ha'aretz*, contained the following question: "What in your opinion is the most important problem facing the country today?" Respondents labeled the first five, in order of importance, as, the economic situation (inflation), the security situation, the peace process (autonomy for the West Bank), social problems, and strikes.[6] Respondents to another survey, reported in *Ma'ariv*, gave answers as shown in table 8–5 in response to the question "What do you think are the most important problems facing the next government?"

Economics and security concerned the Israeli public far more than the social gap or continuation of the peace process in the months of May and June. The issue of security rose in saliency to become more important to the public in June, although the economy and inflation remained their primary concern. The dominance of the security issue in media news coverage during the preceding month may have affected the results of the poll. (There usually is a time lag between the

TABLE 8-5

Public Agenda, May and June 1981

	Most important issue		Second most important issue	
	(percent)		(percent)	
	May	June	May	June
Economics (incl. inflation)	47	49	30	25
Security	31	36	25	31
Social gap	5	9	14	15
Continuation of peace process	5	4	3	3

SOURCE: Hancoch Smith survey in *Ma'ariv*, June 22, 1981.

appearance of an issue in the media agenda and its reflection in the public agenda.)

Begin's role in the security issue was preeminent; he was as clearly present in the public agenda as in the media agenda, even though media coverage of security issues was not discussed in personal terms. The economic situation was foremost in the public mind, however, despite all the media reporting of spectacular security-related events. How did the parties address these findings concerning the two agendas in their propaganda?

Party Agendas

Both major parties fought for their cause on the battleground of domestic issues (see table 8–6); the parties reflected the public's concerns more closely than did the media agenda in May and June. Although the saliency of the security issue increased in the public's mind in response to the events of May, their primary concern still focused on economic issues, especially on inflation.

It is surprising that the Likud did not make more of Begin's success as a peacemaker until the final stage of the campaign. It is more understandable that the Alignment chose to make the domestic failures of the Likud the focus of its advertising campaign, for performance on domestic issues was felt to be the great weakness of the Begin government, as revealed in opinion polls. Much of the Alignment's domestic focus in the last phase of the campaign, however, dealt with the violent conduct of the contest, rather than with substantive issues. Meanwhile, the Likud was pointing to its record of achievement and going unchallenged. If the Alignment felt that Minister of Finance

TABLE 8-6

Party Agenda: Issues in Newspaper and Television Advertising

Party	Issues in Newspaper Ads[a]			Issues in Television Ads		
	Foreign	Domestic	Total	Foreign	Domestic	Total
Likud	34 (18%)	171 (82%)	208[b]	17 (22%)	60 (78%)	77
Alignment	81 (19%)	334 (81%)	418[c]	15 (25%)	51 (75%)	66

[a] Newspaper ad totals do not include organizational advertisements, meeting announcements, or ads referring only to personalities.
[b] Likud newspaper ads include thirty instances of double counting (that is, more than one issue mentioned in a single ad); Likud television ads include twenty-three instances of double counting.
[c] Alignment newspaper ads include twenty-seven instances of double counting; Alignment television ads include thirty such instances.

Yoram Aridor's handling of the economy was unsuccessful (by challenging the credibility of his cost-of-living index in May, for example), it had great difficulty explaining this contention convincingly. A more revealing analysis of what the parties felt would arouse the public can be seen in table 8–7, which classifies the newspaper advertisements of the two largest parties according to the nature of the appeal made by each party. If we compare the percentages in table 8–7 with those of the 1977 campaign, we find certain similarities in the low percentage of ads based on the appeal to frustration (1977: Alignment 7 percent, Likud 5 percent); in the percentage devoted to ads relying on the prestige of famous names to impress voters (1977: Alignment 28 percent, Likud 26 percent); and in the level and imbalance in the unity category (1977: Alignment 5 percent, Likud 33 percent).[7] A striking difference in the Alignment's use of fear as a means of appealing to the voter emerged in 1981: whereas only 15 percent of its 1977 ads used fear as an approach, in 1981, 39 percent of them did. In comparison, the Likud in 1977 based 19 percent of its ads on the fear appeal versus 10.8 percent in 1981.[8]

When the anger appeal (used much more by the Alignment than by the Likud in this year's contest) is combined with the fear category, it becomes apparent that the Alignment campaign in the press was highly charged emotionally. This undoubtedly added to the heated climate of the Begin-Peres confrontation, even though the Likud presented itself as the party of consensus and of hope for the future.

The images of the two rival parties that emerge from this analysis are of an incumbent who was aggressive and vituperative yet prone to speak of national unity and promise for the future, and of a chal-

TABLE 8-7

Appeals in Newspaper Advertisements by Party, 1981

Contents of Appeal	Alignment Number of ads	Alignment Percent of total	Likud Number of ads	Likud Percent of total
Prestige (authority, famous names, lists of supporters)	112	23.1	89	26.0
Discrediting (insult, sarcasm, including cartoons)	65	13.4	81	23.7
Fear (war, danger to democracy, irresponsible leadership, economic and political uncertainty)	189	39.0	37	10.8
Frustration (discrimination, social gap, housing, economic, women)	13	2.7	8	2.3
Unity (consensus, patriotism, nostalgia)	41	8.5	89	26.0
Vision (promises, better future)	0	—	26	7.6
Anger (generalized, against lies and deceptions of opponents)	49	10.1	11	3.2
In group/out group differentiation (old-timers vs. immigrants, builders vs. wreckers, we/they)	15	3.1	1	.3
TOTAL	484	99.9	342	99.9

NOTE: Percentages add up to 99.9 percent in this impressionistic content analysis of election advertisements in the daily press between April 14 and June 30, 1981.

lenger who appeared to be fear-ridden concerning the future, highly emotional, and defensive (note the we/they category as well as the nostalgia note characteristic of the Likud's unity appeal). A review of the events of the campaign illustrates how these two images emerged.

Media Agenda: Image Building

The Alignment's strategy, based on the January polls, was to focus on the failures of the Begin government. As the campaign progressed, it shifted to an all-out attack on Begin himself. When both efforts brought no results and a sweeping Likud victory seemed inevitable, the Alignment turned to the violence issue.

Acknowledging that the prime minister's accomplishment in achieving peace with Egypt was unassailable, the Alignment's campaign propaganda began by emphasizing the domestic issues that, in its opinion, had not been dealt with successfully during Begin's four years in office. In view of the prominence of the economic issue on the public agenda, the economy would have been the proper ground on which to wage the propaganda war, but for two factors: the changing economic environment in the country, which diminished anxiety among Likud supporters over this issue; and the dizzying sequence of events in the international arena involving Israel, which decreased the salience of domestic issues. The month of May was critical in both these respects.

Realizing his vulnerability on his cabinet's domestic record, in January Prime Minister Begin gave his third finance minister the go-ahead for a series of measures designed to change the individual voter's perception of his economic well-being. Tax reductions on a long list of coveted consumer items resulted in a spending spree of major proportions; the reintroduction of subsidies on basic goods gave relief to the Likud's primary constituency, blue-collar and lower-class voters. By the time the large group of undecided voters began making up its mind in June—about 30 percent at the beginning of the month—the results of the changes in economic policy were being felt. This perception of well-being (and of the success of the government's manipulation) is borne out by the 12 percent increase in the standard of living in the first half of 1981.[9] Against this reality, no columnist or editorial writer, no opposition candidate, and no Alignment publicity couched in terms of systems consequences could make a dent in the conviction of the individual Likud supporter that he was doing better than ever before. The Alignment's advertisements warning of economic disaster were not convincing. Its candidate for finance minister, with his professional prescriptions for the national economy, did not speak the language of the Likud voter. When the Alignment switched the focus of its media campaign to Begin in an all-out attack on the prime minister, events conspired at the very same time to put the Likud leader on the front page day after day.

Even before the month of May, the Alignment attack on Begin was in trouble. Ads that were intended to hold him up to ridicule did the reverse: They featured a picture of the prime minister (thus giving him additional prominence) at his most exhortative, on the assumption that this would evoke a negative response from the reader. To Begin's supporters, however, this pose represented Begin at his best, so that the message in the text ("This man cannot be trusted") was totally ineffective.

A number of elements have been suggested to explain the anomaly of support by constituents of Moroccan, Yemenite, Iraqi, and other ethnic origins for this Polish Jewish leader while they so much resented other Alignment leaders of the same background. Begin appeared to them to share their respect for tradition; he seemed to be a patriarchal figure in a largely first-generation immigrant society where modernization has greatly weakened the traditional family structure. The antiestablishment aura still clings to Begin, despite his four years in office, and he assiduously cultivates the resentment of "have-nots" against the old Labor government.

In the campaign, Begin came across to his constituency in language they understood at open-air mass meetings in the small and large towns of Israel. His aggressive, sarcastic, *ad hominem* style evoked an immediate response. The public, aware of the advertising campaign in the press and, later, on television, which attacked the supposedly feeble, despondent, and irresponsible leader, measured this picture against the energetic campaigner before them pounding home his attack on Peres and the Alignment. The media campaign of the Alignment lost its credibility in their eyes.

The Begin image was further strengthened by an incident at the end of April, in which Begin responded vituperatively and most undiplomatically to critical comments made on West German television by Chancellor Helmut Schmidt. Although public opinion abroad responded extremely negatively to Begin's personal attack on Schmidt's past, the effect on Israeli opinion was the opposite: the Likud constituency was galvanized by it, and Begin's rating soared. The feisty defender of Jewish rights was back; this, coupled with his heavy speaking schedule, demolished the image of the sick, despondent leader that the January polls had revealed.

The motif of strength and personal assertiveness played an interesting role in the media presentations of the contending parties. David Levy's Histadrut campaign had been built on the slogan of "the strong man." It is not clear whether this slogan represented compensation for the weakness of his adherents or if it was meant to provide a role model, but the appeal held his voters. The Alignment, not to be outdone, incorporated the strength theme into its parliamentary campaign slogan, "Together for a strong Israel," which can be faulted for building the national image more than building the party's. Be that as it may, the propagandists of both parties evidently felt that the attribute of strength was a vote-getter, indeed essential, in an immigrant society surrounded by enemies.

From May onward, a series of events related to foreign policy again enabled Begin to strengthen his leadership image. The Syrian missile crisis caused a rally-round-the-flag reaction that put him above the poorly articulated criticism of the Alignment. Since war had been averted, Begin could present himself as a responsible leader, heeding the plea of the United States to give diplomacy a chance. Thus, one of the opposition's charges, that Begin could not be trusted with the fate of the nation, was eliminated. Furthermore, the Israeli raid on the Baghdad nuclear reactor in June was grudgingly applauded by Begin's opposition; criticism was made of the timing but not of the act itself. Again, Begin appeared forceful and daring, and his opponents paled by comparison. The Labor strategy to make Begin the issue of the campaign backfired completely.

Public opinion concerning the functioning of the Begin cabinet also changed in the Likud's favor in the wake of this series of events. The Institute of Applied Social Research reported in mid-June that 39 percent of its poll respondents gave the government a good/very good rating, whereas in mid-May the figure was 33 percent and in mid-March only 20 percent. Thus, events not only enabled Begin to restore his old dynamic image but improved that of the government as well. Interestingly, most of the ministers, with few exceptions (Aridor, Meridor), were kept out of sight during the campaign. Begin was the whole show.

The Alignment's newspaper ads included a series attempting to make a comparison between the "capable" team they were proposing for the cabinet and the "incapable" team that Begin worked with. But the ad presented two rows of equally appealing pictures of the candidates under the heading "Our team against theirs" (literally, "These against these"). The ad was so neutral that it was equally effective in arousing sentiment for the Likud team, which by then was benefiting from the positive reaction that Begin had engendered. The Likud then printed a riposte—one of the few occasions it departed from its planned strategy in order to give a direct reply to Alignment propaganda—which was far less balanced and therefore much more effective: The least flattering photographs of the Alignment candidates were presented (in one case a blank was left in order to make fun of a nonentity), and the desired effect on the reader was achieved.

The Alignment's attacks on Begin were prominent in its newspaper campaign. Twenty-two percent of all the Alignment's ads were devoted to attacks on Begin, on his cabinet, and on what was termed "Beginism." Fourteen percent were attacks on Begin only. By contrast, 14 percent of the Likud's ads were attacks on Peres and other leaders of the Alignment (12 percent of those against Peres alone). This focus on personalities added to the acerbic character of the 1981 race.

The Alignment's attempt to build Peres's leadership image had difficulty getting off the ground. Despite a separate advertising campaign by the Citizens for Peres, which ran full-page ads quoting leaders in various fields extolling Peres's abilities, the Likud's constant attack on the Labor leader's credibility was effective. Two of Peres's decisions inadvertently strengthened the impression of indecisiveness and untrustworthiness that he was trying to rid himself of: the choice of Ben-Shahar rather than Ya'acov Levinson for finance minister, and the switch from Haim Bar-Lev to Rabin for defense minister, both in the very last days of the campaign. No media advertising could undo the effect of these self-engendered reversals. Only when Peres adopted an aggressive, determined style in the television debate against Begin did he impress the voters with his leadership ability.

The Alignment devoted almost 10 percent of its advertising to building the Peres image. Twenty-eight percent of its ads compared him with the opposition candidate, most often presenting pictures of both of them in the same ad. The Likud devoted more than 15 percent of its newspaper ads to building Begin's image. Even more interesting is that, of these, 43 percent involved invidious comparisons to Peres, in which only Begin's picture appeared!

Outside Expertise

In an attempt to build the image of the "new Peres," the Alignment hired a number of media consultants from abroad. The Likud had also employed such experts from time to time during Begin's four years in office to help him improve his image overseas. Indeed, the 1981 parliamentary campaign in Israel can be called a test of the relevance and effectiveness of outside media expertise. Both major parties hired American media consultants for the duration of the campaign, the Likud securing David Garth, the Alignment hiring David Sawyer. Although the media gave much attention during the campaign to the presence of these foreign experts, postelection opinion of their efforts was not favorable.

There was sentiment in both parties that advice on strategy was not needed from outsiders. Their major contribution was expected to be on tactics and execution of the media campaign. Even on tactics, however, the advice of the non-Israelis was not always felt to be wise, and at times the foreign consultants were disheartened by the negative reception their advice received.[10] On the technical level, however, the consultants' imprint was more apparent. Especially in the Likud campaign, the degree of coordination between press and TV slogans and themes, and the techniques utilized in the television ads betrayed the American influence.

American television viewers would have recognized Nixon's 1972 use of the "man in the arena" format in the Likud's campaign supporting Finance Minister Aridor.[11] The staging of media events, such as the Fellini-like "dedication" of the Mediterranean—Dead Sea Canal in the Judean desert (the occasion was really only a test drilling for an appropriate site) and, of course, the Begin-Sadat encounter at Ofira, were also Likud achievements. The Ofira encounter was devoid of political significance but presented the Likud with an opportunity to circumvent the ban on showing candidates for office on the regular television news by using the footage for its own propaganda shorts.

Final Phase

Violence Motif

The media campaign was not particularly original or interesting for most of the race: the real contest was in the streets, especially at the mass meetings that Begin addressed. There the atmosphere, as described by foreign as well as local observers, was electric. Begin proved that he could attract crowds and communicate with them as no other politician on the Israeli scene today: Peres's meetings were not only disappointing in that respect, but were the scene of violent behavior by Begin supporters who came determined to prevent Peres from speaking. Chanting "Begin, Begin" and "Begin, the King of Israel," the mostly young and Sephardic Likud supporters used their voices and fists to break up Alignment meetings. When the kibbutz movement decided to send its "troops" in to prevent such activity, and the entire political scene seemed on the verge of explosion, police support was called in. At that point, in mid-June, the Alignment decided to make the behavior of Begin's adherents the main issue for the rest of the campaign, in a last bid to roll back the pro-Likud tide.[12]

The Alignment sent its own camera team to photograph Begin's supporters breaking up an Alignment meeting in Petach Tikva; they also filmed Begin working the crowd at a meeting in Netanya. On June 15 the Israeli radio, less fettered than the television in reporting such events, broadcast an excerpt of the Netanya speech on its morning news program that shocked Alignment sympathizers into realizing that a last-ditch effort had to be mounted to stop Begin. The excerpt, rebroadcast a number of times on the radio and incorporated into the Alignment's television propaganda, revived once again the old demogogic image of Begin. Appearing on Likud television time, Begin denied charges of incitement to violence and called upon his supporters to behave in democratic fashion and let the opposition have its say. The Likud also countered with charges of Alignment violence, but the point had been made. The bullying by Likud supporters against the wearers of Alignment buttons, the destruction of party clubs and vandalization of property where Alignment stickers were displayed (including damage to cars), and the proclaiming of territory (such as the open-air wholesale markets of Jerusalem and Tel Aviv) as off bounds to Alignment supporters led to a backlash of public opinion. The Likud tide was blunted at this point, and the Labor Alignment drew neck-and-neck.

Treatment of the violence issue in the media was massive on the weekend of June 19–20, with all the dailies devoting news stories, features, and editorial comment to the issue. The weekly television news review on Friday night again screened the Petach Tikva footage as part of a broader discussion of the problem of violence. The media agenda was violence. The public agenda that weekend—that is, the topic of conversation in homes and social gatherings on the Sabbath—was also violence. The campaign reached fever pitch at last. Excerpts from the television propaganda of the two parties during the following week typified the viewpoints of the contending camps. The first is an excerpt from a brief talk by Moshe Harif, one of the leaders of the kibbutz movement in the Labor party:

> Last week the Likud conducted a propaganda campaign consisting of shameless lies. This week began a campaign of incitement, of mass emotion, of breaking up meetings, burning clubrooms and attacks on citizens in an attempt to create an atmosphere of fear and intimidation. No. They will not frighten us. The Alignment will continue to explain and convince quietly, confidently, logically. For every clubhouse that will be burned, we will put up two; for every poster torn down, we will put up five. They will not dominate the street because we will be there . . . not with emotional roaring and not with raised fists but with the

strength of quiet belief. Every raised stick and brandished knife only
sharpens the difference between us and them. . . . The movement of
volunteers proves that the people are not terrified, that they recognize
the danger, that the erosion must be stopped. First we must insure that
the Begin regime does not continue, that hooliganism in Israel must
cease. We will return to the authentic Israel . . . today the tomato
throwers are lined up against the tomato growers.[13]

Harif's statement came two days after an assertion by the novelist
Amos Oz on an Alignment broadcast that the philosophical difference
between the two camps could be summed up in the contrast between
"the tree and the path" on one side and "blood and fire" on the other.
Especially toward the end of the campaign, the Alignment's propaganda contained a note of nostalgia for the good old days. Much was
made of the Alignment's claim to represent "beautiful Israel," with the
clear implication that Labor's opponents did not.

The Alignment's stress on the cultural gap between the supporters
of the two parties, their use of we/they terminology, and their claim to
represent the authentic values of the country elicited a sarcastic response from the star of the Likud television propaganda, Sefi Rivlin,
as follows:

Why are they doing this? Why are they trying to incite and frighten
you? Why has the Alignment descended to the lowest level ever of such
propaganda? The answer is simple—once there was a labor movement
with leaders such as Gordon, Tabenkin, and Berl. Today the Alignment
is . . . Shimon Peres. Once the Alignment had a socialist vision—today
it has no path and no manners and no program. Therefore the Alignment is frightening you and doesn't even appeal to your reason. Its fall
began four years ago. Already then the Alignment didn't know how to
make you forget the terrible blunder, the terrible war. . . . The Alignment hasn't learned its lesson . . . again it takes out rusty weapons from
its warehouse of junk, trying to frighten you, brandishing the whip, because it no longer has anything to say. . . . Too bad. Likud will let the
Alignment wallow by itself in the muck.[14]

Here too is we/they terminology, using attack as the best form of defense. Again an attempt is made to saddle Labor with responsibility
for the Yom Kippur War; and again there is liberal use of invective, in
projecting the aggressive Likud.

Nevertheless the violence issue in the media receded in the final
week of the campaign. Cynics claimed that it peaked too soon to
provide Labor with a clear-cut victory. It undoubtedly caused many
wavering Alignment supporters, especially those in the small parties

on the left, to retreat to their own ranks in order to save the "authentic" Israel from Menachem Begin. The deeply emotional appeal was the antithesis of the antidemagoguery line advocated until then by the Alignment.

The "two cultures" split became history when, as the result of an unfortunate off-the-cuff remark by an entertainer at the Alignment's final open-air mass rally in Tel Aviv, the Ashkenazi/Sephardi, or the old-timers and the new immigrants antagonism exploded. Begin seized upon the clash in his closing mass meeting, the papers and party ads were full of it, and the ethnic slur became the basis for a public debate that raged in the media long after the elections were over.

Election Night Coverage

The coverage of election night on television led to a historic flap that embarrassed the Alignment before the watching world. As it had in 1977, television conducted a straw poll of voters as they emerged from the voting booths. Its predictions were based on a sample taken several hours before the polls closed, on the assumption that the responses of early voters would accurately reflect the outcome of the election. Television's first prediction of a neck-and-neck race was corrected—mistakenly—in the Alignment's favor when the first results came in. On that basis, Peres and his supporters held what proved to be a premature victory press conference. Begin, of course, made the most of Peres's mistake, ridiculing him mercilessly in his early morning victory appearance. Actually, neither man knew what the final outcome would be until several days later when the Army vote was counted. The election was decided by a margin of 10,405 votes, and the two largest parties received virtually the same number of seats in the Knesset.[15]

The newspaper headlines on the morning following the election were based on the premature television prediction of the Alignment victory; the afternoon papers were the first to report the Likud's victory in print. Because television went off the air early in the morning while the race was too close to call, it was left to radio to fill the gap between the story on the screen and the story in the papers.

Conclusion

A comparison of the 1977 and 1981 campaigns in the media reveals great similarities in media utilization, little if any innovation in style or format in either press or television propaganda, and an unaddressed need to amend existing anachronistic legislation governing campaign propaganda. Most of the issues raised during the campaign were predictable and had been foreshadowed in the Histadrut elections. The Likud might have made more of the Begin-as-peacemaker theme than it did; the Alignment could have been stronger on Labor's role in building the country and much more focused and economical in its advertising effort. By the end of the television campaign, all the protagonists were repeating themselves, and there was some thought that the public would benefit from a shortened contest in that medium.

It is not known whether Likud supporters were less influenced by the press than Alignment supporters, since they would seem to have been immune to editorial criticism of Begin. (Perhaps they read the news items and skipped the columns.) It is equally impossible, in retrospect, to know which medium—press or television—had a greater role in returning Alignment votes to the fold, thereby producing its great gain in number of Knesset seats (from 32 in 1977 to 48 in 1981.)

In any case, the frequent claim of Begin supporters that he won without the media overlooks the fact that news *events* in May and June gave him overwhelming media prominence. Begin clearly demonstrated that, in the presence of a charismatic leader, the candidate is the campaign. The media had to put him at the top of the news, and the poll data until mid-June seem to indicate that this did have an effect. Lack of editorial support up to this point apparently was not as important as coverage on page one.

Paradoxically, were it not for the massive media treatment of the violence issue in the closing stages of the campaign, there most likely would have been a clear-cut Begin victory instead of a neck-and-neck resolution of the contest. For the Labor Alignment, the only way to rally its supporters to beat back the Begin tide was to use the media, and to pull out all emotional stops. The aptest description of the media's role therefore might well be summed up as "the media giveth, the media taketh away." Having almost given Begin victory by mid-June, the media snatched it from him at the last moment. This would suggest that any candidate, in Israel at least, ignores the media at his peril.

NOTES

1. See Judith Elizur and Elihu Katz, "The Role of the Media in the 1977 Elections," in Howard R. Penniman, ed., *Israel at the Polls: The Knesset Elections*

of 1977 (Washington, D.C.: American Enterprise Institute, 1979), for an explanation of the provisions of the election law.

2. See paragraph 15a of the Election Law [Propaganda] 1959.

3. The 1969 elections were the first in which television was used for campaigning by the parties. The 1973 elections, postponed from October to December because of the Yom Kippur War, were atypical in that all parties agreed to limit their electioneering efforts.

4. I am indebted to Rafi Peled and Elath Brenner for a detailed analysis of the NRP's 1981 election campaign (unpublished paper).

5. The correlation suggested in this paper, however, is impressionistic rather then empirical. Since the three agendas under discussion originate from different sources, the data are not comparable.

6. PORI survey in *Ha'aretz*, June 4, 1981, based on May sampling.

7. See table 9–2 in Elizur and Katz, "The Media in the Israeli Elections of 1977," in Penniman, ed., op. cit., p. 239.

8. Ibid.

9. From figures released by the Central Bureau of Statistics, October 1981.

10. For example, a suggestion to constantly needle Begin about his failure to have the Syrian missiles removed was rejected by Labor tacticians.

11. For the Nixon precedent, see Joe McGinnis, *The Selling of the President* (New York: Penguin Books, 1970), pp. 56–60.

12. Poll results showed that the "undecided" vote in early June was higher than it had been in May (35 percent versus 30 percent, according to Dr. Mona Zemach). The Likud had drawn even with the Alignment by the end of May and it was ahead by mid-June when, according to *Modi'in Ezrachi* polls, it peaked (*Yediot*, June 12 and *Jerusalem Post*, June 28, 1981).

13. Moshe Harif on the Alignment program, June 20, 1981, translated from the Hebrew original.

14. Sefi Rivlin, a popular entertainer, appeared nightly for the Likud in satirical spots devoted almost exclusively to *ad hominem* attacks on opposition politicians. This excerpt is from the night of June 21 (translated from the Hebrew original.)

15. The total vote was 1,954,609 or 78.5 percent of those eligible to vote (*Ma'ariv*, July 8, 1981).

IX

ISRAELI FOREIGN POLICY AND THE 1981 ELECTION

Bernard Reich

Foreign policy and security concerns have been central to the Israeli system since its establishment, and ensuring the nation's existence and security in the face of Arab hostility has remained a primary objective. Nevertheless, such issues have not always played a major role in election campaigns. Foreign policy was not decisive in the 1977 election that brought the Likud bloc and Prime Minister Menachem Begin to power. It was important but was not a contentious issue, and there seemed to be substantial agreement on the foreign and security problems facing the state.[1] In 1981 these matters were debated by the parties, provided a context for the voters' decisions, and seemed to dominate the campaign, especially in its later stages, despite major economic concerns (particularly high and growing inflation rates) and problems within the government itself.[2]

Campaign Themes

The 1981 campaign was a long one, extending over nearly six months, and featured some new techniques transferred from the United States by the two main blocs' political consultants—David Garth for the Likud and David Sawyer for the Labor Alignment. Labor sought to focus the voters' attention on the failures of the Begin government, especially the economy and triple-digit inflation. Security and foreign policy issues seemed to serve the Likud, which trumpeted its peace efforts and the treaty with Egypt.

The Likud

The Likud's campaign reflected Begin's abilities, and he played an active role. He projected a charismatic appeal to large segments of the electorate and made skillful use of his incumbency.

The Likud focused on its achievements during the four years when it led Israel's government (1977–1981) and argued that it had made a number of good starts but needed to continue. It stressed that it was not the party of war (as it had been portrayed by the Labor Alignment) but rather a party that brought Israel both peace and security. The Egypt-Israel peace treaty was the centerpiece, and the treaty's implementation through the normalization process continued the Likud's effort. "The Peace Treaty with Egypt is an expression of an active policy to safeguard the security of the country, the same active policy that includes preventive strikes against the terrorist bases—carried out successfully. And this policy will continue." The Likud also noted its policy of establishing settlements, with the theme "we are on the map" (*anachnu al hamapa*). In the first four years the Likud government established 155 new settlements, of which 55 were in Judea and Samaria (the West Bank); it argued that every one of them strengthened Israel's security, and it pledged to continue its settlements in those areas. It argued that the Alignment, in supporting Shimon Peres's Jordanian option, sought to return 70 percent of Judea and Samaria to Jordan, which would turn these territories over to Yasser Arafat, and that a Palestinian state would be established. Thus the Likud suggested: "This time you are required to choose: the security of Israel or a Palestinian state."[3] In the debate with Peres televised just before election day, Begin summarized the perspective of the Likud in these terms:

> Jerusalem . . . a united city, not given to any partition, without two mayors, without two sovereignties–rather, one mayor, a Jew, one sovereignty–Israeli–the capital of Israel totally under Israeli sovereignty . . . ; not to turn over any part of Eretz Yisra'el to Jusayn or to Arafat–which means to Arafat. No, we will not turn it over. It is our country, our homeland. We want to live in peace and mutual respect with the Arabs and we will give them autonomy, even under our sovereignty, certainly. However, Eretz Yisra'el is the homeland of the Jewish people. . . . We will, of course, increase the number of settlers in Judea, Samaria and Gaza. We have established 144 settlements, but one can still add houses and increase the population. They will live in peace with their Arab neighbors.[4]

The Likud also sought to reverse the "one against the other" comparison campaign in which Labor had sought to portray its candidates as superior to those of the Likud. The Likud suggested that Begin should be preferred to Peres ("who changes his mind twice a week") and Yitzhak Shamir to Eban (who was linked with the "blunder"—*mechdal*—government implicated in the failures associated with the Yom Kippur War). The summary argument was that "the *Ma'arach* wants you to believe again in the same people who brought the *mechdal*."[5]

Labor

Labor focused on the failures of the Begin government (which Labor urged the voters to measure carefully) and on the candidates and their relative merits (suggesting the quality of Labor's people and the failures of Begin's team). "The Likud is a threat to democracy." Labor's main target was Begin. The theme was "you cannot depend on Begin," and the party suggested that it was forbidden to place the defense of Israel in the hands of such an unreliable man.[6] Labor sought to depict Ariel Sharon (the prospective minister of defense) as an antidemocratic figure[7] and summarized its position with the comment that there was a "pressing need to provide Israel with responsible, experienced, innovative leadership."

The negative approach to Begin contrasted with a positive portrayal of Peres, as a leader who could improve Israel's international relations, especially with François Mitterrand, the newly elected president of France. Voters were reminded of Peres's role in establishing the Israel-France connection in the 1950s, which helped to secure arms for Israel, and of Peres's accomplishments in other diplomatic arenas, in establishing Israel's aviation industry, and in the field of atomic energy. His role in strengthening the Israel Defense Forces (IDF) while he served as defense minister was highlighted. The factual recital was bolstered with "endorsements" by various national figures, current and past—the most significant being that of "founding father" and first prime minister and defense minister David Ben-Gurion, whose protegé Peres had been.

Labor summarized its position with the argument that the 1981 campaign rested on four main issues, including "the vital urgency of assuring Israel's future as a Jewish State, democratic and secure within defensible borders. The permanent absorption of 1.25 million Palestinian Arabs, as advocated by Begin, will eventually turn Israel into a second Lebanon, while his autonomy programme is bound to bring about a Palestinian State."[8]

Labor focused on the question of the West Bank and the need to ensure continuation of the peace process with Egypt. Peres noted that Labor would be willing to withdraw from the West Bank and the Gaza Strip (unlike the Likud, especially if it had backing from the National Religious party [NRP]). These territories would be transferred to a Palestinian-Jordanian state and would include the majority of the Palestinians. Labor would discuss this matter with Palestinians who were prepared to join the discussions, to recognize Israel, and to reject terrorism. The Jordanian option was seen as the method of achieving a solution focusing on the West Bank and the Gaza Strip, and Peres made clear his opposition to the Palestine Liberation Organization (PLO) as a terrorist organization committed to the destruction of Israel. Labor has focused on the concept of "territorial compromise." It seems prepared to give up a portion of the territory, but only a portion, in agreement with Jordan and the Palestinians.

The concept of a "Jordanian option," often mentioned but rarely explicitly, is based on the assumption that there is an integral connection between the Palestinians in the West Bank and the Gaza Strip and the Palestinians in the Hashemite Kingdom of Jordan. Labor's willingness to relinquish portions of the West Bank is based on what it has called "moral and Jewish values."[9] Labor opposed both the Likud policy of annexation of the West Bank and Gaza Strip and the PLO policy of establishing an independent and sovereign Palestinian state in those areas. It offered instead the policy of compromise, which was, in its view, the only realistic alternative, since it would give each party something from the process. Such a compromise would involve Israel, Jordan, and the inhabitants of the territories. In Labor's perspective, not all of the territories would be returned, and Israel would retain some areas necessary for security reasons.[10]

Other Parties

The Likud and Labor overshadowed the other parties and dominated the campaign, especially as it related to foreign policy questions. The other parties devoted their attention primarily to religious matters (particularly the NRP and Agudat Yisrael), to ethnic and personal appeals (especially Tami), and to more specific concerns (such as revocation of income tax, Arab issues, and so forth). Telem and Tehiya (headed by Moshe Dayan and Yuval Ne'eman, respectively) included foreign policy and security themes as important segments of their public appeals, as did NRP.

Telem (the movement for national renewal) argued that "Israel must have security within defensible borders" and that "ways must be found, and quickly, to reinforce the process of active peace-making with Israel's neighbors."[11] To achieve these ends, it was argued, "Israel needs Moshe Dayan's courage, experience and political realism during the crucial years that lie ahead." Telem noted that it would try to achieve "continuation of the peace process on the basis of the Camp David accords."[12] It summarized its position in these terms: "Self-rule for the Arabs of Judea, Samaria and the Gaza Strip, without the imposition of Israeli citizenship; the maintenance of the Israel Defence Forces wherever necessary for Israel's security; and the continued settlement of Jews in these areas either on State-owned land or on land purchased from its owners."[13]

Dayan suggested on a number of occasions that he was closer personally, and on the issues, to Labor than to the Likud, and his main objection was to Labor's proposal that an accommodation with Jordan be reached in stages. He wanted the IDF to retain control of the hills of the West Bank because he regarded this as the fulcrum of Israel's eastern defense line. At the same time he noted that, in his view, Herut still aspired to annex Judea and Samaria (and the Golan Heights)—a move he regarded as political folly. "I left the government because they didn't want to implement the autonomy."[14]

Tehiya, the Israel Renaissance party, focused its concern on the land of Israel. A party of true believers, it was established after the signing of the Camp David Accords and the Egypt-Israel peace treaty primarily by defectors from the Likud who firmly believed that Begin had sold them out by these two actions and that there was a need for Israel to retain full possession of all the territories occupied in the June war.[15]

The foreign policy sections of the National Religious party's political platform called for "finding ways within the framework of the peace agreement with Egypt to make it possible for the Sinai settlements to remain in Israeli hands": it proposed legislation to prevent removal of settlements from Judea, Samaria, Gaza, and the Golan and recommended that "suitable conditions be found for extending Israeli law to the Golan."[16] On the issue of the autonomy negotiations, at which NRP leader Yosef Burg led the Israeli team, the NRP noted that Israel must insist that responsibility for security—both internal and external—remain in Israeli hands in Judea, Samaria, and Gaza and that the "existence, expansion, and development of the Israeli settlements, as well as the right to set up more settlements, be safeguarded." [17]

The Campaign Environment

During the latter months of the campaign, various foreign policy and security issues provided a context for the voters as they prepared to determine their choices. These issues diverted attention from domestic ills and allowed Begin to portray himself as a decisive defender of Israel's interests. [18]

The Lebanese Missile Crisis

The Lebanese missile crisis developed in late April but had a long and complex background. The Lebanese civil war had erupted in 1975 and Syria had become involved as early as 1976. By performing a peace-keeping role with Arab League sanction, Syria, it seemed "understood," would be subject to limitations, among them that it would not deploy ground-to-air missiles in Lebanon. Israel provided support for Christian forces, especially those of Major Saad Haddad in the south, flew reconnaissance missions over Lebanon, and periodically attacked Palestinian positions in retaliation for strikes into Israel. The relatively quiescent situation began to collapse early in 1981 when Phalangist militiamen clashed with Syrian and Palestinian elements. In the escalated conflict Syria used helicopters against the Phalangists, and Israeli Phantom jets eventually shot down two of them, on April 28. Syria subsequently moved SAM-6 antiaircraft missiles into the Bekaa Valley of Lebanon, and Israel warned that the missiles should be removed or its air force would eliminate them. [19] Syria's response was to increase its missile and troop concentrations in Lebanon.

Israel accepted an American mediation effort by special envoy Philip Habib. Begin was willing to give diplomacy a chance but indicated that Israel would not indefinitely tolerate the missiles in Lebanon. The military option remained a probable alternative. [20] The Lebanese/Syrian missile crisis became a matter of election controversy. The opposition charged that Begin sought to use it for political advantage, [21] and the matter was debated both in the Knesset and at election rallies. Begin sought to focus on the security factor and on Israel's need for unimpeded access to Lebanon's skies for surveillance and for air strikes against Palestinians in Lebanon. The Likud also complained that the opposition acted irresponsibly in attacking Begin on this issue at a time when Israel should present a united front to the enemy. Labor and some of the other parties attacked Begin's comment that Israel had been prepared to strike against the missiles on April 30 but that poor weather conditions had prevented the raids. Criticism centered on his revelation of the air force's operational circumstances.

Menachem Begin and Syrian President Hafez Assad were both able to turn the crisis to their own domestic political advantage. For his part, Begin not only was able to demonstrate his willingness to allow Habib and, by extension, Reagan to defuse the situation and prevent conflict but also took actions to demonstrate his resolve; for example, he sent Israeli aircraft to attack Palestinian targets and some SAM missile batteries of Libyan origin. Polls showed an improvement in Begin's electoral standing that was apparently linked to his actions.

The Sadat Summit

In early June Egyptian President Anwar Sadat held a meeting with Begin (at the latter's invitation) for the first time in almost a year and a half at Ofira (Sharm-el-Sheikh). The summit meeting boosted Begin's position, especially among voters committed to neither Labor nor the Likud, but contributed little to the Egyptian-Israeli peace process. In a joint communiqué emphasizing the achievements toward peace, Sadat and Begin agreed that the peace process would continue as they had earlier said it would, and Sadat agreed with Begin that the status quo that had existed before the introduction of Syrian missiles in the Bekaa Valley of Lebanon had to be restored. The points in contention included the duration of the Habib mission and the Israeli raids on the PLO in Lebanon. In their press conference, both men repeated their well-known and longstanding (and mutually contradictory) positions regarding Jerusalem. Sadat, however, seemed to identify himself with Begin in opposition to Syria's actions in Lebanon, a rather curious phenomenon that would have its impact on the Israeli voter. Although cynical Israelis referred to it as "an election show,"[22] the overall effect of the summit was positive, viewed from Begin's perspective.

The Iraqi Reactor Strike

On June 8 the government of Israel announced: "Yesterday the Israeli Air Force set out to attack the Osirak nuclear reactor, which is near Baghdad. Our pilots fulfilled their assignment in its entirety. The reactor has been completely destroyed. All our planes returned safely to their base."[23] The rationale for the strike was that the reactor was meant to produce atomic bombs. "The target for these bombs was Israel." Thus "a danger to the existence of the Israeli nation had been created." The government decided to act without further delay to ensure Israel's security. It had to act before the completion of the reactor and its activation (before its becoming "hot").

A negative reaction, worldwide in scope, followed. The United States condemned the attack, temporarily suspended the delivery of F-16 aircraft to Israel, and joined in a United Nations Security Council resolution "strongly condemning" the raid. Labor charged that electoral considerations had entered into Begin's decision to strike the reactor at that time. Begin and Peres became involved in a nasty dispute.[24] Peres had written to Begin on May 10 urging him not to strike—subsequently he argued that he meant only not to strike on that date, because it was the day of the French elections. Begin argued that Peres opposed the raid "in principle."[25]

Begin appeared to gain support as a result of the raid. In a public opinion poll conducted between June 15 and June 18, the Likud continued to forge ahead of Labor, "apparently on the strength of the raid against the Iraqi nuclear reactor."[26] The results projected the Likud with forty-nine seats and Labor with thirty-seven. The destruction of the reactor had an electrifying effect on the Israeli voter as it conjured up images of threat and of Israeli capability. A euphoria was created that seemed likely to assist Begin's position in the election, despite criticism from the United States (and from the United Nations) and the U.S. decision to suspend the delivery of F-16 aircraft to Israel. Although the circumstances and the timing were debated (the question of whether the reactor would go "hot" sooner or later), few questioned the raid itself. Begin and his supporters declared the raid to be in the national interest and insisted that it had been necessary for Israel to act when it did. Moshe Arens, then chairman of the Knesset Defense and Foreign Affairs Committee and a director of the Likud election campaign noted: "We were in a race against time—any postponement would have opened us to a worst-case scenario. The scientific risk was paramount. Our intelligence told us that the reactor would become hot between July and September. . . . There was serious danger in any further delay."[27] When asked whether the raid had been an election device, Arens noted: "He didn't need it. Besides, if it hadn't been successful, the whole thing could have boomeranged."[28]

Labor charged that the operation was timed with the elections in mind. Labor claimed the attack was "premature," since there was still time for political moves to defuse the issue before the use of a military option. Peres accused Begin of "subordinating the most vital national security matters" to electoral considerations and flayed Begin for "unprecedented chattering on nuclear matters."[29] Chaim Herzog, a senior Labor party leader, evaluated Begin's actions in these terms: "It's not by coincidence that Begin likes to create crises." He observed that Begin was trying to divert attention from Israel's economic crisis and from other regime failures and was "succeeding reasonably well in doing it" by "calling people names and following the politics of attack" and by creating an atmosphere in which "it becomes unpatriotic to oppose him."[30] In contrast to Labor's criticism, Yuval Ne'eman of Tehiya generally supported Begin's position. He argued that Begin had exhausted the "French option" and was justified in ordering the raid.[31]

The Begin-Peres Television Debate

The campaign reached its end almost anticlimactically with a televised debate on June 25 between Begin and Peres in which each sought to summarize his positions and perspectives.[32] In noting the achievements of his four years in office, Begin began with "the peace treaty between Israel and Egypt . . . a revolutionary event in the position of the State of Israel in the Middle East." There was, however, also the "effective and practical defense of the people."

Peres noted that the peace process began, under a Labor government, with the disengagement of forces in 1974, a process that, Peres stressed, Begin had opposed. He also pointed out that the autonomy discussions were still pending and endangered the peace process. He sought to focus the debate on the failures of the Begin tenure, with emphasis on economic issues (especially inflation). "These were the four most difficult years ever experienced by the State of Israel."

Benefits for Begin

Begin seemed to gain support as a result of the various foreign policy/ security issues and the government's responses to them, whereas Labor seemed plagued by misadventure. In addition to the acrimony between Peres and Yitzhak Rabin, Peres seemed unable to generate much "spark" for Labor's efforts. Peres's reported secret meetings (in March) with King Hassan of Morocco and with a brother (Mohammad) of Jordan's King Hussein (Peres neither confirmed nor denied

the reports) were perceived as a blunder, since he seemed to be usurp-
ing the government's foreign policy position. The original omission of
Rabin from the proposed Labor government (and the inclusion of the
dovish Haim Bar-Lev along with Abba Eban) appeared to be errors of
calculation. Rabin was included in the prospective Labor government
at the last minute. In a press conference on June 25, Peres announced
that Bar-Lev would serve as deputy prime minister and Rabin as minister of defense. Despite the known animosity between Peres and
Rabin, the latter agreed to participate because of his view that there
was an overriding national need for Labor to resume its control of the
government of Israel. The overall impression, however, was that foreign policy issues worked to the advantage of the Likud.[33] They diverted attention from domestic problems to the sphere where Begin's
stand appealed to voters more than Labor's equivocations and its criticisms of Begin.

Begin's Second Administration

The elections returned a Likud-led coalition government to power in
Israel, but one different from its predecessor in the participation of
parties and of personalities and in policy perspectives. The Likud's
margin of victory was narrower than in 1977, and the two major blocs
(the Likud and the Labor Alignment) emerged approximately equal
in parliamentary strength (between them they won nearly 100 of 120
seats in the Knesset) while the small parties lost votes and parliamentary representation. Begin was able to form a government with a
number of small but politically potent parties. The Knesset approved
his coalition of the Likud, the National Religious party, Agudat Yisrael, and Tami, controlling sixty-one seats, on August 5, 1981.

The eighty-three clause coalition agreement and the government's
official program (also endorsed by the Knesset in its August vote) provided some insight into the policy perspectives of the new government,
although that policy was affected by numerous additional factors.

Program and Policy Perspectives

The new government's formal positions were contained in the program submitted to and approved by the Knesset on August 5, 1981.
That program was rather general and not very dissimilar from its
predecessors. The document spoke of the right of the Jewish people

to the land of Israel and of the central importance of efforts to achieve peace. The peace treaty between Israel and Egypt was hailed as a historic turning point. The government committed itself to diligent observance of the Camp David Accords and to "work for the renewal of negotiations on the implementation of the agreement on full autonomy for the Arab residents of Judea, Samaria, and the Gaza District." At the same time the government noted that "the autonomy agreed upon at Camp David means neither sovereignty nor self-determination. The autonomy agreements set down at Camp David are guarantees that under no conditions will a Palestinian state emerge in the territory of Western 'Eretz Yisrael.'" It also stated that, at the end of the stipulated transition period, "Israel will present its claim, and act to realize its right of sovereignty over Judea, Samaria and the Gaza District." In the interim, Israel's settlement efforts will continue as a "right" and as an integral part of Israel's security.

Protection for the Arabs of the territories was mentioned. The Golan Heights and Jerusalem received particular attention. "Israel will not descend from the Golan Heights, nor will it remove any settlement established there. It is the Government that will decide on the appropriate timing for the application of Israeli law, jurisdiction, and administration to the Golan Heights." Finally, the program declared: "Jerusalem is the eternal capital of Israel, indivisible, entirely under Israeli sovereignty. Free access to their holy places has been and will be guaranteed to followers of all faiths." [34]

Begin elaborated on the views expressed in the program in his presentation to the Knesset. He noted that Israel had adhered to the Camp David Accords and that the autonomy talks had been stopped by Egypt "with no justified reason." In reviewing U.S.-Israeli relations, he began with "the declaration of the President of the United States that Jewish settlement in Eretz Israel is not illegal" and suggested that this statement confirmed Israel's view. He was pleased that "now, from the lips of the highest authority in the United States, we have heard an unequivocal declaration that Jewish settlement is not illegal." Begin stressed: "Of great importance is the announcement, reiterated a number of times by the President of the United States, that Israel is a strategic asset to the United States in the Middle East, that Israel is a friend and ally of America, that Israel performs an important role in blocking Soviet expansionism."

Begin commented that there was no written and signed alliance between the two states but suggested that if the United States were to propose to Israel that the two countries sign a written defense pact, "I shall recommend to my colleagues in the Government to sign such an agreement." He believed that the United States should take the initiative in suggesting such an arrangement. Begin also spoke about the general areas of concord between the two states and especially joint defense of freedom and democracy. Yet although he accentuated the positive overall nature of the relationship, Begin spoke also of "practical negative developments": the suspension of the supply to Israel of F-16 aircraft in the wake of the bombing of the Iraqi reactor and the raids in Lebanon and the proposed sale to Saudi Arabia of additional equipment for the F-15s already on order and of AWACS aircraft.[35]

The formal government program was further amplified by the eighty-three-clause agreement signed by the coalition partners on August 4, 1981. It retained in force all of the provisions of the Ninth Knesset coalition agreement and focused heavily on religious matters. Foreign policy and related issue areas were not considered, an omission that reflected the domestic priorities of the coalition partners and the relative concord among them on foreign policy and security issues.

The NRP has been a member of virtually every coalition government and prides itself on this fact. The party is also proud that, as a result, it has been able to secure significant concessions concerning religious matters. It continues to see its mission primarily in such terms, although it has an interest in foreign policy and security issues; Yosef Burg, a longtime party leader and a member of virtually all of Israel's governments, has served as Israel's senior negotiator in the autonomy talks. The NRP is in far greater accord with the Likud than with Labor on the major policy issues facing Israel, both domestic (especially religious) and foreign (especially occupied territories—particularly the West Bank).

There is also a strong feeling within the NRP that Begin is far more committed on the religious question and on the future of the West Bank and Jerusalem than Peres or any other Labor Alignment leader. Agudat Yisrael's leadership has a similar perspective on the efficacy of coalition participation, and its main (if not sole) focus remains religious. Tami's agenda cannot be separated from the personal views and ambitions of Aharon Abu-Hatzeira, its founder and leader, although the party continues to articulate its grievances against Israel's Ashkenazi-dominated establishment. The policies of the Begin government were no doubt affected by the positions taken by the religious parties but the policies were probably more a function of the views of the government's major figures.

Begin's views concerning the West Bank and Palestinian autonomy (as well as most other issues) have been conditioned over a long period by numerous historical events and tend to be ideological. He has been a devoted follower of Vladimir Zeev Jabotinsky, who believes, with the Zionist revisionists, that the West Bank and even part of the east bank (that is, Jordan proper) were originally part of Palestine. Begin views his position as one of commitment to principle and to the survival of Israel and of the Jewish people. Begin's ideological proclivities are reinforced by his practical beliefs. He has little direct, personal knowledge or understanding of the Palestinians under Israeli administration. Begin does not view Palestinian terrorists in the same light as the Jewish freedom fighters of the Mandate period.

Begin's perspective on the Camp David process and the autonomy accords was derived from his previous experience with those efforts—he believes that what Israel, Egypt, and the United States agreed to should be implemented and not altered. He sees the autonomy plan as deriving from proposals he advanced to Egypt and the United States at the end of 1977. In line with the agreements, he was willing to include Jordan and representatives of the Palestinians in future negotiations (as called for in the Camp David Accords) but continued to oppose any dealings with the PLO on the grounds that it was a terrorist organization committed to the destruction of Israel. In this matter he had strong support in many quarters in Israel, especially in the ruling coalition and among its constituencies.

Begin's political skills, as clearly demonstrated during the 1981 election campaign, were an important factor in his government's programs. The Likud was a clear loser according to public opinion polls in January 1981 (by a ratio of about fifty seats for Labor to twenty for the Likud), but by June the Likud was able not only to increase its support to forty-eight seats but also to emerge as the party designated to form the government. Begin was able to take advantage of developments to increase voting support for his bloc.

Begin's skill was complemented by his increased control of the Likud and of the coalition. In the Likud he no longer faced a confrontation with Ezer Weizman, who did not participate in the election. The coalition was more ideological and probably less pragmatic than that established in 1977, given the absence of Weizman, Moshe Dayan, and Yigael Yadin, and did not have strong opposition within its councils. It did not have the Democratic Movement for Change (DMC) and Yigael Yadin, with whatever moderating influence they may have had on the prime minister and on the policies of the government.

Dayan and his new Telem party were of minor political consequence and were outside government, although Telem members (especially Mordechai Ben-Porat and Yigal Hurvitz) are thought to be sympathetic to Likud foreign policy perspectives on issues relating to the conflict. Dayan's death further reduced the potential strength of Telem opposition and its role as a moderating force. Telem joined the coalition after Dayan's death, but Ben-Porat resigned from his post as minister without portfolio in January 1984. Initially Begin gained passive support from the right-wing Tehiya (Renaissance) party[36] on crucial foreign policy issues on which he took a hard-line position, since the party's ideology was even more strident on these matters. Tehiya, for example, had argued for revision of the treaty with Egypt to stop the withdrawal from Sinai and it tried to prevent the dismantling of the settlements in the Rafiah salient. It could be expected to support Begin against dovish parties and positions.

Begin's position was also strengthened by the fact that he continued to have strong support from the Israel Defense Forces,[37] the youth, and the Sephardic communities. More than one-third of the voters in 1981 were under thirty years of age, and that segment of the population is growing in proportion. Polls indicated a strong preference among young voters for Begin, the Likud, and the right wing in general. They also preferred a hard-line foreign policy. This preference may well have been a result of Israel's occupation of Arab territory for more than fourteen years; many Israelis under the age of thirty did not remember well what Israel was like in its pre-1967 borders. Today Judea and Samaria are places that many young people associate with the pioneering spirit and with their own military service rather than with the occupation of "Arab territory."

Begin was joined in the government by two men who held strong views on foreign policy and security issues and probably harbored doubts about the Camp David process and about significant West Bank concessions: Foreign Minister Yitzhak Shamir and Defense Minister Ariel Sharon.

Sharon brought with him to the ministry the baggage of a long (and distinguished, if not legendary) but tempestuous military career and a short period as a politician. He became minister of defense despite some misgivings (apparently some were felt by Begin and others within and outside the Likud as well as in the defense establishment) in part because he had a reputation for imprudence and was regarded as ambitious. He served in the previous Begin government as minister of agriculture and as head of the ministerial committee on settlement affairs, a post that gave him responsibility for increasing settlement in Judea and Samaria (as well as in pre-1967 Israel). He worked to this end with great initiative and argued that the West Bank settlements were primarily designed to serve Israel's security needs. In his four-year tenure he helped to increase the Jewish population of the West Bank by some 400 percent. Millions of dollars were spent for housing, roads, and other requirements of the settlements. Sharon regards the establishment of settlements in the territories as logical and not as an obstacle to peace. He felt that objections to them came more from the opposition Labor party than from Israel's negotiating partners.

In his first speech as defense minister, Sharon told the Knesset on August 10, 1981, that Jordan was a "Palestinian state" and that Israel would not allow the establishment of another Palestinian state on the West Bank. Sharon regards Begin's autonomy plan as more far-reaching than any ever suggested by an Arab state. Sharon has noted, "With Arab autonomy we are giving up what is ours." [38]

Soon after taking office, Sharon inaugurated a policy toward Arabs living in the territories under Israeli administration that was seemingly designed to improve relations between Israeli administrators and Palestinian residents by relaxing conditions and improving the atmosphere and attitudes. Ultimately the goal was to identify and to establish a dialogue with Arab leaders willing to cooperate with Israel on resolution of the autonomy issue. Sharon sought to create a situation in which potential Arab partners to the negotiations would not remain silent from fear of Palestinian terrorist groups, and he tried to increase the influence of moderate spokesmen. One of the overriding objectives was to create a suitable atmosphere for including the inhabitants of the territories in the peace process. (It was described as a policy of receptiveness and openness to the Arabs of Eretz Yisrael.)

Sharon reportedly became aware of the need to establish an infrastructure of leaders in the territories with whom it would be possible to hold a dialogue that would help find political solutions to emerging problems, including that of autonomy. To complement this dialogue, he announced his intention of meeting with Arab notables from the territories to become better acquainted and to create a basis for mutual trust. At the same time he adopted a hard line on the question of PLO links with the territories. West Bank mayors and other leaders were warned against any contact with PLO officials during trips abroad and against issuing any public statements supporting the PLO. The military government banned the receipt of money from the Joint Jordan-PLO Committee in Amman.

Sharon believed that the retention of the Golan Heights and the West Bank and Gaza were integral to his security concept, as was continued Israeli settlement in these areas. In office he indicated his intention to integrate the settlements into a massive local defense system—well organized and cooperating closely with the military. He appeared to believe that the peace agreement with Egypt would have to be scrupulously maintained, with no erosion of either the normalization process or the postpeace military status quo.

Foreign Minister Yitzhak Shamir, who replaced Begin as prime minister in 1983, had a virtually religious belief in Zionism. He joined the Irgun—the military arm of Jabotinsky's Revisionist party—in 1937 and later left with the faction led by Avraham Stern and helped to establish Lehi (Lohamei Herut Yisrael—Israel Freedom Fighters—popularly known as the Stern Gang). After Stern's death, Shamir was one of a committee of three that ran Lehi. He later worked for the Mossad and joined Herut in 1970. His views on foreign policy are complex, if rarely expressed. In the Knesset he abstained on the Camp David agreement vote, in part because it provided for withdrawing the Sinai settlements. He believes that Israel should maintain its presence on the West Bank and sees Israel's 1967 frontiers as indefensible. He has suggested that a softer stand than that adopted by the Likud would probably help the autonomy talks go more smoothly "but at the expense of our vital interests."[39] He has supported the Egypt-Israel peace treaty, although he disagrees with some of its clauses, and believes that Israel must work within its framework. He believed there was a risk in giving up Sinai, but it was done for the sake of peace, which he sees as essential. He would like normalization to be faster and smoother but recognizes that there are obstacles. Shamir's views on autonomy are best summed up in the following comment: "We are very flexible, and we have already reached the limit of the concessions we are able to make. Do not forget that in Camp David we have paid a tremendous price for the peace. And I don't think that anybody is entitled to ask from us more sacrifices and more risks."[40]

Moshe Arens, former chairman of the Knesset committee on defense and foreign affairs, was appointed ambassador to the United States. He believed that the right of Israelis to live in the land of Israel did not end at the Green Line (that is, the 1967 frontiers of Israel) but included Judea and Samaria, where settlement serves to fulfill historic desires and security considerations.[41]

Begin's views were compatible with the perspectives of this group. Everyone, including Begin, believed in settling the West Bank (or, preferably, Judea and Samaria) to serve the purpose of creating a Jewish presence in historic Eretz Yisrael. Settlement would, of course, also prevent the establishment of a Palestinian (read PLO) state. At the same time neither Begin nor his closest advisers wanted the peace process with Egypt to collapse, since it was a major (and often mentioned) achievement of the first Begin government.

Policy Continuity

The success of the Likud in the elections and of Menachem Begin in forming a new coalition government suggested that many of the policies and trends that had characterized Israel during the preceding four years and had formed the positions of the Likud (and its coalition partners) during the campaign would continue during the second Begin government. The new government soon began to act in support of its perspectives, and in the first months after its endorsement by the Knesset indicated the nature and direction of its approach. The issues of war and peace—the Arab-Israeli conflict in its various manifestations—and relations with the United States continued to be the focal points of Israel's foreign and security policies.

Initially, the government concentrated on relations with Egypt—including normalization, the withdrawal from Sinai, and the autonomy talks concerning the future of the West Bank and the Gaza Strip—which became more complex with the assassination of Anwar Sadat in early October 1981 and the succession of Hosni Mubarak to the presidency of Egypt. Soon after the endorsement of the government, Begin met with Sadat for their eleventh meeting in four years, in Alexandria, Egypt, to consider the normalization process and the autonomy talks, which had earlier been suspended by Sadat. Since Camp David, Israeli policy had centered on the peace process with Egypt, and Begin's reelection campaign identified the peace treaty as his major foreign policy accomplishment. Under the terms of that agreement, Israel was required to complete its withdrawal from Sinai in April 1982, to dismantle its strategic facilities, and to remove its settlements from the peninsula.

The certainty of Israel's commitment to withdrawal from Sinai became a matter of speculation and conjecture after the Likud's return to power; some observers suggested that Israel would not meet its obligations while others seemed confident of the Begin pledge. The peace process enjoyed wide support in Israel, although there were misgivings concerning, and organized opposition to, the requirement of total withdrawal from Sinai and the dismantling of the settlements.

After Sadat's assassination, Israel closely watched and carefully gauged Egypt's position and its capacity to remain on the course Sadat had set. Some Israelis sought to modify Israel's policy on the assumption (or in the hope) that change would occur in Egypt. Militant Jewish settlers in northern Sinai accelerated their campaign to force the Israeli government to abrogate the Egypt-Israel treaty and to cancel the scheduled withdrawal.

Begin provided reassurances that Israel's commitment was firm and that it would honor its obligations. In an instructive interview in *Ma'ariv* on September 28, 1981, he said: "We signed a peace treaty and we will fulfill everything stipulated in that treaty. Personally, there is nothing more painful than the commitment we undertook . . . to evacuate the settlements. . . . The government, the Knesset and the people made their decision. Threats, violence and violent opposition cannot influence us in the least." Ultimately, all obligations concerning Sinai were fulfilled.

The autonomy talks were resumed in late September 1981, though not as a result of substantive changes in Israel's or Egypt's position. At the time when the talks had been suspended, the negotiations had made some progress in translating the Egypt-Israel peace treaty and the Camp David Accords from paper to reality. On peripheral and essentially technical matters, substantial agreement had been reached, but central problems remained unresolved. Israel maintained the view that its autonomy proposals did not require change.

The West Bank remained a far more complex problem than Sinai had been. It involved territory more central to Israel and had substantially more settlements and settlers, the latter with considerable political power. The West Bank (in Israel called Judea and Samaria to reflect the biblical and traditional names of the territory) was part of the original Palestine Mandate, whose partition in the 1920s to create Transjordan was never accepted by the Revisionist Zionist movement of which Begin is the ideological heir. Begin saw the West Bank as an integral part of Israeli sovereignty and as liberated territory. He said, on the program "Issues and Answers" on May 22, 1977, "I believe that Judea and Samaria are an integral part of our sovereignty. It's our land. It was occupied by Abdullah [King of Jordan] against international law, against our inherent right. It was liberated during the Six-Day War when we used our right of national self-defense, and so it should be. . . . You annex foreign land. You don't annex your own territory. It is our land. You don't annex it."

Although Begin's perspective has strong support within Israel, that support is not unanimous. At the same time there is a national consensus in Israel that total withdrawal from the West Bank (and from other occupied territories) is unacceptable, primarily because of security considerations. The lines established after the 1967 war significantly enhanced Israel's security position. The ascendancy of the Begin government in 1977 and its return to power in 1981 did not alter the security perspective but added elements to the arguments concerning retention of the West Bank. These included an ideological commitment to Jewish rights in Judea and Samaria as parts of the historic homeland—as a part of historic Eretz Yisrael.

There were other elements that affected the West Bank and were not important considerations in Sinai. Sinai did not involve religious symbolism, and there were no significant holy sites for which there was or is a Jewish-Israeli longing. There was no perceived danger that Sinai would become an independent Palestinian state, whereas the autonomy talks were seen as possibly opening the door to the creation, on Israel's border, of an independent Palestinian state of questionable motive and virtue. Opposition to such a state came from both the Likud government and the Labor-dominated opposition. Israelis see a PLO-dominated West Bank state as a threat to Israel's security and its very existence. The broadest and most articulate consensus in the Israeli system continues to center on opposition to the creation of a Palestinian state and to negotiations with the PLO.

For Begin and his government, autonomy was seen as primarily administrative, with Israel responsible for the security of the area. Israel continued to argue that autonomy should be confined to the inhabitants of the territories but not extend to the actual territory. In addition to limiting the self-governing authority in size and power, Begin has reiterated his intention to press Israel's claim of sovereignty over the West Bank and Gaza after the five years of autonomy and his determination never to tolerate a Palestinian state in those areas. Israel saw an agreement on autonomy as a practical solution to the status of the Palestinian Arabs, one that was responsive to Israel's need for security, to Egypt's wish to adhere to the Arab cause, and to the Palestinian Arab's desire to control their own affairs. Thus the autonomy scheme remained the basis for the Israeli position, and there was no identified need to move beyond that position to allow the creation of a Palestinian state in the West Bank and Gaza. The link between the Palestinians and Jordan was articulated by Foreign Minister Shamir on October 5, 1981, in a speech to the Foreign Policy Association in New York City in these terms: "The irrefutable fact is that Jordan is a Palestinian Arab state in everything but name."[42]

Although the government's policy concerning the settlements in the

territories was not fully articulated at the outset, it seemed logical that
the government would continue its efforts to develop Israel's presence
through the construction of settlements and the encouragement of
people to move to the areas. This program would follow the general
approach adopted during the first Begin administration when Sharon,
then minister of agriculture, concentrated on settlement construction,
mostly in locations of strategic importance. Herut doctrine viewed Judea and Samaria as an integral part of Eretz Yisrael and settlements
there as a natural and inalienable Jewish right. Apart from security
considerations, settlements reaffirm a claim to Jewish sovereignty in
Eretz Yisrael. Israel's presence, both structures and settlers, was substantially increased, and the policy would be continued. Such issues were soon overshadowed by the 1982 war in Lebanon and by its
aftermath.

The continued presence in Lebanon of the Syrian missiles that had
been moved there during Israel's election campaign receded into the
background during the fall and winter of 1981. The Habib mission
achieved a cease-fire, although it failed to secure resolution of the
problem, and Israel made clear its view that the presence of the missiles and continued PLO attacks against Israeli and Jewish targets
worldwide would not be tolerated indefinitely. In a news conference
on November 9, 1981, Defense Minister Sharon noted: "We prefer to
solve it by political means. We will try first every political way that will
be possible. We have patience. We are not in a hurry. But we are not
going to leave this situation forever. We have been promised that steps
would be taken a long time ago. Nothing has been done since. . . . If
that does not work, Israel will have to act."[43]

On June 6, 1982, Israel launched a major military action against the
PLO in Lebanon. Operation Peace for Galilee sought to remove the
PLO military and terrorist threat to Israel and to reduce the PLO's
political capability. The war and its aftermath have remained major
elements of Israeli foreign and security policy since that time and
have become major factors in Israel's relations with the United States.

Relations with the United States

Relations with the United States remain an important factor in Israeli
politics and foreign policy. The United States and its policies were a
campaign theme, and on a number of occasions the media suggested
that the United States expected and "hoped for" a victory by Peres
and the Labor Alignment, since this, it was believed, would facilitate

United States efforts in the region, particularly with regard to the autonomy talks and the broader peace process.

Relations between the Begin and Reagan administrations were complex and variable, reaching high and low points at various times. Israel and the United States clashed over divergent interpretations of the regional situation, of the peace process, and of Israel's security needs. Israel struck at the Iraqi reactor and at PLO positions in Beirut during the summer of 1981 and took action on other issues when it believed that its national interest was at stake—even when it understood that its stance would lead to clashes with the United States. The United States strongly opposed the Israeli raid on the Iraqi reactor, questioned the Beirut raids, and postponed the delivery of F-16 aircraft to Israel. On less central questions Israel was prepared to defer to the United States.

Various substantive issues emerged, including disputes about settlements in the occupied territories and Israel's concern about a perceived pro-Saudi tendency in U.S. policy. That trend was made manifest, in part, by arms supplied to Saudi Arabia (including F-15 enhancements and AWACS).

The proposed sale of AWACS and other military equipment to Saudi Arabia, which had aroused Israeli concern and opposition in the spring of 1981, became a major factor in the fall as Congress debated the issue. Israel opposed the sale, but it was approved, and Israel was dismayed. Israel had been placed in a no-win situation, with negative results if it opposed the sale and the president was defeated and negative results if it did not actively oppose the president and he won, thereby increasing Arab (especially Saudi) military capability against Israel. Israeli anxiety was heightened when the administration seemed to suggest that a peace plan put forward in August by then Crown Prince Fahd of Saudi Arabia had some merit. Israel viewed the proposal negatively. It lent credence to the Israeli perspective of a "tilt" toward Saudi Arabia in U.S. policy.

In an effort to mitigate the effects of the sale, Reagan sought to reassure Israel that the United States "remains committed to help Israel retain its military and technological advantages."[44] Israel was drawn to the proposal of strategic cooperation originally discussed during the earlier Begin visit to Washington and reiterated in Reagan's post-AWACS letter. On November 30, 1981, the United States and Israel signed a "Memorandum of Understanding on Strategic Cooperation." "The parties recognize the need to enhance strategic cooperation to deter all threats from the Soviet Union to the region." The agreement called for joint naval and air exercises in the eastern Mediterranean and labeled the Soviet Union a threat to the region. The view was that the United States and Israel would cooperate in response to Soviet or Soviet-controlled threats and that the agreement was not directed against any Middle Eastern state or group of states. Working groups were to negotiate the details of implementation. For the Begin government the agreement constituted an important milestone, suggesting improved relations with the United States and some mitigation of the negative effects of the U.S. sale of the AWACS and other advanced weapons systems to Saudi Arabia. The opposition raised various objections, offered no-confidence motions in the Knesset, and sought to downplay the success of Begin and Sharon, but their efforts failed.

A number of foreign policy themes and issues seemed to come together in December 1981, when the government of Israel, in keeping with its perspectives and campaign themes, decided to alter the status of the Golan Heights. On a number of occasions, Begin and other spokesmen for the Likud made clear that Israel was prepared to negotiate with Syria but would not agree to withdraw ("to come down") from the Golan Heights or to remove any settlement from it. In presenting its policy guidelines to the Knesset in August 1981, the new government noted, in paragraph 11: "Israel will not descend from the Golan Heights, nor will it remove any settlement established there. It is the government that will decide on the appropriate timing for the imposition of Israeli law, jurisdiction and administration on the Golan Heights." On December 14, 1981, the government presented to the Knesset the Golan Heights Law, whose primary clause stated: "The law, jurisdiction and administration of the State shall apply to the Golan Heights." The rationales were many but centered on historical and security factors and on the refusal of Syria to recognize Israel's existence and to negotiate with Israel for peace. The Knesset subsequently endorsed the government's proposal, the government gaining some support from the ranks of the Labor opposition.

The action generated a swift reaction in Washington. U.S. spokesmen stressed that the United States had been given no advance warning and opposed the decision to change the status of the Golan through unilateral action. Statements of displeasure and condemnation were accompanied by U.S. support for a United Nations resolution of condemnation and by U.S. suspension of the agreement of understanding on strategic cooperation. Israel was "stunned" by the extent of the U.S. response, and its strongly negative reaction included Begin's castigation of the U.S. ambassador.

Although the exchanges concerning the Golan decision exacerbated tensions in the relationship, the main watershed was the war in Lebanon, with associated developments that called into question various aspects of the links between the two states and posed major dilemmas for Israeli foreign policy. The war in Lebanon led to clashes between the United States and Israel concerning the nature and extent of the war actions and the U.S. effort to ensure the PLO's evacuation from Beirut. The initial U.S. involvement to secure the PLO's evacuation was soon supplemented by the decision to return to Beirut after the massacres at the Shatilla and Sabra refugee camps, thus beginning the lengthy involvement of U.S. Marines in the turmoil of Lebanon. The war also led to the Reagan fresh-start initiative, which sought to reinvigorate the Arab-Israeli peace process by taking advantage of the opportunities presented by the situation in Lebanon at the end of the summer of 1982.

The Reagan initiative presented Israel with a major policy dilemma. It saw the proposals as detrimental to its policies and rejected the initiative. That action, coupled with the massacres at the Shatilla and Sabra camps, resulted in a sharp deterioration in Israel's standing in American public opinion and further disagreements with the Reagan administration concerning the situation in the Middle East. After the failure of Hussein to join the peace process, however, and with the increased Soviet involvement in Syria, the Lebanon-Israel accord of May 1983, and the Syrian-Soviet opposition to it, relations between the United States and Israel became more positive. Relations appeared to have come full circle by the summer of 1983, when the two states seemed linked by a congruence of policy that included recognition of Israel's strategic anti-Soviet value and its desire for peaceful resolution of the Arab-Israeli conflict as well as parallel views concerning Lebanon and its future. This development comported with Reagan's initial perceptions of Israel and its position in the Middle East and suggested that there would be a period of positive relations between the United States and Israel—a trend that received explicit expression in the December 1983 agreement between Reagan and Shamir for closer strategic cooperation between the two states.

The Shamir Government

Menachem Begin's decision to resign as prime minister of Israel on September 16, 1983, brought to an end a major era in Israeli politics. His tenure as prime minister (1977 to 1983) was stormy, marked by significant accomplishments and major controversies. The major achievement, for which Begin shared the Nobel Prize for Peace with President Anwar Sadat of Egypt, was the Egyptian-Israeli peace treaty of 1979, which resulted from the Sadat initiative and the Camp David Accords. For Begin and for Israel, the treaty was a momentous but difficult accomplishment. It brought peace with Israel's most populous adversary and significantly reduced the military danger to the existence of Israel by neutralizing the largest Arab army, with which Israel had fought five wars. It was also traumatic, however, given the extensive tangible concessions required of Israel, especially the uprooting of Jewish settlements in Sinai. Operation Peace for Galilee—the war in Lebanon—in June 1982 occasioned debate and demonstration within Israel, resulted in substantial casualties, and led to Israel's increased international isolation and major policy clashes with the United States. The war was a factor in Begin's decision to step down from office.

The major foreign relationship continued to be that with the United States, and it underwent significant change during Begin's tenure. It was often tempestuous, as the two countries disagreed on various aspects of the regional situation and the issues associated with resolution of the Arab-Israeli conflict. Nevertheless, U.S. economic and military assistance and political and diplomatic support rose to their highest levels.

On October 10, 1983, the Knesset endorsed the government and its programs, and Yitzhak Shamir became the prime minister of Israel. The government was the same as its predecessor except for the absence of Begin and the appointment of Pessah Grupper as minister of agriculture to replace the late Simcha Ehrlich. Shamir retained the foreign affairs portfolio.

Shamir's initial effort was to reconstitute the government on the same terms that had been associated with the outgoing government, although certain changes were essential. His administration's program has been general and has not been very dissimilar from those of its predecessors. In his presentation to the Knesset, Shamir paid tribute to Begin, promised "to continue along the course he charted," and said that his government would be bound by the basic principles and the coalition agreement of the previous government as submitted to the Knesset in 1981. He paid tribute to the IDF and noted that "Israel's security situation is immeasurably better than it has ever been at any time since we renewed our independence." He attributed this state of affairs to the peace with Egypt, to the removal of the threat of terrorism from Lebanon, and to "a desire to maintain quiet along the border" with Jordan. He identified Syria as a hostile and aggressive neighbor.

In connection with the quest for peace, Shamir stressed the agreements with Egypt and Lebanon. He noted a "chilly attitude" but restated Israel's desire to cultivate good relations with Egypt. He urged Egypt to return to the autonomy negotiations and called on Jordan and the Arabs of Judea, Samaria, and the Gaza District to join the talks. "It must be clear to all that the Camp David Accords are the only document agreed on by all and, therefore, the only way to continue the [peace] process." [45]

With regard to Lebanon, Shamir said that no one should think that any settlement could be reached there unless the May 17, 1983, Lebanese-Israeli agreement was implemented. Israel would not agree that any state of the "Rejection Front" should have the right to veto an agreement between Israel and a neighboring country. He said that Syria's "massive military presence" in Lebanon increases the danger that Lebanon will once again serve as a base for attacks on Israel. Hence, the sooner Syria accedes to Lebanon's demand and withdraws its army, the better it will be for Lebanon and for the prospects of peace and stability in the entire region. Shamir said that

> the relations of trust, friendship and close cooperation between ourselves and the United States are vital for us and for the stability of the whole Middle East. This closeness stems from both common values and a tradition of mutual sympathy between the two peoples, as well as from a complex of shared interests which have stood the test of time and events in our region. The Government of Israel will do all it can to foster and deepen our ties with the United States in all fields of endeavor. [46]

Shamir noted that the differences in political positions that appear at times between Israel and the United States are a "natural and understandable phenomenon" and do not cloud the atmosphere of friendship and the strong alliance that characterizes the relations between the two states.

Israel and the Shamir government faced a range of foreign policy issues that continued to coalesce around aspects of the Arab-Israeli conflict (including Lebanon) and relations with the United States. Although Israel's military position in Lebanon improved with the IDF's redeployment from the Shuf Mountains to the Awali River, it did not guarantee the security and safety of Israeli forces, as was demonstrated by bombings and other attacks against Israeli positions. Israel's major goals in Lebanon have not been achieved, and even the May 17 agreement has not been implemented. The potential resurgence of the PLO, despite its internecine warfare, has raised concern about terrorist strikes. Syria's Soviet-supported belligerence and intransigence, its growing control of the PLO, its might (it has the largest Arab army, now that Egypt has reduced strength), and its increased and sophisticated arms supply from the Soviet Union have further complicated the situation. No clear means of responding to these challenges has been readily identified by the government.

The involvement of the United States in Lebanon, and the attacks on U.S. forces and positions in Lebanon and elsewhere in the region, provided the context for improved relations between the United States and Israel after Shamir took office. Shamir and Defense Minister Moshe Arens visited the United States at the end of November 1983, at Reagan's invitation, to discuss the various elements of bilateral relations and other regional problems. Upon his return to Jerusalem after the visit, Shamir noted that the meeting had been "one of the finest hours in U.S.-Israeli relations. . . . We have good grounds to be satisfied with the attitude of America's leaders. With America's help, I hope we shall be able to overcome all our difficulties, both military-political and economic."[47]

The major foreign policy problems were addressed during the meeting, although they were not resolved, as the "positive" visit focused on the areas of current mutual concern to the two states— that is, on issues revolving around the problems of Lebanon—and demonstrated the extent to which the concerns and policies of the two states had become congruent. The need to reinforce the Gemayel government and to rebuild Lebanon as a free, independent, and sovereign state, with a reconstructed economic infrastructure, to force the withdrawal of all foreign forces, and to provide an army capable of supporting the government's position seemed to be an area of agreement between the two leaders. Syria and the Soviet Union were viewed as the forces promoting instability and seeking to prevent or obstruct these goals. Both were identified as threats to peace and stability.

Shamir noted on "Good Morning America" on November 30, 1983: "I think as we and the United States now have the same goals to stabilize the situation in Lebanon, to reach a withdrawal of all foreign forces from Lebanon—to get—to insure the security of our northern border, we have to act together in order to reach these goals. And, for this purpose, we need a close cooperation. . . . It's a close cooperation between two countries who have the same goals, the same policy in this region, and some identical interests." He told "CBS Morning

News," on December 1, 1983, that "this visit was a satisfying visit, a successful visit. We found ways to strengthen our cooperation with the United States, and I think that it will contribute to peace and stability in the Middle East."

This coincidence of perspective and objective led the two governments to achieve wide-ranging agreement on closer coordination and policy. At the same time the major issues of discord in the relations between the two governments, which focused on the West Bank and Gaza and on the Reagan fresh-start initiative, were not addressed in any meaningful way. The United States and Israel do not agree on these matters, and the likelihood of their clashing is probable if negotiations on these issues are begun.

Future Prospects

With the inauguration of the Shamir government, the foreign policy of Israel entered a new phase already heralded by the heavy costs to Israel of its extensive involvement in Lebanon and by the Kahan Commission's report, which achieved the termination of Sharon's tenure as defense minister and brought Arens to that crucial position from his post as ambassador to the United States. The new administration (Shamir continued to hold the foreign affairs portfolio) approached many foreign and security policy issues from a perspective similar to that of the Begin-Sharon team, but its style and the new circumstances in which it had to operate have suggested that there may be alterations in Israeli foreign policy. From a broad perspective, however, the uniqueness of this phase will probably be less profound than its continuity. The Arab-Israeli conflict in its various manifestations and Israel's relations with the United States will continue to be at the center of Israel's foreign and security policy concerns.

NOTES

1. See Bernard Reich, "Israel's Foreign Policy and the 1977 Parliamentary Elections," in Howard R. Penniman, ed., *Israel at the Polls: The Knesset Elections of 1977* (Washington, D.C.: American Enterprise Institute, 1979), pp. 255–282.

2. Earlier the identified priorities of the electorate were oriented toward inflation and the economy. A "mood of the nation" public opinion poll conducted at the beginning of February identified economy/inflation as the main problem affecting the voters (58.8 percent). Although defense was the next most often identified problem (7.9 percent), the peace process received but a

2.1 percent rating, and foreign policy and *hasbara* (information) only 1.9 percent. The poll was conducted by the Modi'in Ezrachi Applied Research Centre for the *Jerusalem Post* and was reported in *Jerusalem Post*, international ed., March 1–7, 1981.

3. *Jerusalem Post Magazine*, June 12, 1981, p. 4. In a speech to the Likud unification conference, which subsequently unanimously elected him as the Likud's candidate for the premiership, Begin listed the Likud's achievements during his four-year term as prime minister and identified the peace treaty with Egypt as the most important of them. Text in *Foreign Broadcast Information Service (FBIS)*, May 11, 1981, p. I1.

4. From the debate as broadcast on Israel television, June 25, 1981, in *FBIS*, June 26, 1981, p. I9. On May 7 Begin spoke at Ari'el (a West Bank settlement) before a crowd of 35,000. He vowed no withdrawal from the territories. "I, Menahem, the son of Ze'ev and Hasia Begin do solemnly swear that as long as I serve the nation as prime minister, we will not leave any part of Judea, Samaria, the Gaza Strip and the Golan Heights." He warned that the Jordanian option (as proposed by Peres) meant surrendering to the terrorists and to "Arafatism" the mountain ridge of Samaria on which Ari'el is situated. "We want to live with the Arabs of Eretz Yisra'el as neighbors with mutual respect, but we will not surrender part of it to foreign sovereignty." Prospective minister of defense Ariel Sharon noted that the Likud had established 144 settlements during the past four years and said he hoped that, by the end of the next four years, "we will have quintupled the number of Jews living in Judea and Samaria" (*Jerusalem Post*, May 8, 1981, pp. 1, 2). Abba Eban's strong criticism of this perspective may be found in "What Kind of Israel," *Jerusalem Post*, May 29, 1981.

5. See, for example, the advertisement in *Yediot Aharonot*, May 22, 1981.

6. It was noted that, without consultation, Begin had committed Israel to an unprecedented military commitment—he pledged that the Israel Air Force would aid the Christians in northern Lebanon. "The undeniable fact is that Menachem Begin without authority, in an unprecedented move, committed Israel militarily. This was done in an irresponsible manner. Without prior consultation or reflection, without relying on any process of decision making, he committed the Israel Air Force to support the Christian forces in northern Lebanon. He thus placed a Syrian or Falangist finger on the trigger of the Israel Defence Forces. This man cannot be relied upon to bear the responsibility for the conduct of Israel's defence affairs" (*Jerusalem Post*, June 1, 1981).

7. See, for example, *Jerusalem Post Magazine*, June 5, 1981, p. 20.

8. This theme was repeated in numerous newspaper ads. See, for example, *Jerusalem Post*, June 2, 1981.

9. During the Begin-Peres television debate broadcast of June 25, Peres commented: "The Alignment explicitly states that the width of Israel's defense, the range of Israel's defense, must stretch from the Jordan River to the sea, and neither Katyushas nor Arab soldiers will be allowed to go into Judea, Samaria, and Gaza. . . . On the other hand, we have a second problem: There are 1.3 million Arabs. If the Herut Movement and Begin annex these 1.3 million Arabs to Israel, Israel will not be a Jewish state but rather be a binational state—maybe it will become Palestinian. This would be the end of the Zionist enterprise" (quoted from *FBIS*, June 26, 1981, pp. I7–I8). For further elaboration of these perspectives, see Shimon Peres, "A Strategy for Peace in the Middle East," *Foreign Affairs* (Spring 1980), pp. 887–901; and Shimon Peres, "Building Peace in the Middle East," *AEI Foreign Policy and Defense Review*, vol. 3, no. 1 (1981), pp. 14–19.

10. For elaboration of this perspective of territorial compromise, see Haim Bar-Lev, "To Each What Is Vital," *Jerusalem Post*, international ed., April 5–11, 1981.

11. Campaign ad, *Jerusalem Post*, international ed., June 14–20, 1981.

12. Ibid.

13. Ibid.

14. *Jerusalem Post*, June 19, 1981.

15. Ne'eman has said: "We will not join any government that does not stop the withdrawal from Sinai and prevent the uprooting of the settlements in the Rafiah Salient. We are not for abrogation of the treaty with Egypt, but we will insist on its revision" (*Jerusalem Post*, international ed., June 7–13, 1981).

16. *Jerusalem Post*, June 25, 1981; *FBIS*, June 25, 1981.

17. *Jerusalem Post*, June 25, 1981; *FBIS*, June 25, 1981.

18. After a visit to Saudi Arabia in April 1981, during which arms sales were discussed, West German Chancellor Helmut Schmidt stated that Germany had a moral commitment to "the Palestinians who escaped or fled from the West Bank." Israel protested to the German government. Begin attacked the German position and subsequently called Schmidt a hypocrite, observing that he sought to forget the German crimes against the Jewish people and charging him with being interested only in selling weapons at high prices and buying oil cheaply (*Jerusalem Post*, international ed., May 10–16, 1981). In the course of an interview, Begin commented that Schmidt had served in the German army during World War II and that he was "a good officer, a good warrior in the German Army until he was taken prisoner by the British. He has never violated his personal oath of loyalty to Führer Adolf Hitler" (*FBIS*, May 8, 1981, p. I5). Begin also attacked French President Valery Giscard d'Estaing: "It is known for a fact that this man does not have any principles whatsoever, only to sell arms to the Arabs and buy oil from them" (*FBIS*, May 8, 1981, p. I5). For further elaboration of Begin's comments, see his Independence Day interview for Israeli radio (May 7, 1981), in *FBIS*, May 8, 1981, pp. I4–16.

19. In early May Begin said that if Syria did not remove the missiles from Lebanon, "the Israeli Air Force will be given an instruction to operate—let nobody either in Israel or abroad doubt this—and when our air force operates it achieves results" (speech delivered at the Likud unification conference in early May, in *FBIS*, May 11, 1981, p. I1).

20. In an Independence Day interview, Begin responded in these terms to a question concerning a peaceful solution to the crisis on the northern border: "There is a chance that the problem will be solved either peacefully or in other ways . . . if this dispute is not solved through the diplomatic efforts by the United States and by many other countries, we will not be able to tolerate, under any circumstances, the positioning of those missiles on Lebanese territory and we will do what we have to do" (interview broadcast on Israeli radio, May 7, 1981, in *FBIS*, May 8, 1981, p. I1). In the television debate with Shimon Peres, Begin said: "Mr. Habib is here. We let him have time. . . . The political process should be exhausted. If the missiles are not removed by diplomatic moves, we will use military means to remove them completely from Lebanon" (ibid., p. I6). The debate was broadcast on June 25, 1981, and appears in *FBIS*, June 26, 1981.

21. See, for example, Shimon Peres's interview broadcast on Israeli radio May 29, 1981, in *FBIS*, June 2, 1981, pp. I4–16.

22. In their June 25 election debate, Peres noted, "Because of the elections, Mr. Begin invited As-Sadat 3 days prior to the bombing of the reactor and put him in an intolerable and unnecessary situation" (Israeli television, June 25, 1981; *FBIS*, June 26, 1981). See also Peres's comments to Israeli television on

May 28, in *FBIS*, May 29, 1981, pp. 16,17, and Peres's interview broadcast on Israeli radio May 29, 1981, in *FBIS*, June 2, 1981, pp. 16–18. Begin's rationale was articulated on IDF Radio May 28, in *FBIS*, May 29, 1981, pp. 12–14.

23. *FBIS*, June 9, 1981, p. 11.

24. See, for example, their exchanges on Israeli radio as published in *FBIS*, June 11, 1981, pp. 13–16.

25. The text of the letter was published in the *Jerusalem Post*, June 11, 1981.

26. The poll was conducted by the Modi'in Ezrachi Applied Research Centre for the *Jerusalem Post*.

27. Arens also noted: "We tried for two years to make the French and the Italians change their plans, and to get the United States to intervene to stop the Iraqi program. The announcement by the Socialists in France that they would stand by the past commitments was an important factor. Last September, when the Iranians tried to bomb the reactor and failed, the French and Italian experts left Iraq. There was a five months' hiatus. Then, in February, the French returned" (quoted in Robert Shaplan, "Letter from Israel," *New Yorker*, June 29, 1981, pp. 85–86). Arens also commented: "In my opinion, it was a situation of there being no other alternative. There was no way for a sensible decision, a decision based on concern for the security of the people of Israel, that could in any way have been different. This operation should have been performed and as soon as possible" (Arens interview on IDF Radio, June 9, 1981 in *FBIS*, June 10, 1981, p. 113).

28. Shaplen, "Letter from Israel," p. 86.

29. *Jerusalem Post*, international ed., June 14–20, 1981. See also Peres's comments on IDF Radio, June 9, 1981, in *FBIS*, June 10, 1981, pp. 113–114. In contrast to Peres, who was at first reticent in commenting on the attack, Rabin expressed his appreciation to the IDF and to the air force pilots for their success in the daring operation while withholding comment about the timing of the operation. Abba Eban also praised the IDF and the air force but suggested that the proper thing would have been for the operation to be determined by the new government after the June 30 elections.

30. Quoted in Shaplen, "Letter from Israel," p. 86. In his election debate with Begin, Peres noted: "As regards the reactor, I have no doubt that Iraq wants a nuclear bomb. I have no doubt that Israel must act against the nuclear bomb. I have fundamentally different opinions regarding the best way to prevent Iraq from having a nuclear bomb but I will not go into this" (*FBIS*, June 26, 1981, p. 11).

31. See Shaplen, "Letter from Israel," pp. 86–88.

32. For the full text of the debate as broadcast on Israeli television, see *FBIS*, June 26, 1981, pp. 11–19.

33. In an interview published in *Al-Hamishmar* on June 26, 1981, Peres commented on the link between developments and the election in these terms: "It is obvious today that the meeting with President as-Sadat in Ofira, three days before the bombing of the Iraqi reactor, was also intended for election purposes. The downing of the two helicopters . . . also happened."

34. "Fundamental Policy Guidelines of the Government of Israel As Approved by the Knesset on 5 August 1981," text provided by Israel Information Centre, Jerusalem.

35. In a speech to the Knesset, Begin spoke of a number of other international issues and expressed the hope that relations between Israel and France would improve with the election of François Mitterrand, whom he described as "a friend of Israel"—in marked contrast to Begin's election campaign comments about Mitterrand's predecessor. His comments concerning the Soviet

Union elicited attention: "We are in favour of the normalization of relations between ourselves and the Soviet Union. Our regimes are different; let each go its own way. However, normal relations are possible even between countries which maintain regimes that are fundamentally different." The initiative, however, would have to come from the Soviet Union, which had broken relations with Israel in 1967. No further elaboration was provided.

36. Tehiya is a party of true believers focusing on the Land of Israel with an ideological fervor reminiscent of Israel's political parties in the early years of independence and before. It is composed of both religious and secular elements and appeals strongly to Israel's youth. It has a component from Gush Emunim, and two prominent leaders of the Gush (Hanan Porat and Gershon Shafat) helped to found it and work actively for it. Various secularists and secular-oriented groupings are also involved. Tehiya includes old associates of Begin from the Mandate period underground. Former Herut member of the Knesset Guela Cohen is a prominent member and was joined by Knesset member Moshe Shamir. Various Land of Israel movement personalities have also joined. Tehiya's origins trace to the Camp David Accords (which party members would like to see revised in favor of a more hard-line stance) and the peace treaty with Egypt, which called for a total withdrawal by Israel from Sinai and commitment to autonomy for the Palestinians. Tehiya's members were traumatized by the accords and the treaty and believed that Begin had sold them out. The party's head is Yuval Ne'eman (a physicist from Tel Aviv University), a leading nuclear scientist with a longstanding role in the defense establishment. He firmly believes that Israel needs to retain all of the occupied territories.

37. In the 1981 elections the Likud received approximately 37.1 percent of the vote, and the Alignment secured 36.6 percent. Tehiya achieved the third highest proportion (6.3 percent). See *Jerusalem Post*, July 6, 1981. Much of this vote reflects the high proportion of eighteen- to twenty-one-year-old conscripts in the IDF.

38. *Ha'aretz*, July 14, 1978.

39. *Newsview*, May 31, 1981, p. 14.

40. Ibid.

41. See, for example, *Ha'aretz*, April 7, 1978. Arens voted against the Camp David Accords in the Knesset.

42. Quoted in *New York Times*, October 6, 1981.

43. Quoted in *New York Times*, November 10, 1981.

44. Quoted in *New York Times*, October 30, 1981.

45. See note 34.

46. "Statement: Address by Prime Minister Yitzhak Shamir in the Knesset Announcing the Formation of the Government, 10 October 1983," Israel Ministry of Foreign Affairs, Information Division, Jerusalem.

47. *Jerusalem Post*, international ed., December 4–10, 1983.

X

BEGIN'S TWO-YEAR GOVERNMENT

Daniel J. Elazar

Menachem Begin came to life for the election campaign and demonstrated once again what an awesomely effective politician he is in the Israeli context. He then continued to demonstrate his political skills in the negotiations surrounding the formation of a governing coalition as well. For a brief time, the religious parties perceived themselves to be even stronger than the number of seats they won because of the 48–48 tie between the Likud and the Ma'arach and began to present extraordinary demands. Begin succeeded in quashing those demands to which he was opposed by refusing to give in to them and by threatening to call new elections.

While the new government had the formal support of only 61 of the 120 members of the Knesset, it turned out to be even stronger in certain ways than Begin's previous government because there was less variance in views on key issues among the coalition partners than there had been before. This was especially true of the key figures in the government. Begin, Yitzhak Shamir as foreign minister, and Ariel Sharon as defense minister represented a far more united team than Begin, Dayan, and Ezer Weizman four years earlier. The power of Yoram Aridor and David Levy in their respective ministries of finance and housing also added to Begin's strength.

Moreover, Menachem Begin knew how to govern in the sense that he treated a majority of one as if it were a landslide, and was not inhibited by a small margin. (One of the problems of Shimon Peres is that he has acted in just the reverse fashion. He was never able to act as if he were the leader of his party, despite his overwhelming majority within its caucuses.) After the Israeli withdrawal from the rest of Sinai in April 1982, Tehiya and Telem joined the government in order to help prevent a withdrawal from Judea, Samaria, and Gaza, raising its margin of support in the Knesset.

The Evacuation of Eastern Sinai

Begin and his government went through the excruciatingly painful process of evacuating the eastern Sinai area on schedule, engaging in direct confrontation with settlers in the area and their supporters who conducted a physical struggle, at times violent, against their evacuation. Ariel Sharon, who was appointed defense minister in the second Begin government despite Begin's own strong reservations regarding his appropriateness for the post (Begin was quoted as saying that, as minister of defense, Sharon would not hesitate to send tanks to surround the Knesset and stage a coup if he thought he could get away with it), played a double game. On one hand, he instructed the Israel Defense Forces (IDF) in the area to allow opponents of the withdrawal from other parts of the country to cross into the Sinai through IDF controlled areas, while on the other hand he fully implemented the government's evacuation policy. The best explanation for his seemingly contradictory behavior was that he, like many others in the government, wanted an appropriate but limited confrontation in Sinai so as to make it impossible for any Israeli government to evacuate settlements in Judea, Samaria, and Gaza in the future.

Indeed, most of those actively opposing the Sinai evacuation were members of Gush Emunim or settlers from the territories who also saw the Sinai as a place to make their stand so as to prevent future concessions by the Israeli government in historic Eretz Yisrael. The end result was a curiously Israeli kind of confrontation. Regular Army officers applied for leaves of absence, took off their uniforms, and, as civilians, joined those holding out in the settlements. The demonstrators were under IDF siege until the very end and were only removed by a military assault, but the assault was played out according to rules that kept it virtually bloodless, with people fighting with their fists rather than with weapons. Even Meir Kahane's *Kach* contingent, who threatened to blow themselves up in their bunker, were ultimately evacuated peacefully. Tears were shed on all sides as the assault was successfully concluded. The settlements, including the city of Yamit, were leveled, and the settlers and their supporters were evacuated to the other side of the international border. People from both sides embraced each other, weeping. The civilians went back to their other pursuits, including their own settlements in the territories, and the handful of soldiers on leave put their uniforms back on and went back to their regular duties. Sad, even tragic, as the whole business was, it was a tremendous reaffirmation of the health and solidarity of Israeli society and of the strength of its democratic institutions. The most uncomfortable note in the process was the huge compensation which the government agreed to pay the evacuees, about which there was a great deal of discomfiture in the rest of the country.

With the evacuation completed, the Egyptians sent an ambassador to Tel Aviv, but the peace rapidly became a cold peace and no more. The Egyptians indicated that they were not interested in more than correct relations and, after Sadat was assassinated, his successor, Hosni Mubarak, used every pretext to reduce their scope in his efforts to begin a rapprochement with the rest of the Arab world. Israelis flocked to Egypt while the Egyptians did not (or were not allowed to) flock to Israel in turn. An Israeli interuniversity office to promote scientific research and cooperation with Egyptian scientists was established in Cairo, but very little else emerged in the way of active links between the two countries. When Israel invaded Lebanon two months after the withdrawal from Sinai, the Egyptians withdrew their ambassador. He had not returned by the end of 1983 and, in fact, the Egyptians have indicated he will not do so "without the approval of the Egyptian people" even after the Israeli withdrawal from Lebanon.

The Likud's Domestic Agenda

On the domestic front, Begin's second government was at once more single-minded, more experienced, and more rapacious in pursuit of control over the bureaucracy than his first. It was single-minded in its pursuit of an Eretz Yisrael embracing the entire land west of the Jordan, and in its efforts to weaken if not destroy the PLO. It was more experienced in its handling of domestic affairs, particularly the economy, industrial development, and intercommunal relations.

The new government was more rapacious in that it sought to entrench itself further in the public offices of the country. The desire of the Likud party faithful, particularly those of Herut, to gain offices was manifest from the very first in 1977, but that appetite, if anything, had grown. More people had risen within the party to the point that they were confident they could handle these jobs. As the way in which

Labor-oriented bureaucracies worked to frustrate government policies had become apparent, the pressure to strengthen Likud representation in all facets of public life increased.

This effort to fill public positions was not simply a matter of spoils. Israel still has not fully accepted the idea of a neutral civil service. The jobs of civil servants are protected by law, but the civil servants themselves are barely required to maintain neutrality. After more than a generation of Labor rule, during which party ties were of crucial importance in obtaining public positions, Israel's public sector was thoroughly dominated by people who owed allegiance to the Labor Alignment. During the first four years of Likud rule, most incumbents made little effort to conceal their Labor ties, and in many cases they continued to use their offices to advance Labor's interests in opposition to those of the government in power. The Likud, therefore, felt that it had to make as many personnel changes as it could in government offices, in the national institutions, and in public organizations and public companies simply to protect itself and to advance its policies.

Operation Peace for Galilee

Even before completing the withdrawal from Sinai, the Begin government had turned its attention to the strength of the PLO presence in Lebanon. That presence had two implications. Most directly, the PLO had begun intermittent massive shelling of Jewish settlements in the Galilee. Given the size of the country and the range of the new PLO arms, this action threatened almost the entire region, obviously an intolerable situation from the Israeli point of view. Moreover, the apparent regularization of the PLO military forces, which this development seemed to reflect and which was given maximum publicity by the PLO itself, suggested to the Palestinian Arab residents of Judea, Samaria, and Gaza that the balance of power was shifting in their favor and the time had come for them to more actively demonstrate their hostility to the Israeli occupation.

The renewed activity of Arab residents was further stimulated by the somewhat draconian policies of Defense Minister Ariel Sharon, who, despite a series of initial promises to respect Arab rights and a formal move to transfer authority from a military to a civil government in the territories, actually raised the level of military intervention in the daily life of the Arab townsmen in an effort to strengthen Arab forces hostile to the PLO. The end result was much increased

tension in the territories and heightened expectations of the local inhabitants that the PLO might indeed be able to deliver them from the
Israelis.

A brief war between Israeli forces and the PLO around the time of
the 1981 elections ended in an indirectly negotiated cease-fire, which
the PLO kept along the Lebanese border. The cease-fire, however,
was violated by Arab terrorists, under PLO direction or otherwise, on
Israel's eastern border with Jordan, which had been at peace since before the Yom Kippur War, and through a series of assaults on Israeli
government officials in Europe. By January 1982, Sharon had decided that Lebanon should be invaded and the PLO concentration
there wiped out. While he was able to persuade Begin of the necessity
of this course of action, other members of the Begin government, notably Interior Minister Yosef Burg of the National Religious party
and, apparently, Housing Minister David Levy as well, managed to
prevent the necessary cabinet approval. The matter was brought up
repeatedly in the six months between January and June, but each time
it was rejected. It was not until June, when Palestinian terrorists shot
and critically wounded Israel's ambassador to Britain in London, that
Sharon was able to carry the day with the government.

Israel's Operation Peace for Galilee, as it was named, began at mid-
night on June 6 and quickly escalated into a full-scale war. The PLO
"army" turned out to be much less than its publicity notices indicated,
and the IDF quickly cleaned out southern Lebanon and, following
Sharon's grand strategy, advanced on Beirut. At that point the war became the focus of a series of controversies, external and internal.
American support, which was principally offered by then Secretary
of State Alexander Haig, over the opposition of Defense Secretary
Caspar Weinberger, diminished drastically as Israel passed the 25-
mile line in its advance northward. Haig, who had apparently indicated his tacit support for the Israeli invasion on the assumption that
it would only secure southern Lebanon, resigned as secretary of state,
and the American government pressured Israel to lessen its military
effort, thereby leading to a protracted "siege" of the PLO in Beirut
that brought about the PLO's evacuation in early September.

In the interim, in Israel proper, the same set of events led to the
emergence of opposition to the war, especially by the Labor Alignment and its supporters. Sharon's obvious adventurism and his desire
to clear the PLO and the Syrians from all of Lebanon, the fact that
expected Lebanese Christian cooperation failed to materialize, and
the mounting Israeli casualties strengthened this opposition. The

Christian Phalangists, who were supposed to join Israel in the effort, sat back and let the Israelis do their fighting for them. From the beginning, Israel received negative publicity when PLO sympathizers succeeded in getting their version of the war into the Western media. The situation deteriorated further during the "siege" of Beirut when Israeli air and artillery attacks caused civilian casualties while seeking to hit the PLO, who, in their usual way, were shielding their troops behind the local civilian population. That the extent of the casualties and destruction caused by the IDF was greatly exaggerated by the PLO and the media did not become known until later. Finally, Israelis had become used to short wars and this one stretched beyond anything since the War of Liberation in 1948–49.

Matters came to a head after the PLO evacuation of Beirut when Christian Phalangists, taking advantage of the IDF victory, massacred Palestinian civilians in the Sabra and Shatilla refugee camps, virtually under the eyes of the Israelis. Several hundred Palestinians (the exact number will never be known) were killed before the Israelis managed to get the Phalangists out of the camps. This was followed by a strong reaction against Israel throughout the world and against the Israeli government within Israel itself. While Begin rejected the world's protests in typical Begin fashion, seeing them as illegitimate in the wake of the Holocaust and interpreting them as motivated by anti-Semitism, the Israeli public's demands could not be so easily rejected. After a brief five-day attempt to avoid appointing a formal investigatory commission with full powers, the Begin government was forced to give in to public opinion, which was manifested in various ways, ranging from a demonstration of several thousand antigovernment Israelis in Tel Aviv on the Saturday night following the massacre to a revolt within the government itself by its Sephardic members and the National Religious party ministers.

Who Really Brought About the Massacre Investigations?

Nothing could have done more to tarnish Israel's world image in the wake of the tragic Phalangist massacre of Palestinians in Beirut than the massive demonstration of several hundred thousand Israelis in Tel Aviv a week after those terrible events. Nevertheless, sophisticated observers of Israeli politics knew that what brought Menachem Begin to accept a full-scale investigatory commission was not that gathering—which Begin interpreted as strictly a Labor opposition ploy—but the opposition which he incurred within his government and ruling coalition. Not only did one minister, Yitzhak Berman, resign in what was essentially an individual act, but the National Religious party (Mafdal) leadership in its entirety came to the threshold of resigning. This threat extracted a promise from Begin that the right thing would be done, and in effect it forced Defense Minister Ariel Sharon to go on national television and announce that he was for a full-fledged investigatory commission.

Even more important in bringing about the investigation was the revolt of the Sephardic members of the government. David Levy, deputy prime minister and minister of housing and absorption, the strong man of the Herut party organization, made his outrage over the massacre and his dissatisfaction with the defense minister's explanation eminently clear from the first. Indeed, he had strongly opposed Sharon's policies during the entire summer and even before. He was joined by Aharon Uzan of Tami, the Abu-Hatzeira-led party that broke away from the Mafdal in 1981 to mobilize North African Sephardic voters on a platform combining communal aspirations and Jewish tradition. Most vocal of all was Mordechai Ben-Porat, who succeeded Moshe Dayan as the head of Telem and whose letter to the prime minister publicly calling for a proper investigatory commission stated the central question that needed to be answered. Indeed, of the Sephardim in the cabinet, only Justice Minister Moshe Nissim remained silent, as he invariably has done on all issues, speaking out only at the end in connection with the execution of the cabinet's decision.

While no one who understood the Sephardic population of Israel should have been surprised by all of this, it helped give the lie to the kind of myth propagated by certain Ashkenazim, particularly intellectuals of the Labor camp, who suggest there is a difference in moral character between "easterners" and the Ashkenazic "westerners." It may be reassuring to those Labor intellectuals, who perceive themselves as having become a minority in the country, to create a self-serving myth that they are somehow superior to the new majority, and that whatever the country's problems, they are the result of government by the representatives of the "great unwashed." It also happens to be an utterly false mythology. On the issue of the Beirut massacre, no differences could be detected between the responses of the Sephardim and Ashkenazim. The overwhelming majority of all Israelis were shocked, horrified, and desirous of a full investigation.

It was noted that few Sephardim were visible at the huge demonstration led by the Alliance in Tel Aviv on June 25. While that assumes that Sephardim look sufficiently different from Ashkenazim as to stand out among hundreds of thousands of demonstrators, it is probably true that they were underrepresented at what was, in essence, an opposition rally. Given Sephardic hostility toward the opposition, they could not bring themselves to be present. Moreover, since most of Sephardic power was with the existing government, they were able to make that power felt more effectively in ways other than by participating in a demonstration.

A Turning Point for the Sephardim?

Nevertheless, the way the Sephardim spoke out may indeed be a turning point in Israeli politics. The massacre was an issue in which the Sephardim in the coalition could find an independent voice and did not need to remain deputies of Begin, Sharon, and Shamir. Once found, that independent voice is not likely to be stilled on other issues. Indeed, within the month, David Levy and Aharon Uzan led the opposition within the cabinet against the dissolution of El Al, against Transport Minister Haim Corfu and Finance Minister Yoram Aridor. Moreover, they forced a compromise decision on the issue.

For the first time, David Levy began to be considered seriously as a possible successor to Begin, a far cry from the public perception of him in 1977 when the Begin government took office and the country abounded with David Levy jokes similar to Polish jokes in America. Indeed, a year later he emerged as Yitzhak Shamir's principal rival for prime minister after Begin resigned. Whether or not the deputy prime minister is ready for such an assignment at this particular moment or could win the post were the opportunity to present itself again in the near future is another question. But he has become a serious contender.

At the same time, in the Labor party the fight between Shimon Peres and Yitzhak Rabin was barely papered over, and it was widely known that behind them there were three or four others ready to join the fight for position and potential office. Peres's rapid embrace of President Ronald Reagan's plan for Israeli withdrawal from Beirut did not help him to convince the unconverted; many of those who might have agreed with his stance felt that it was unseemly for the leader of the opposition to take that stance the way he did. Begin, in response, reminded Israelis of the way in which his party, when it was in opposition, remained loyal to the government in power on similar foreign policy issues, in contrast to the Peres approach. Right or wrong, it was an effective argument.

Peres made a brilliant speech in the Knesset to open the debate over how to respond to the Beirut massacre. On that podium his best qualities shone forth, but they were not enough to overcome what happened off that platform. In a subsequent appearance in Kiryat Shmona, where he had been warned that hecklers would try to prevent him from speaking, he was indeed prevented from appearing. This episode helped him only with his existing constituents. Everyone else, led by President Yitzhak Navon and Prime Minister Begin, condemned what they perceived as an effort by a faltering Peres to deliberately provoke a tiny minority of the disaffected, most of whom were Sephardim, in order to put all Sephardim in a bad light.

When all is said and done, the Labor camp has become Israel's Bourbons, learning nothing and forgetting nothing. Americans are likely to note that their penchant for nostalgia for a world that never was and the program that they are advocating as a result are reminiscent of the politics of the so-called White Anglo-Saxon Protestants (WASPs) in the United States in the years just prior to World War I. When confronted by the realities of an immigrant population beginning to come to political power, the WASPs sought refuge in a distorted attempt to go back to what were presumed to be the good old days of the early republic and that ended up in Prohibition and Isolationism, as part of a moral crusade to cleanse the American "great unwashed" of that time. It brought the WASPs to political disaster in the United States of two generations ago, and it is bringing the Labor camp to disaster now.

Yitzhak Navon is the one bright light on the Labor horizon. The then-president of Israel shone forth in the aftermath of the Beirut massacre as a strong beacon to the country and the world. It is hard to overestimate the importance of what Navon did in speaking out as president to coalesce and crystallize the overwhelming Israeli opinion about what needed to be done. Indeed, this was only an additional manifestation of how he quietly raised the importance of the presidency as a moral force on the Israeli scene. While other presidents may have been more distinguished as scholars, scientists, or intellectuals, he was the best at "presidenting," and since this was perceived by one and all, he became and remains extraordinarily popular.

Needless to say, this brought calls from many corners of the Labor camp that Navon be brought in by the party to replace Peres at the head of the party's ticket. No doubt he weighed that alternative among others, since his term as president expired in April 1984. Navon returned to active politics, but contrary to the expectation of some, he did not seek the leadership of the Alignment.

There is, of course, no guarantee that Navon can magically restore Labor's voting majority. Those who pushed for his candidacy were Ashkenazim, many of whom had earlier supported Yigael Yadin's ill-fated Democratic Movement for Change, and who believed that Navon, as a Sephardi, would attract other Sephardim to his banner. Many Sephardim outside of the Labor camp saw this as a move that could discredit Navon and that would not persuade them to abandon the Likud or NRP to support a still-insensitive Labor party.

Begin and Sharon: The Crisis of Confidence

The Beirut massacre shook public confidence in Begin and ended any confidence the public may have had in Sharon. The Prime Minister seems to have implicitly understood this: witness the fact that he virtually ceased to appear in public or speak out in any way after that fateful Rosh Hashana. Sharon also understood it but his tactic was to appear everywhere to try to rebuild his shattered position. Begin sought a way to jettison Sharon, whose defective character had become apparent to one and all, even to those who admire his talents. He found it in the report of the Kahan Commission, which conducted the investigation.

While the people lost confidence in the Begin government, they would have voted to reelect Begin and his coalition, had the elections been held, principally because they did not see Labor or any other party as a reasonable alternative. For most voters, the election would have rested upon negative choices, as have the last two, a vote for the least displeasing. Here, too, there was little distinction between Sephardim and Ashkenazim. There were those who voted Labor because they were repelled by Begin. Despite the television images of many Sephardic voters (mostly teens) chanting "Begin, King of Israel," most Sephardim voted for Begin because they were repelled by Peres and Labor, not because they had any great confidence in Begin.

Little of this has been reflected in the polls because of the way the pollsters ask their questions. If one asks people for whom would they vote, or a simple question such as "Are you satisfied with the present government?", then the answers are invariably going to show a higher level of support than is really the case. With regard to the first question, even largely dissatisfied people intended to vote for Begin, for the aforementioned reasons. In the case of the second, satisfaction with the government depends on more than one aspect of its performance. Even so, the public opinion poll surveys show that support for the Begin government had dropped.

In the interim between the massacres and the Kahan Commission report, Begin maintained a dignified silence, compounded by his grief at the death of his wife and no doubt reflecting his own moral discomfort at what happened in the two camps. His appearance before the investigating commission showed him at his best—Menachem Begin, the democrat and constitutionalist, playing his role in strengthening the legitimate and vital instruments of constitutional government. Ariel Sharon, on the other hand, worked frantically to restore his image and status—appearing everywhere, engineering situations in which he had to be well-received, seeking bogeymen against whom only he could defend Israel, while trying to play a statesman's role in bringing peace to Israel's northern border. The more he tried, the less worthy of public confidence he seemed. He lost his ministry in the aftermath of the commission report but was retained in the government, either because Begin felt he had to or to neutralize Sharon by preventing him from attacking the government from the outside.

Problems in the Coalition Ranks

Only a new election could have cleared the air. No doubt Begin would have gone to the polls confident that he would have been returned, but he was held back by his coalition partners, who remained properly fearful that they would suffer additional setbacks, as reflected in the polls. Ironically, the "good guys" in this whole business had lost the confidence of many of their voters for other reasons, while support for the seemingly culpable ones apparently increased. Again, this was because voters make their decisions at the polls in response to a whole complex of issues, including the character and personality of those for whom they are asked to vote, and in the case of the smaller parties, the party leaders do not have the confidence of sufficient numbers of their potential publics.

As of this writing, the problems which existed since the 1981 elections remain real ones. The NRP is in particularly difficult straits. Its three leaders, Interior Minister Yosef Burg, Education Minister Zevulun Hammer, and Deputy Foreign Minister Yehuda Ben-Meir, have all lost the confidence of many potential Mafdal voters, each in his own way. Burg is perceived as a man who will do anything to hold his cabinet seat. He, indeed, was the weakest in speaking out against the prime minister and on behalf of an investigatory commission, and his weak response was perceived as being part of an overall syndrome of not wanting to be out of office.

Zevulun Hammer is in an ambiguous position. He won a great deal of support from the nonreligious public as well as his religious constituency for his courageous stand and for subsequently speaking out against the tendency to emphasize the land of Israel over the people of Israel. Indeed, he is considered one of those who helped restore the role of religious Jews as the consciences of the nation. He is also rated as one of the best education ministers that Israel has ever had and is the government's most popular minister according to the public opinion polls. On the other hand, over the years he has lost the confidence of the NRP rank and file in much the same way that Shimon Peres has lost the confidence of his. The internal politics of trying to advance within the party led him to lose credibility, especially with the Sephardi voters in the Mafdal who represent a majority and who were particularly instrumental in raising him to the party leadership.

Ben-Meir, as Hammer's loyal partner in all of this, has the image of a political deal-maker among all segments of the population. To the extent that he has been publicly identified as making the deals for Hammer, he suffers doubly.

The party leadership has been challenged from the right by Yosef Shapira, former head of Bnei Akiva, the party's youth movement, and by Rabbi Haim Druckman, the party's leading Land of Israel militant. It may be challenged by a group of Sephardim who are centrist in their political orientation and could be the strongest supporters of Hammer's new stance, were they to have confidence in him personally. Should Hammer and Ben-Meir be able to overcome these difficulties, particularly by bringing the Sephardim into positions of real power, they could rebuild the party and emerge as very strong figures in Israeli politics overall. However, there are few, if any, signs that they will be able to do so, because of intraparty constraints, despite their concerted efforts to enunciate a more moderate NRP position on the foreign policy and security questions of the day. If Hammer has the strength of character to break out of his present fix, it will be a sign that he is ready for bigger and better things. If not, he will simply remain a coalition partner, perhaps on a more limited basis.

Conflicts within Agudat Israel

Agudat Israel has also been thrown into something of a crisis by
events, although its voting strength is not likely to decline since its
rank and file vote *en bloc* as their leadership directs. The crisis is within
the leadership itself. The party always has tended to be more compromising with regard to the future Israeli presence in Judea, Samaria,
and Gaza, but the Lebanon operation, the Beirut massacre, and resultant world response led to a split between those who are in every respect "doves" and who see the present government's policies as provoking the Gentile world and thereby endangering the Jewish people,
and those who would still like to see the continuation of a Jewish presence in the administered territories, even if not endorsing the position
of the present government. Moreover, the economic crisis of late 1983
has placed the party in an exposed position with regard to its demands on the state treasury. Finally, in the municipal elections of
1983, the Sephardic members of AI in Jerusalem broke away to run
their own list (the Sephardic Torah Guardians), in response to the
heavy discrimination against them in a super Ashkenazic party where
Yiddish remains the language of business at the higher echelons. In
an upset, the Sephardic Torah Guardians won three seats on the city
council and indicated that they were considering running a list in the
next Knesset elections.

Lesser Parties

Tami at the Crossroads

By the summer of 1983, Tami, when confronted by serious choices a
year earlier, had made the wrong ones. Hence it had not grown and,
indeed, was fighting for its life. Its leader, Aharon Abu-Hatzeira, was
serving a prison term as a result of his conviction for misuse of public
funds. In the fall, the economic crisis gave it some measure of hope as
it seized the populist issue of protecting the weaker elements in the
society against the government's belt-tightening economic measures.
Thus, none of the smaller coalition parties wanted to go to the polls in
the near future. All would have liked more time to improve their
fortunes.

A New Center Party?

No doubt the most publicly courageous of the cabinet members following the Beirut massacre was Minister of Energy Yitzhak Berman, a leader of the Liberal party within the Likud. Berman actually resigned his cabinet position as a result of the massacre and voted against the government in the Knesset, endorsing a full investigation. He was supported by his young Liberal colleague, Dror Zeigerman, and there was talk that the two of them would try to form a new center party to compete with the Likud and the Labor Alignment.

In principle, a center party should do well, since most Israeli voters today are centrists by inclination. But no such party is in the offing. The best name they could come up with to lead the party is former Defense Minister Ezer Weizman, formerly of Herut, who was cut down by Begin in the latter half of the Likud's first term of office, and who has since been out of active politics. Weizman would no doubt be delighted to make a comeback, but he is not sufficiently popular with the public, most of whom perceive him as a very amiable fellow but not of stern enough mettle to be prime minister and represent Israel in negotiations with friends and foes alike, both of whom are pressing Israel forcefully to make concessions which few Israelis want to make.

Moreover, Weizman has no real support among the Sephardim, where he is simply perceived as another member of the old Ashkenazi establishment. True enough, some of the leaders of Tami, particularly among their anti-Begin diaspora sponsors, periodically push for a Weizman-Tami-Liberal linkage to create a center party. Negotiations to that effect go on sporadically but they do not appear to have any visible support from other Israeli party leaders.

Events move so rapidly in Israel and the Middle East that it would be unwise to rule out a Labor victory, were something else to happen like the Beirut massacre. Failing that, however, Labor is condemned to the wilderness by its own hand. No center party is likely to emerge, and the Likud is likely to continue dominant if not particularly popular. Therefore the real question becomes, who will dominate the Likud for the foreseeable future?

From Begin to Shamir: The Implications of Herut's Succession Struggle

Menachem Begin's decision to resign from his post as prime minister brought to the surface long latent questions about the future of Herut, the party he had founded and dominated for thirty-five years. Fore-most among these questions was whether Herut would be able to con-tinue functioning as a united party or whether it would fragment into quarreling factions in the absence of Begin's leadership. Herut's ability to face up to its first major post-Begin challenge—choosing his suc-cessor—gives us an indication of the party's viability and direction in the near future. The party's choice of Foreign Minister Yitzhak Shamir over Deputy Prime Minister David Levy provided Herut with a smooth transition which left only surface scars among the top leader-ship and indicated that Herut's membership still adheres closely to the basic positions pursued by Begin. Whether he had fully intended it or not, Menachem Begin submitted his resignation two weeks after his seventieth birthday (according to the Western calendar), thereby ful-filling a longstanding promise. Whatever the reasons behind it, the fact of the resignation coming at a time when the Prime Minister was obviously incapable of continuing to function was a salutary act. Even more salutary was the way in which the Likud came together to choose his successor, fairly, democratically, and with grace.

For years the political pundits emphasized the likelihood that the Likud and even Herut would fall apart once Begin departed from the scene. They claimed that the party was so much his creature that it could not survive the loss of his personal leadership. Begin's author-ity over Herut had been so complete that during his tenure he was approved time and again as party leader by acclamation, without a general vote in the central committee. The only challenges to Begin's control of Herut—by Shmuel Tamir in 1964 and by Ezer Weizman in 1977—were both crushed, with the result that Begin emerged stronger than before. Moreover, Begin was careful not to groom any successors and, indeed, to cut down any potential rivals within his party. Those who suggested that Herut had acquired a wider base, particularly in the years since their first electoral victory in 1977, and a group of potential contenders worthy of the title, despite the Prime Minister's best efforts, were looked upon with great skepticism.

Even without Begin's encouragement, by June of 1982 there were five contenders for his job. Within the government itself, Defense Minister Ariel Sharon was the most aggressive in his pursuit of the office and presumably the most popular member of the government other than Begin himself. Rumor had it that Foreign Minister Yitzhak Shamir was Begin's choice. Finance Minister Yoram Aridor, secretary-general of the Herut Party Executive and architect of the 1981 Likud victory, who opened the floodgates of consumption in Israel, saw him-self as one who could almost buy his way into the prime ministership.

Housing Minister David Levy, the strong man of the Herut Party organization, was just becoming a contender, as his talents began to be recognized by ever-wider segments of the public. Finally, Moshe Arens, then Israel's ambassador to the United States, had quietly launched his pursuit of the office by building up a cadre of supporters within the party.

The Peace of Galilee operation proved to be the graveyard for the political ambitions of Ariel Sharon. As it became apparent that his reach had exceeded his grasp, his popularity began to decline, and then to plummet after the Lebanese Christian massacre of the Palestinians in September 1982. While he will never give up his striving for the prime ministership, he was effectively knocked out of contention by his own mistakes. In the meantime, Sharon had succeeded in knocking Shamir out of contention at the time by eliminating him from the foreign affairs aspects of the Lebanon operation early in its course. Sharon seized control of the negotiations surrounding the Lebanese conflict, leaving Shamir nowhere to be seen.

In the fall of 1982, despite murmurings against his policy, Aridor still thought he was in the running, although, in fact, the added economic burdens of the Lebanese operation had already sealed his fate. David Levy's stand with regard to the necessity for a full-fledged investigation of what happened in Sabra and Shatilla, plus the information that reached the public about his earlier stand in the Cabinet trying to limit the extent of the Lebanese operation, made him a serious contender in the eyes of the public for the first time, but still not one strong enough to assert a clear claim to the office.

Then in February 1983, the removal of Sharon from the post of defense minister in the wake of the Kahan Commission report opened the door for the fifth contender, Moshe Arens, to return to Israel to replace Sharon at the Defense Ministry. Given his own ambitions, Arens clearly had to be considered a contender from that moment on, but because he was not a member of the Knesset (he had to resign to accept the ambassadorship) he could not be an active contender until the next elections. Arens strengthened his position as a result of his extraordinarily effective performance in the Defense Ministry from his first day in office. In the meantime he also brought Shamir back into the picture by convincing Begin to send the foreign minister to Washington to try to resume the U.S.-Israel dialogue which had suffered so much all during that fall and winter. In one fell swoop, Arens undercut Sharon's last possible power position and brought in Shamir as his preferred interim candidate until he could make his own bid.

Meanwhile, Aridor's antagonistic behavior during the doctors' strike further weakened his public image, virtually eliminating him from contention. His situation continued to worsen as the economy went from bad to worse as a result of his policies. So it was well-nigh inevitable that, when Begin announced his resignation, Shamir and Levy should appear as the two leading contenders for the succession.

What followed was no surprise on one level, but a very pleasant surprise on another. On the first level, Arens, looking to protect his future against a competitor whose relative youth and strong party position would have made him very difficult to remove once he was in the prime minister's office, and Sharon and Aridor, both hoping that their fortunes would be reversed in the future, all united behind Shamir, whose age and lack of party base made him an ideal interim candidate in their eyes to hold the position until one of them was ready to make his move.

The above three cabinet ministers joined all of the other Herut ministers, except for Levy himself, in support for Shamir's candidacy. In fact, Shamir attempted to gain a unanimous endorsement from the Herut ministers in order to present a *fait accompli* so that no election would be necessary. Thus, a massive coalition confronted David Levy and his supporters. Levy, however, held out against his fellow ministers and forced the decision into the nine-hundred-member central committee.

The significance of Levy's action reached beyond the immediate framework of his contest with Shamir. In effect, it marked the culmination of a process of internal democratization within Herut. This process had begun in 1977, when the party decided to choose its Knesset delegation by a vote of the four-hundred-member party convention rather than by decision of the fifteen-member appointments committee. Levy's persistence meant that Herut's central committee had to conduct the first secret ballot leadership vote in the party's history.

Levy had reason to believe that his chances of winning the vote were favorable. Because of his years of experience as head of the party's Histadrut faction, he enjoyed a strong measure of popularity within the central committee. Indeed, during the 1981 party convention Levy had outpolled Shamir and had been chosen as number two man on the party list. Furthermore, in the months preceding Begin's resignation, Levy's abilities as deputy prime minister had earned him the reputation of an effective manager of domestic policy.

Shamir, however, enjoyed many advantages over his rival. Foremost among these was the strong support he received from his fellow ministers, who used their influence to obtain votes for Shamir in the central committee. A further advantage was Shamir's expertise in foreign affairs in contrast to Levy's inexperience in that field. Moreover, Shamir's experience as commander of Lehi (*Lohamei Herut Yisrael*— the Stern group) during the prestate struggle for independence earned him the support of Herut's old guard of underground fighters. Finally, Shamir's hard-line positions regarding the administered territories and the Palestinian question drew the hardliners to him rather than to the more moderate Levy.

Before the voting, the two candidates took pains to indicate that regardless of the outcome they both would be able to continue working together in the same cabinet. Each candidate offered the post of deputy prime minister to his opponent in the event of victory.

The party leaders decided that the best way to resolve the competition between the two candidates was through an open, free, and fair election in which all factions and subfactions of the party would have the opportunity to vote. The contest was conducted according to the rules, in the best sense of the term, and in such a way that the party and relationships among its leaders would be minimally damaged. Issues were confronted directly and attacks on persons were avoided. When the election was held, Shamir with his grand coalition won by almost a two-to-one margin, which surprised many, but, in fact, demonstrated what great strength Levy had developed over the years, especially in light of his starting point as the butt of crude jokes reflecting his Moroccan origins. Most important of all, good relations were preserved among all the participants, so much so that in the aftermath of the vote, Shamir could ask Levy to undertake the task of putting together the coalition which he needed to form a government.

Herut came out of the succession struggle much strengthened as a party and in the eyes of the discerning public. It had demonstrated its capacity to govern by having a leader who knew when to resign, others waiting to take up his responsibilities, and a way of conducting its affairs that was in the best traditions of democratic government. Herut looked especially good when contrasted with the Labor party, where the struggles between the party leader and the contenders for his position remained as messy and self-defeating as ever.

Although both candidates succeeded in ensuring that their contest provided an essentially smooth transition for Herut, it would be incorrect to claim that the Levy/Shamir competition left no rifts within the party. The precise nature of those rifts, as well as Shamir's ability to hold together a troublesome coalition in the face of daunting economic and international problems, remains to be seen. For now, however, Herut has emerged intact from the most serious challenge in its thirty-five-year history and has demonstrated its continued viability in the post-Begin era.

While Shamir may have garnered support for his candidacy because many expect him to be an interim figure, it is unlikely that he has accepted the task in that spirit. He is very much his own man, one who immediately demonstrated his intention to govern as if his majority were secure (as did Begin), a sure sign of leadership capability. He has been, at one and the same time, tougher than his predecessor in some ways and more conciliating in others. We have already seen some signs of both.

Shamir's efforts to bring the Labor Alignment into a national unity government in the fall of 1983 was genuine and, apparently, he was most forthcoming in his discussions with Labor. The idea fell through because of Labor's insistence that the Likud, for all intents and purposes, repudiate all of the policies its governments have pursued since 1977 and go back to the policy positions of Labor prior to the 1977 elections—an obvious impossibility and, even more than that, something of an affront to the Likud as the governing party. Nevertheless, Shamir's speech to the Knesset presenting his government was full of conciliatory nuances, suggesting that he is not likely to bait and provoke the opposition in the way Begin liked to do, but would seek to work with them, especially in matters of vital common interest to Israelis.

On the other hand, since he is less of a formalist and can be more flexible, Shamir is likely to be even tougher in foreign policy matters when he feels Israel's basic security interests are threatened. But he will be tough in a quieter and more soft-spoken way. This was made evident almost immediately by the Shamir-Arens trip to Washington and the resultant agreement with the Reagan administration for U.S.-Israeli "strategic cooperation," which signalled a new "era of good feeling" in relations between the two countries. Shamir also made a surprise visit to the Israeli troops in Lebanon shortly after assuming the reins of government, something which Begin had not done and which attracted much favorable attention in Israel.

At the same time, Shamir confronts serious economic problems, which he has inherited and which are not amenable to rapid resolution. Nor is the Shamir-Levy contest over. Levy extracted a promise from Shamir that he be given the foreign minister's portfolio when the latter relinquished it, but Shamir, under pressure from Levy's rivals to keep him out of that position, seemed in no hurry to do so. This angered Levy, who tried to raise the issue publicly in November 1983 but backed off when the media response was unfavorable. As of April 1984 there was a truce between the two men, but in the way of politics, how long it will last is uncertain.

Political rivalries being what they are, such competition is part and parcel of the democratic process—indeed, a sign of health in a democracy. What is most important in the larger picture is that the rivalry is being conducted with decency and grace, as it had been all along.

The State of Democracy in Israel

As Menachem Begin, last of the famed founders of Israel, passes from the scene, what are we to make of the state of Israeli democracy? The last year of Begin's government was a very difficult one for Israel in terms of the immediate events which the Israelis confronted. Overall, however, it was a year in which the people's full commitment to democratic politics was revealed, so much so, that despite the real tensions in Israeli society on the political and social levels, on the constitutional level the foundations of Israeli democracy emerged strengthened. The year presented a number of serious challenges to Israel's constitutional tradition, and in every case the challenges led to a strengthening of that tradition through renewed commitment to the unwritten rules of the game of democratic politics in Israel, even sharpening some of those rules. Each affair was typical of Israeli democracy—a bit noisy and quarrelsome, with the introduction of a lot of seemingly extraneous issues, in full public view, with something less than elegance, and in the end, a result which somehow vindicated the democratic process. Israel's constitution, like Britain's, is not written in a single document although, also like Britain's, it is based upon a set of constitutional documents. These include the Proclamation of Independence of the State, seven basic laws, the covenant between the State and the World Zionist Organization/Jewish Agency, the Harari resolution enacted by the Knesset in 1950 establishing the process of constitution-making, and perhaps one or two other pieces of legislation. The essence of Israel's constitution, again like that of the British, is its ancient constitutional tradition, as adapted to contemporary conditions. The last year of the Begin government revealed much of that ancient tradition and the way in which its adaptations have been successful.

A number of milestones that affected Israeli democracy during that year have already been noted. The public response to Sabra and Shatilla, which within one week brought about a complete change in the government's stated policy in the appropriate democratic direction, was as fine a demonstration of the power of public opinion as seen anywhere. The result of that change, namely the investigation itself, further strengthened Israel's democratic tradition, with Menachem Begin himself doing his share both behind the scenes and in his public testimony. The commission's report, unlike previous state investigating commissions of equal magnitude, did not pull any punches. The government implementation which followed, at first all that some wanted, met the commission's requirements and, certainly in retrospect, did the job required of it.

In the process there occurred the tragedy of Emil Grunzweig's murder and the injuring of other Peace Now demonstrators by other Jews opposed to the antigovernment demonstrations. This tragedy led to an abrupt halt in the demonstrations and counterdemonstrations on the part of both opponents and supporters of the government. The actual spilling of Jewish blood was the catalyst needed, however, tragically, to bring about a lessening of the confrontation within Israeli society. The greatest fear of all sensible Israelis is that the exacerbated factionalism of Israeli society will lead to Jew raising hand against Jew—the kind of violence which, in Jewish historic memory, is associated with the destruction of the Second Temple, when the great revolt against Rome was accompanied by internal civil wars among the various ideological parties within the Jewish community. Avoidance of the repetition of such a situation is placed first on the agenda of every Israeli government. Thus the tragic event sent shock waves throughout Israeli society, far beyond the issue which caused it. The very act seemed to have had a sobering effect on all segments of the Israeli public and, tragic as it was, probably hastened Begin's implementation of the report and the resolution of the tensions surrounding it. Once again, the Zionist consensus asserted itself to bring about a common solidarity against such violence.

Another milestone came early in March when new chief rabbis of the national Rabbinate had to be elected. The two incumbents wanted the Knesset to change the law in midstream to allow them to stand for reelection for another five-year term, but the Knesset refused and the election was held according to the existing statutory requirement. In a country where in the past laws have frequently been changed to suit the convenience of the ruling coalition, this, too, was a major step in strengthening the constitutional condition of rule of law which all Israelis endorse in principle.

In late March a new president was elected (Yitzhak Navon having decided not to stand for a second term). The Likud and the Labor Alignment each put up candidates. The Likud candidate was Professor Menachem Elon, a Supreme Court justice and distinguished scholar of Jewish law. The Labor Alignment candidate was Chaim Herzog, a member of the Knesset and distinguished public leader. Despite the government support for Elon, the Knesset proceeded to follow the letter of the law and hold a secret ballot in which Herzog, far better known in the country because of his far more impressive record of public service, won. While either candidate would have been excellent and the merits of the result could have been fairly argued, the public response was highly positive since they wanted Herzog and, most importantly, they wanted the Knesset to be free to choose without being under party discipline.

The final milestones were Menachem Begin's resignation, the successful transfer of the leadership within the Herut, and then the government which followed, described in the previous pages. Thus as the Begin era ended, Israel stood strengthened, not only externally as a result of its peace with Egypt, but also by the increased internal strength of its democratic system.

APPENDIX

KNESSET ELECTION RESULTS, 1949–1981

Compiled by Richard M. Scammon

Results of the Election to the Tenth Knesset, June 30, 1981

	Votes	Percentage	Seats
Total eligible	2,490,014		
Total voting	1,954,609	78.5	
Invalid ballots	17,243	.9	
Valid ballots	1,937,366		
Likud	718,941	37.1	48
Alignment (Labor)	708,536	36.6	47
National Religious Party	95,232	4.9	6
Agudat Yisrael	72,312	3.7	4
Democratic Front	64,918	3.4	4
Resurrection (Tehiya)	44,700	2.3	3
Israel Tradition Movement (Tami)	44,466	2.3	3
Movement for State Renewal (Telem)	30,600	1.6	2
Change-Center Party (Shinui)	29,837	1.5	2
Citizens' Rights	27,921	1.4	1
Others	99,903	5.2	—
			120

SOURCE: Results of Elections to the Tenth Knesset, Special Series No. 680, Central Bureau of Statistics, Jerusalem, 1981.

Distribution of Seats, First through the Tenth Knessets, 1949–1981

The columns headed 7th–10th for the top rows are grouped under the label **Labor Alignment**; the Herut/Liberal columns for the 6th–7th Knessets are grouped under **Gahal** and for the 8th–10th under **Likud**.

Party	1st 1949	2nd 1951	3rd 1955	4th 1959	5th 1961	6th 1965	7th 1969	8th 1973	9th 1977	10th 1981
Mapai	46	45	40	47	42	45	56	51	32	47
Achdut Ha'avoda			10	7	8					
Mapam [a]	19	15	9	9	9	8				
Rafi [a]						10				
Democratic Movement for Change									15	
Herut	14	8	15	17	17	26	26	39	43 [b]	48
Liberal [c]	7	20	13	8	17					
Independent Liberal [d]	5	4	5	6		5	4	4	1	
United Religious	16									
National Religious		10	11	12	12	11	12	10	12	6
Agudat Israel		5	6	6	4	4	4	5	4	4
Poalei Agudat Yisrael					2	2	2		1	
Communist [e]	4	5	6	3	5	4	4	4	5	4
Citizens' Rights								3	1	1
Arab lists	2	5	5	5	4	4	4	3	1	
Others [f]	7	3				1	8	1	5	10

[a] Rafi was formed by David Ben-Gurion after he broke with Mapai in 1965. In 1968 the majority of its members joined the Labor Alignment.

[b] This figure rose to 45 shortly after the election, when Shlomzion (here included under "Others") joined the Likud.

[c] General Zionist through 1959.

[d] Progressive through 1959.

[e] The Communist figure represents Communist party seats in the First through the Fifth Knessets. In 1965 and 1969 the figure includes one seat for the "old" Jewish-oriented party (Maki) and three for the "new" Arab-oriented group (Rakah). In 1973 and 1977 the figure is for the latter only), in 1977 and 1981 under the name Democratic Front for Peace and Equality.

[f] Four small new parties are included under "Others" for 1981. For further identification see Shinui, Tami, Tehiya, and Telem in the Glossary of Parties.

SOURCE: Results of Elections to the Tenth Knesset, Special Series No. 680.

GLOSSARY OF

POLITICAL PARTIES

Listed in order of votes cast.

Likud. The ruling parliamentary block which maintained control in the 1981 elections. The Likud was formed in 1973 by the combination of Herut, the Liberals, and La'am. It is dominated by the Herut (Freedom) Party, which, under the leadership of Menachem Begin, developed from the underground guerrilla organizations, the Irgun Zvai Leumi and the Stern Group. The 1981 Likud campaign stressed the continuing peace process with Egypt, the settlement program in the Occupied Territories and Galilee, and improvement in social conditions.

Ma'arach. The Ma'arach, or Alignment, is a parliamentary block which was formed in 1969 by a combination of the Labor Party and Mapam. The Labor Party was itself established in 1968 by the merger of three parties: Mapai, Achdut Ha'avoda, and Rafi. Mapam, or the United Workers' Party, broke away from one of the three precursors of the Labor Party, Mapai, in 1948. Regressing from the pioneering militant socialism of the early years, the Ma'arach now presents a moderate left-of-center viewpoint.

National Religious Party. The NRP was founded in 1956 by the merger of two religious parties, Mizrachi (Spiritual Center) and Hapoel Hamizrachi (Workers of the Spiritual Center). The party seeks to incorporate traditional Orthodox Jewish ideals with a pioneering and pragmatic approach. In the 1981 campaign, the NRP stressed the principle of combining religion and nationhood, Torah and State.

Agudat Yisrael. In contrast to the NRP, Agudah originally opposed statehood and remains an ultra-Orthodox party advocating the reception of Torah and Jewish law in the State of Israel. The Agudah stressed both its commitment to the "fortification of the bastion of Judaism," by the promotion of pro-religion laws, and its support for the improvement of social conditions.

Democratic Front for Peace and Equality. This list first stood in the 1977 elections, having developed from the Arab Communist Camp.

Tami. This list appeared for the first time in the 1981 elections. Essentially an ethnic and religious grouping, Tami stressed the importance of tradition and cultural origins.

Tehiya. A right-of-center party, Tehiya stresses the biblical Jewish claim to "Eretz Yisrael," and the importance of the Jewish cultural heritage to the State. Tehiya therefore stood against withdrawal from Sinai and against an autonomous regime for the West Bank.

269

Telem. Dominated by its leader, Moshe Dayan, Telem, or the State Revival Movement, first appeared in 1981. Its campaign relied heavily on the personal appeal of Dayan.

Shinui. Shinui was formed as a center party in 1968 by members from the right and left. Its principal aims in 1981 included a policy of territorial compromise in the Arab-Israeli conflict. On the home front, Shinui promised to pay particular attention to human rights and to reforms in the electoral and party systems and in local and state government.

Citizen's Rights Movement. A breakaway from the Labor Party, emphasizing civil rights, particularly women's rights.

Poalei Agudat Yisrael (PAY). This party holds somewhat more moderate views on religious matters than does Agudat Yisrael, but tends to reflect a more left-wing stance in social and economic spheres.

Independent Liberals. This list was formed by those members of the Liberal Party who broke away in 1965, refusing to accept the Liberal Party's alliance with Herut. Most of the Independent Liberals are former members of the Progressive Party, one of the two parties which joined to form the Liberal Party in 1961.

United Arab List. The establishment Arab list, leaning in political sympathies toward Labor.

Development and Peace. Successor of the one-man list of Shmuel Flatto-Sharon, the French millionaire wanted by the French authorities, now expanded, however unsuccessfully, to two candidates.

Shelli. Left-wing list claiming to stand for peace with the Palestinian Arabs and equality between Jews and Arabs.

Arab Brotherhood. The Arab Brotherhood, or Ahva, was a small Arab list which did not succeed in gaining any seats.

Immigration. A nonaligned independent grouping in favor of promoting Jewish immigration to Israel.

Kach. An extreme right-wing party dominated by its charismatic leader, Rabbi Meir Kahane. Kach is militantly nationalistic, supporting deportation of the Israeli Arab population, and upholding the biblical claim of the Jews to the whole of "Eretz Yisrael."

Independence. A list dedicated to the abolition of income tax as the cure for all Israel's ills.

Yisrael Ahat. This list advocated electoral reform to place the emphasis on the individual candidate, together with a broad platform of social reforms concerning such areas as education, working women, soldiers, and the general closing of the social gap.

Arab Citizens' List. Small list concentrating on the improvement of social conditions for Israel's Arab population.

Retired. List for the promotion of the interests of retired citizens.

Ihud. List spreading the message of unity and social justice.

Ya'ad. Ya'ad placed particular emphasis on social problems, and stressed the importance of solutions based on youth and education. In foreign relations, Ya'ad favored territorial compromise as a means of solving the Middle East conflict.

Otzma. Headed by the holder of the "Mr. Israel" title, this list presented a "nonpolitical" platform stressing the importance of individual effort and initiative.

Ohalim. A nonaligned list committed to combating the failures of the welfare system, and to improvement in social conditions.

Revocation of Income Tax. A one-man list devoted solely to the abolition of income tax.

Amcha. A list taking a particular interest in domestic affairs, Amcha's campaign stressed the need to curtail waste in public expenditure and to achieve the integration and independence of Israeli society.

Youth List. A two-man list promoting the interests of Israeli youth.

Council for a Changing Society. This list concentrated on the necessity to work toward a solution to Israel's sociological problems, working to bridge the gap between Ashkenazim and Sephardim, and between the religious and the secular.

Yozma. Essentially the small businessman's list. Yozma emphasized the importance of individual initiative and independence in business and commerce.

CONTRIBUTORS

Asher Arian is Professor of Political Science at Tel Aviv University. His books include *The Choosing People*, a study of the Israeli electorate, *Hopes and Fears of Israelis* (with Aaron Antonovsky), and *Israeli Politics*.

Avraham Brichta is a Senior Lecturer in Political Science at Haifa University. He is author of numerous articles on electoral systems and legislative recruitment in Israel, as well as of a book, *Demokratia Ubechirot*.

Daniel J. Elazar is President of the Jerusalem Center for Public Affairs, Senator N. M. Paterson Professor of Political Studies at Bar Ilan University, and Director of the Center for the Study of Federalism at Temple University. Among his many published works are *Governing Peoples and Territories*, and, with Stuart Cohen, *The Jewish Polity—From Biblical Times to the Present*.

Judith Elizur currently holds a joint appointment in the Department of International Relations and in the Institute of Communication at the Hebrew University of Jerusalem.

Ilan Greilsammer teaches comparative politics in the Department of Political Studies at Bar Ilan University, and is a Fellow of the Jerusalem Center for Public Affairs. He is author of several books and articles, mainly concerned with political parties in Israel and in Europe, and also on the process of European integration. His main publications include a book on the history of the Israeli Communist Party, *Les Communistes Israeliens*, and, on relations between the European Community and Israel, *L'Europe et L'Israel*.

Samuel Krislov is Professor and Chair of Political Science at the University of Minnesota. He has been visiting professor at numerous universities, including Tel Aviv University, where he inaugurated the Keating Memorial Lectureship. Among his publications are *The Supreme Court and Political Freedom* and *Representative Bureaucracy*.

Bernard Reich is Professor of Political Science and International Affairs at George Washington University in Washington, D.C. He was a Fulbright Research Scholar in Egypt in 1965 and a National Science Foundation Postdoctoral Fellow in Israel in 1971–72. He has served as a consultant to various U.S. government agencies. Among his numerous publications are *Quest for Peace: United States-Israel Relations and the Arab-Israeli Conflict*; *The United States and Israel: Influence in the Special Relationship*; and *Israel: Land of Tradition and Conflict*. He is coeditor of *Government and Politics of the Middle East and North Africa*.

Shmuel Sandler is a Senior Lecturer in the Department of Political Studies at Bar Ilan University, and a Fellow of the Jerusalem Center for Public Affairs. He is currently Visiting Professor at the University of British Columbia. He has published various articles and books on American foreign policy, Israeli politics, and the West Bank, including *Israel, The Palestinians and the West Bank—A Study in Intercommunal Conflict*, with Hillel Frisch.

Efraim Torgovnik is a Professor in the Political Science Department at Tel Aviv University and is a Fellow of the Jerusalem Center for Public Affairs. He has written numerous articles on public policy and urban management as well as on Israeli politics, with particular emphasis on electoral politics, party structure, and factions.

INDEX

Abu-Hatzeira, Aharon, 9, 10, 11, 25–26, 96, 106, 118, 119, 122–23, 135, 170, 190, 197, 224, 250, 256. *See also* National Religious party; Tami

Achdut Ha'avoda, 39, 45, 65, 114, 150, 172. *See also* Labor Alignment

Advertising. *See* Newspapers; Press; Radio; Television

Agudat Yisrael party, 9, 12–13, 72, 77, 98–99, 105, 107–25, 150, 216, 222, 224, 256

Akzin, Benjamin, 19

Alef (Citizens for Peres), 145

Alignment. *See* Labor Alignment

Allon, Yigal, 39, 42, 45, 46

Aloni, Shulamit, 8, 32, 191

Arabs, 129, 131; voting behavior, 13–14, 99–100. *See also* Druse; Palestinians; Territories

Arafat, Yasser, 89, 144, 167, 214

Arbeli-Almoslino, Shoshana, 136

Arens, Moshe, 82, 180, 220, 228, 238, 259, 262

Aridor, Yoram, 51, 52, 73, 205, 207, 244, 251, 258–60; economic policy of, 15–16, 73, 91–92, 94, 142, 145, 146, 201; Herut, 28, 257–63

Army. *See* Israel Defense Force

Ashkenazim, 128–58, 224, 250, 253; campaign 1981, 140–47; cleavages, 36, 41, 47–48, 57–59, 123, 129–30, 133–38, 256; Democratic Movement for Change, 30; demographics, 130–33; party images, 152–55; political ideology, 147–52. *See also* Ethnicity

Assad, Hafez, 180, 219

AWACS, 176, 198, 224, 233

Ball, George, 161

Bar-Lev, Haim, 3, 4, 52, 56, 90, 141, 206, 222

Begin, Menachem, 4, 9, 38, 43, 56, 80, 114, 117–18, 134–35, 159, 162–85, 251; autonomy plan, 55, 119, 148; Camp David Accords, 52, 65, 73, 98, 119, 183; coalition with religious parties, 124–25; ethnic appeal, 4; election campaign, 89–95; first government, 15–16; foreign policy, 15, 98, 165, 170–85, 219–35; Gahal party, 69–70; Herut and, 28, 65–67; Iraqi nuclear plant, 53, 73, 94, 146, 147, 219–21, 224; Irgun and, 65; Jewish Democratic leadership, 11–13; media, 188–211; peace treaty with Egypt, 15, 51, 52, 65, 73, 98, 143, 214, 223; resignation, 235, 257–58, 265; Likud and, 52, 76–77, 173; support for, 73, 76–77, 123–25, 156, 186–88, 204–05, 207; television debate, 94, 206, 221; two-year government, 244–65. *See also* Israeli/U.S. relations; Likud

Beit Berel, 46

Ben-Gurion, David, 38–39, 44, 45, 56, 66, 67, 69, 83, 112–14, 117, 134, 135, 160, 169, 170, 173, 215. *See also* Labor Alignment

Ben-Meir, Yehuda, 10, 117, 118, 255

Ben-Porat, Mordechai, 226, 250

Ben-Shahar, Haim, 3, 144–45, 206

Berman, Yitzhak, 250, 257
Bnei Akiva movement, 25, 255. *See also*
  National Religious party
Brandeis, Louis, 181
Brzezinski, Zbigniew, 167
Burg, Yosef, 10, 25, 118, 119, 170, 217,
  224, 248, 254–55

Callaghan, James, 183
Campaign advertising. *See* Newspapers;
  Radio; Television
Campaign issues: ethnicity, 128–58; foreign policy, 159–85, 219–35; Palestinian autonomy, 148; violence, 93–94,
  126, 145–46, 207–10
Campaign results, 95–96
Camp David Accords, 52, 64, 65, 73, 81,
  83, 98, 119, 123, 148, 165–66, 169,
  183, 188, 217, 223. *See also* Israeli/U.S.
  relations
Candidate selection, 18–35; Central
  Elections committee, 18; phases of,
  18–19; nature of process, 19–30;
  proportional representation, 19–22;
  Sephardim and, 25–26. *See also* Cen-
  tral Elections Committee; Democratic
  Movement for Change; Labor Align-
  ment; Liberal party; Likud; National
  Religious party
Carter, Jimmy, 162, 165–85. *See also*
  Camp David Accords; Israeli/U.S. rela-
  tions; Peace Treaty with Egypt
Central Elections Committee, 18, 190.
  See also Candidate selection
Chapman, Brian, 170
Church, Frank, 165, 169
Citizens' Rights and Peace movement, 8,
  94, 95, 100, 191
Clifford, Clark, 163, 168
Cohen, Geula, 55, 81, 188, 197
Communist party. *See* Rakah
Corfu, Haim, 251

Dayan, Moshe, 4, 14–15, 26, 32, 39, 40,
  44, 51, 52, 69, 71, 72, 76, 80, 83, 98,
  142, 165, 175–76, 188, 190, 197, 216–
  17, 225, 244, 250; Six-Day War, 38–
  39. *See also* Telem
Democratic Movement for Change, 36,
  42, 43, 58, 64, 71, 72, 73, 92, 118, 121,
  138, 170, 172, 175, 189, 190, 225, 253;
  candidate selection, 19, 29–30; Amnon Rubinstein, 29, 92, 118; Shinui,
  29; Yigael Yadin, 29, 71, 92, 118. *See
  also* Labor Alignment
Druckman, Haim, 25, 26, 31, 75, 118,
  119, 255. *See also* National Religious
  party
Druse, 29–30, 100, 129, 131

Eban, Abba, 39, 41, 172, 215, 222
Economy, 77–80; as campaign issue,
  15–16, 51, 91–92, 94, 101, 142, 199–
  203; cost of living, 73, 78; inflation, 15,
  73, 78, 142; taxes, 15, 73, 91. *See also*
  Yoram Aridor; Simcha Ehrlich; Yigal
  Hurvitz
Egypt. *See* Begin; Camp David Accords;
  Mubarak; Peace treaty; Sadat
Ehrlich, Simcha, 26, 27, 51, 83, 188, 236;
  economic policy of, 77–79
Ein Vered, 82
Eisenhower, Dwight, 163
Eitanim, 25
Elazar, Daniel, 31, 172
Election analysis, 96–98
Elections: financing of, 42; law govern-
  ing, 187, 189–90
Electoral system, 18–35. *See also* Candi-
  date selection; Proportional repre-
  sentation
Elon, Menachem, 265
Eretz Yisrael Hashlema movement, 66
Eretz Yisrael Hayafa, 58
Eshkol, Levi, 38, 39, 69, 114
Ethnicity, 128–58; cleavages, 36, 41,
  47–48, 57–59; party support, 27, 28,
  122–25; voting patterns, 122–25. *See
  also* Ashkenazim; Sephardim
Etzel, 28, 65. *See also* Irgun Tsevai Leumi
Etzioni, Moshe, 93
European Economic Community (EEC),
  183

Fahd, Prince, 233
Fisher, Max, 181
Flatto-Sharon, Samuel, 97
Ford, Gerald, 165, 169, 174
Foreign policy, 213–43; as campaign
  issue, 198–200, 205. *See also* AWACS;
  Camp David Accords; Iraqi nuclear
  plant bombing; Lebanon; Peace treaty
  with Egypt; Sadat; Syria
Free Center, 29, 71
Friedman, Milton, 77, 78
Fundamental Law of the Knesset, 18. *See
  also* Candidate selection

Gahal party, 67, 68, 69–70, 71, 81, 151
Galili, Yisrael, 39
Gaon, Nissim, 11, 171
Garth, David, 171, 206, 213
Gaza, 38, 40, 70, 98, 148, 216, 217, 223,
  228. *See also* Israeli/U.S. relations;
  Territories
Gemayel, Amin, 238
General Federation of Labor. *See*
  Histadrut
General Zionist party, 68–69

Geyelin, Philip, 182–83
Giscard d'Estaing, Valery, 183, 198
Golan Heights, 38, 70, 98, 217, 223,
    228–32. *See also* Israeli/U.S. relations;
    Territories
Goldwater, Barry, 164
Grunzweig, Emil, 264
Grupper, Pessah, 236
Gush Emunim (nonparty pressure
    group): 25, 44, 75, 82, 105–106, 116,
    117, 118, 119, 245. *See also* National
    Religious party

Habib, Philip, 56, 165, 178, 198, 218–19,
    232. *See also* Israeli/U.S. relations
Haddad, Saad, 218
Hagana, 66, 135
Haig, Alexander, 248
Hakibbutz Haartzi movement, 24
Halpern, Rafael, 196
Hammer, Zevulun, 10, 11, 25, 80, 115,
    117, 118, 254–55
Hapoel Hamizrachi, 109, 114–15
Harif, Moshe, 45, 46, 54, 208–09
Hassan, King, 221–22
Hassan, Mohammad, 221–22
Hawkins, Paula, 169
Hertzbert, Arthur, 181
Herut (Freedom) movement, 51, 65–67,
    80–82, 116–17, 134–35, 151, 257–
    63; candidate selection, 26, 28, 33; for-
    eign policy, 66–67, 170; Likud affilia-
    tion, 7–8, 90, 114. *See also* National
    Religious party
Herzog, Chaim, 39, 53, 221, 265
Histadrut (General Federation of Labor),
    39, 41, 44, 49, 72, 134, 157, 204; elec-
    tions to, 69–70, 86–87, 91, 142–43,
    186–88, 211; Likud affiliation, 27, 77,
    86–87
Horowitz, Dan, 111
Humphrey, Hubert, 164, 182
Hurvitz, Yigal, 51, 79–80, 83, 91, 141,
    142, 188, 226. *See also* Economy
Hussein, King, 144, 221–22, 235

Ichud Hakvutzot Vehakibbutzim move-
    ment, 44, 45
Inflation. *See* Economy
Iraqi nuclear plant bombing, 53, 60, 61,
    73, 94, 146, 147, 177–79, 198. *See also*
    Israeli/U.S. relations
Irgun Tsevai Leumi (Etzel), 65, 66,
    134–35
Israel Defense Forces (IDF), 172–73,
    179, 215, 217, 226, 236, 237, 245, 249
Israeli/U.S. relations, 159–85, 213–43

Jabotinsky, Vladimir, 11, 65, 225, 228
Jackson, Henry, 180
Jaring, Gunnar, 70
Johnson, Lyndon, 164, 180
Jordan, 55, 66, 144, 148, 180, 236–37
Judea and Samaria. *See* West Bank

Kach, 245
Kahan Commission, 180, 239, 249–51,
    253–54, 259
Kahane, Meir, 196, 245
Katz, Shmuel, 81
Katzav, Moshe, 7
Kennedy, Edward, 167, 168
Kennedy, John, 163–64
Key, V. O., 20
Kibbutz Hameuchad movement, 44, 45
Kubbutzim, 32, 44, 45, 154–55, 157
Kirkpatrick, Jeane J., 178
Kissinger, Henry, 164–65, 173–74, 180
Klutznick, Philip, 166–67

La'am, 8, 26, 65, 71, 79, 80, 81, 83
Labor Alignment (*Ma'arach*), 13, 36–63,
    70, 117; advertising, 55–56, 57, 58;
    Arab electoral support, 14, 99–100;
    background, 37–43; campaign issues,
    48–59, 140–41; campaign results,
    95–96, 98; campaign strategy, 51–53,
    140–47; campaign violence, 57–59,
    60, 95, 146, 207–210; candidate selec-
    tion, 5–6, 14, 19, 22–24, 31, 32, 33;
    defection of Dayan, 52; decline of,
    1–9, 19, 42–43, 151, 157; economic
    policy of, 43, 77; ethnic cleavages, 2–7,
    36, 41, 47–49, 133; foreign policy, 55,
    56, 60, 89, 91, 159–85, 215–16, 220–
    21; Histadrut elections, 87, 187; im-
    age, 188–89; Jordanian option, 55, 89,
    91, 143, 144; media, 2, 186–211; Meir
    and, 38, 41; opinon polls, 48–51, 52,
    136, 141, 142, 186–87; Peres, 6, 23–
    24, 42–43, 44–47, 52, 53, 54, 121,
    141; Rabin, 42–43, 44–47, 52, 54, 77,
    141; scandals, 42–43, 141
Lahat, Shlomo, 87
Lamifne faction, 25, 32, 114, 118. *See
    also* National Religious party
Lebanon, 56, 99, 198, 218–19, 238,
    248–49. *See also* Israeli/U.S. relations
Lehi (Lohamei Herut Israel), 28, 65, 228.
    See also Herut
Levinson, Ya'acov, 46, 206
Levy, David, 7, 11, 48, 51, 79, 80, 90–91,
    136, 143, 187, 204, 244, 248, 250, 251,
    257–63; Herut, 7, 28, 257–63
Lewis, Flora, 179, 182
Lewis, Samuel, 179
Liberal party, 65, 66, 70, 80–81, 82–83,

90, 151; candidate selection, 26–28,
31, 32, 33; history of, 67–69; Likud
affiliation, 90
Lijphart, Arend, 116
Likud, 64–106; background, 40, 41, 43,
65–72; campaign issues, 64, 72–73,
82, 83, 91–92, 140–42, 143; campaign
results, 96–101; campaign strategy, 64,
89–92, 140–47, 177; campaign violence, 93–94, 95, 128, 146, 207–210;
candidate selection, 19, 26–28, 32;
coalition, 8–9, 222–29, 254–55; economy, 75, 77–80, 94, 141–42; domestic
agenda, 246–47; foreign policy, 75,
94, 159–85, 214–15; Histadrut, 27,
77, 86–87, 143, 186; history of, 65–
72; image, 72–88, 188–89; internal
discord, 80–83; media, 83, 92, 186–
211; National Religious party and,
117–19; opinion polls, 64, 73, 74,
81–88, 141–42, 186–87; Sephardic
support, 6–8, 73–74, 90–91, 122–25,
133–34. See also Begin; Camp David
Accords; Herut; La'am; Liberal party;
Peace treaty with Egypt
Likud V'tmura, 25, 31, 32
Linowitz, Sol, 164–65
Lissak, Moshe, 111

Ma'arach. See Labor Alignment
McCloskey, Paul, 161
McGee, Gale, 169
McGovern, George, 164, 165
McHenry, Donald F., 168
Mafdal. See National Religious party
Magen, David, 7
Mapai Labor party, 38, 39, 66, 67, 68–
69, 70, 110, 134–35, 150, 169, 172. See
also National Religious party
Mapam party, 14, 39, 89, 160; candidate
selection, 22–23, 24, 32, 33
Massacres. See Kahan Commission;
Sabra/Shatilla Massacres
Mathias, Charles McC., 161
Media. See Advertising; Newspapers;
Radio; Television
Meir, Golda, 38, 41, 42, 68, 114, 164,
172, 173. See also Labor Alignment
Meridor, Ya'acov, 92, 196, 205
Meshel, Yeroham, 93, 143
Mitterrand, François, 215
Mizrachi, 107–15
Moda'i, Yitzhak, 27, 28, 82
Moshav movement, 32
Movement for National Religious Re-
vival, 118
Moyers, Bill, 168
Mubarak, Hosni, 246

Nasser, Gamal Abdel, 172
National Religious party, 8, 32, 72, 73,
75, 77, 105–25, 169, 197, 216–17,
249, 250, 254–55; candidate selection,
19, 25–26, 33; decline of, 9–11, 19,
96, 97, 99, 105–107, 128, 171; es-
trangement from Labor, 117; Jewish
Democratic synthesis, 11–13; Sephar-
dic support, 10–11, 25–26; Six-Day
War, 115–17. See also Aharon Abu-
Hatzeira; Herut; Lamifne; Likud
V'tmura; Tami; Young Guard
Navon, Yitzhak, 39, 152, 252–53, 265
Nawi, Eliahu, 5–6
Ne'eman, Yuval, 82, 197, 216–17, 221
Nelson, Gaylord, 165
Neturei Karta (Guardians of the Wall),
109
Newspapers, 84, 187; campaign report-
ing, 198–200; political advertising,
190, 191–96, 205–06
Nissim, Moshe, 27, 250
Nixon, Richard, 163, 164, 165, 182, 183

OPEC, 160, 172
Operation Peace for Galilee, 232, 236,
247–49, 259
Opinion polls, 2, 43, 79, 83–88, 136,
141, 142, 148, 176, 186–88, 199, 200–
01, 202, 205, 219, 220, 253–54, 255;
Dahaf, 76, 171; Hebrew University Institute for Applied Social Research, 85,
205; Knesset, 87; Labor Alignment,
2, 49–51, 52, 56; Likud, 72–75, 79,
81–88, 226; Modi'in Ezrachi Institute,
64, 81, 84, 85, 86. See also Newspapers
Oren, Mordechai, 160
Oz, Amos, 209

Palestine. See Palestinians; Territories
Palestine Liberation Organization (PLO),
75, 166, 167, 176, 177, 179, 216, 219,
225, 227, 229, 231, 232, 233, 235, 238,
247–49. See also Yasser Arafat
Palestinians, 55, 89, 99, 119, 160, 162,
175, 215. See also Israeli/U.S. relations
Palmach, 135
Pat, Gideon, 26
Peace treaty with Egypt, 15, 51, 52, 64,
65, 72, 75, 82, 98, 143, 203, 213, 216,
217. See also Israeli/U.S. relations
Peres, Shimon, 3, 4, 6, 14, 76, 89, 93,
121, 123, 143, 178, 179–80, 182, 204,
215, 244, 251; debate with Begin, 206,
221; feud with Rabin, 24, 44–47, 52,
54, 141, 221–22; Labor Alignment
and, 6, 23–24, 39, 42–43, 56, 204
Poalei Agudat Israel party (PAY), 105,
120

Political advertising, 2, 54, 186–211. *See also* Newspapers; Press; Radio; Television
Political parties. *See* names of individual parties
Political violence, 93–94, 128, 146
Porat, Hanan, 197
Press, 16, 46, 83, 171, 186–211. *See also* Newspapers; Radio; Television
Progressive party, 69. *See also* Liberal party
Project Renewal, 16; press coverage of, 16
Proportional representation, 19–22, 32. *See also* Candidate selection; Electoral system
Public opinion, 41, 48–51, 52, 56, 72–73, 74, 75, 83, 159, 162–63, 173, 205, 208, 249, 264. *See also* Opinion polls

Rabin, Yitzhak, 4, 76, 90, 93, 162, 164, 172, 173–74, 181, 184, 206, 251; feud with Peres, 24, 44–47, 52, 54, 141, 221–22; Labor Alignment and, 23, 42–43; scandals, 42–43, 141, 175. *See also* Israeli/U.S. relations
Rabinowitz, Yehoshua, 41, 42
Radio, 94, 208
Rafi, 26, 38, 39, 44, 70, 152
Rakah (Israeli Communist party), 98, 99, 135
Raphael, Yitzhak, 118
Ratz, 32
Reagan, Ronald, 160, 176, 179, 182–83, 184, 251. *See also* Israeli/U.S. relations
Religious parties, 105–25; Likud coalition, 124–25; 1981 elections, 121–24. *See also* Agudat Yisrael; National Religious party; Tami; Tehiya
Reston, James, 175
Rivlin, Sefi, 209
Rokach, 32
Rubinstein, Amnon, 29, 32, 92, 118. *See also* Democratic Movement for Change

Sabra/Shatilla massacres, 179, 235, 249, 252. *See also* Kahan Commission
Sadat, Anwar, 53, 61, 64, 74–75, 81, 143, 159, 166, 172, 176, 177, 207, 219; assassination, 229, 230, 246; Camp David Accords, 52, 64, 65; peace treaty, 52, 64, 65, 98, 143. *See also* Israeli/U.S. relations
Safire, William, 180
Sapir, Pinchas, 40, 41, 42
Sarid, Yossi, 196
Sartori, Giovanni, 43
Saudi Arabia, 176, 198, 224, 233
Sawyer, David, 171, 206, 213

Schmidt, Helmut, 146, 177, 183, 198
Seidel, Hillel, 65
Seligman, Lester, 28
Sephardim, 33, 128–58, 250–53, 255; Begin popularity with, 4, 122–25, 204, 207, 226; campaign 1981, 123, 140–47, 204, 207–11; cleavages, 36, 41, 47–48, 56–59, 129–30; Democratic Movement for Change, 29; demographics, 130–33, 171; Herut, 28; party images, 152–55; political ideology, 3–8, 25–26, 27, 28, 47–48, 73–74, 90–91, 122, 133–38, 147–52. *See also* Ethnicity
Settlements. *See* Gaza Strip; Sinai; Territories; West Bank
Shamir, Yitzhak, 82, 83, 92, 215, 226, 228, 231, 244, 251, 258–63; government of, 235–39; Herut, 28
Shapira, Moshe Haim, 115, 255
Sharett, Moshe, 67, 68
Sharir, Avraham, 26
Sharon, Ariel, 8, 56, 65, 70, 72, 75, 95, 118, 180, 215, 226–28, 244, 245, 247, 248, 250, 251, 253–54, 258–60. *See also* Sabra/Shatilla massacres; Settlements
Shelli, 94, 98, 100, 122, 191
Shinui (Change), 29, 32, 94, 98, 100, 122. *See also* Democratic Movement for Change
Shitreet, Meir, 7
Shlomzion party, 8, 72, 95
Shultz, George, 179–80
Sinai Peninsula, 38, 55, 67, 118, 122–23, 162, 166, 173; peace treaty with Egypt, 15, 82, 98; settlements, 40, 82, 229–30, 245–46; Six-Day War, 38, 172–73. *See also* Territories
Sisco, Joseph J., 165
Six-Day War, 38, 39, 40, 115, 117, 144, 172
Stern, Avraham, 228
Stevenson, Adlai, 163
Stone, Richard, 169
Strauss, Robert, 165
Syria, 56, 198, 205, 219, 235, 237, 238

Tami party, 7, 9, 10, 11–12, 26, 32, 60, 96, 97, 98, 99, 100, 106, 119, 123, 125, 135, 170, 190, 216, 225, 250, 256. *See also* Aharon Abu-Hatzeira
Tamir, Shmuel, 71, 92, 258
Tehiya, 8, 26, 32, 82, 83, 97–98, 105–06, 123, 190, 197, 216, 221
Telem, 8, 14–15, 26, 32, 98, 190, 216–17, 250. *See also* Moshe Dayan
Television, 2, 43, 83, 151, 159–60, 196–97; allocation of time, 187, 189–90;

Television (*continued*)
  Begin/Peres debate, 94, 206, 221; campaign and, 56, 57, 146–47, 171, 189–90, 196–98; Labor Alignment, 2, 54, 55, 57, 58; Likud, 83, 92, 94; polls, 43
Territories, 15, 40, 119; Six-Day War, 38, 115. *See also* Gaza; Golan Heights; Sinai; West Bank
Toon, Malcolm, 174
Truman, Harry, 163
Tzeirim. *See* Young Guard

Uzan, Aharon, 250, 251

Vance, Cyrus, 167, 168
Voters. *See* Electorate

Watt, James, 180, 181
Wattenberg, Ben, 165
Weber, Max, 20
Weinberger, Caspar, 248
Weizman, Ezer, 51, 52, 64, 70, 72, 76, 80, 82, 142, 165, 181, 188, 257, 258
Weizmann, Chaim, 68
West Bank, 40, 72, 98, 115–16, 148, 171, 183, 216; settlements, 75–77, 116–17, 166, 167–68, 214, 217, 226–32; Six-Day War, 38. *See also* Ariel Sharon; Israeli/U.S. relations; Territories

Will, George, 179
Workers. *See* Herut; Histadrut

Ya'acobi, Gad, 39
Yachdav, 46, 60
Yadin, Yigael, 29, 71, 72, 92, 118, 189, 225, 253
Yagouri, Assaf, 196
Yanai, Nathan, 31
Yarkoni, Amiram, 88
Yehoshuah, Avraham B., 58
Yom Kippur War, 41–42, 70, 71, 95, 149, 160, 172–73, 180, 209, 215, 248
Young, Andrew, 167, 181
Young Guard (Tzeirim), 9, 10, 12, 25, 31, 32, 83. *See also* National Religious party

Zariski, Raphael, 20
Zeigerman, Dror, 257
Zemach, Mina, 87
Zionism, 107, 111, 115–16, 120, 122, 124–25, 134, 147, 225; Arab electoral support, 13–14; Herut, 65–66, 82; Labor Alignment, 4, 37, 58; Likud, 82. *See also* Agudat Yisrael; Mizrachi
Zurabin, Eliezer, 196